Media Matters in Landscape Architecture

Published by Applied Research and Design Publishing, an imprint of ORO Editions.

Gordon Goff: Publisher

www.appliedresearchanddesign.com

info@appliedresearchanddesign.com

Author: Karen M'Closkey and Keith VanDerSys

Book Design: Office of Luke Bulman with Haiyu Zhou

Project Manager: Jake Anderson

10 9 8 7 6 5 4 3 2 1 First Edition

ISBN: 978-1-957183-67-1

Prepress and Print work by ORO Editions Inc.

Printed in China

AR+D Publishing makes a continuous effort to minimize the overall carbon footprint of its publications. As part of this goal, AR+D, in association with Global ReLeaf, arranges to plant trees to replace those used in the manufacturing of the paper produced for its books. Global ReLeaf is an international campaign run by American Forests, one of the world's oldest nonprofit conservation organizations. Global ReLeaf is American Forests' education and action program that helps individuals, organizations, agencies, and corporations improve the local and global environment by planting and caring for trees.

Novato, California

Media Matters in Landscape Architecture

Karen M'Closkey
Keith VanDerSys

Introduction

> [Mediation] is not the neutral process of the interaction of separate forms, but an active process in which the form of the mediation alters the things mediated, or by its nature indicates their nature.[1]
> —Raymond Williams

> To say that a medium matters is not to say that it played a causal role. The medium is in the middle, indispensable to what is going on, but neither the actor nor the acted-upon.[2]
> —John Durham Peters

It is well understood that *media matters* to the practice of landscape architecture: the ways in which the conditions of any landscape are measured, drawn, and modeled have fundamental repercussions for how a design is formulated in response to those conditions, just as changing ideas about landscapes and environments lead to changes in their representation.[3] The word "medium" derives from the Latin *medius,* or "middle," "midst or intervening space."[4] As outlined below and addressed in the following chapters, the concept of environmental media, which is the focus of this book, is multifaceted and has several distinct yet overlapping definitions relevant to landscape architecture. On the one hand, environmental media are the materials of the natural world, many of which are fundamental to the "palette" of landscape architecture, such as plants, water, and soil. On the other hand, environmental media encompass communication about "the environment"—that is, the various images and texts that convey information about environmental issues such as pollution, biodiversity loss, and climate change to the public. Another conception of environmental media, however, refers to media that are not simply used to communicate about or represent landscapes but instead consider their role in how we come to know or produce ideas about landscapes and environments in the first place.

While these different meanings are interdependent, the latter framing of environmental media emphasizes how the creation and interrelationship

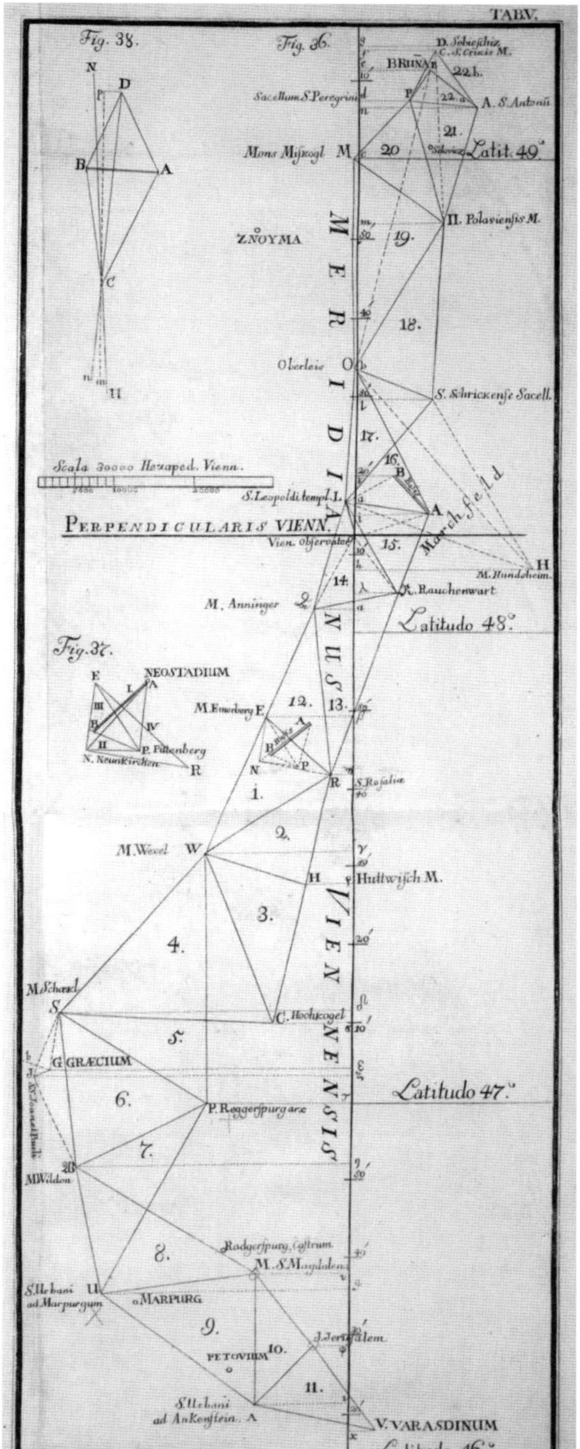

The first triangulation chain survey of the Habsburg Empire. Conducted in 1763 by Joseph Liesganig.

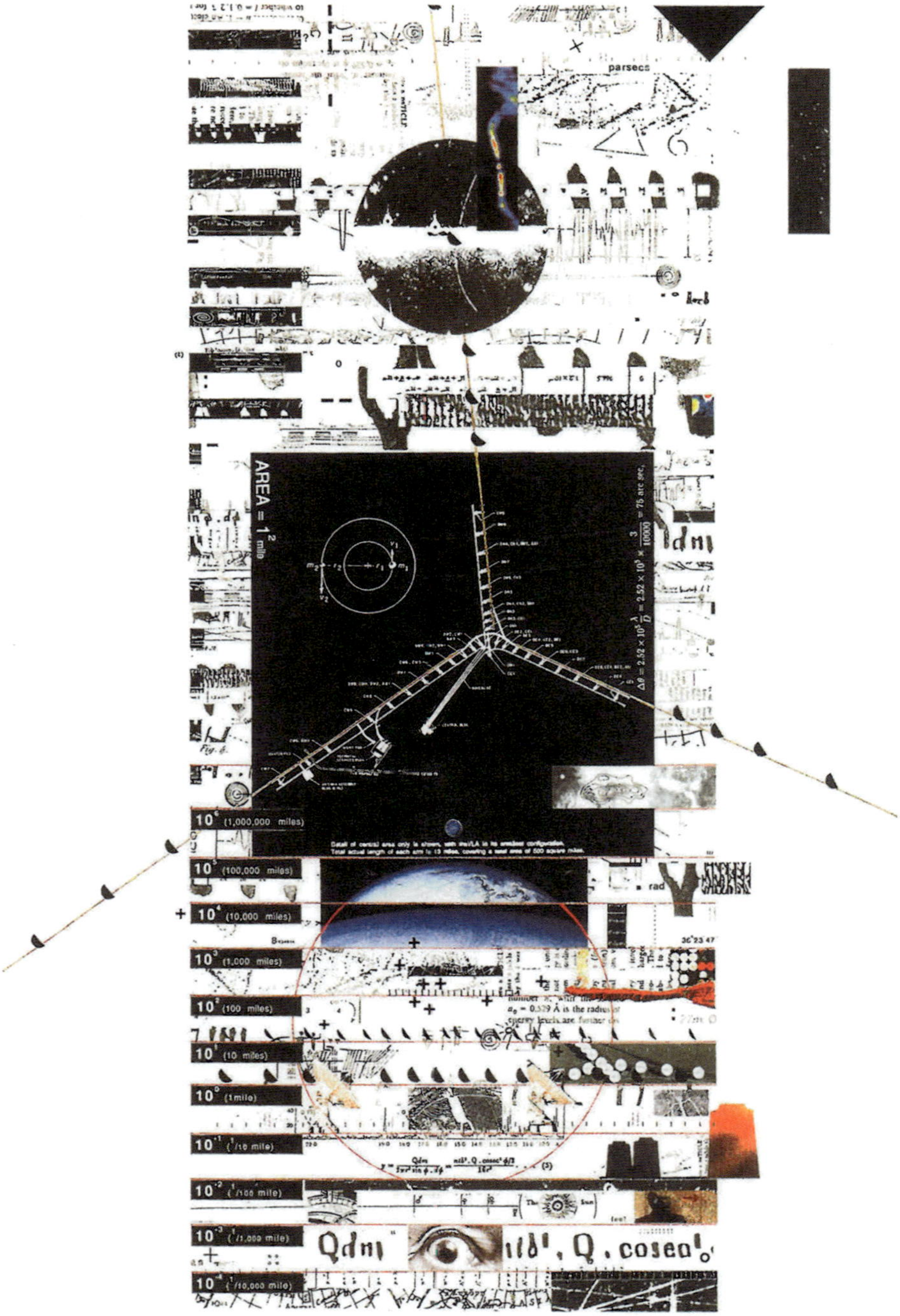

James Corner, *Powers of Ten I*, 1996.

of data, models, and images serve as intermediaries through which ideas about landscapes or environments emerge. Thus, many of the media highlighted in the following pages refer to those that are "infrastructural," which, according to philosopher John Durham Peters, "are media that stand under."[5] Infrastructural media, as we intend here, are distinct from (though entirely dependent on) media infrastructures. There are many foundational and contemporary texts about technology in relation to landscape infrastructures, including railways, roads, dams, and airports. Over the last two decades, an increasing number of texts have focused on the rapid expansion of digital media infrastructures, such as data centers, transatlantic cable networks, GPS, and others. While many of the authors in this book draw attention to digital media as key to the projects and practices they highlight, they do not focus on the hard infrastructure and significant environmental impacts required for digital media to function, such as increased energy and water consumption, mining, and e-waste.[6] As important as these infrastructures are to the shaping of physical landscapes, this book considers various media for their crucial role in data collection, modeling, and image-making, which shape landscapes in different, albeit less obvious or immediate ways.

The opening sentence of "Eidetic Operations and New Landscapes" by landscape architect James Corner reads, "Landscape and image are inseparable. Without image, there is no such thing as landscape, only unmediated *environment*."[7] One quickly recognizes the problem with the phrase *unmediated environment*, which Corner himself addresses in a footnote:

> To the degree that the term *environment* has assumed many meanings and values...it is true to say that environment, too, in its various mediated forms, has become just as much a subjectively constituted and as sensible an *idea* as *landscape*.[8]

This book expands on the footnote in many ways; many of the chapters address the relationship between "landscape" and "environment" rather than treating them as distinct or as background, foreground, or ground for the other. In this introduction, we occasionally use the two terms together. Although they express different ideas and entities with different histories and are therefore not interchangeable, the material conditions to which they refer are inextricably linked and mutually influential, enmeshed in the physical world.

The reciprocal formation of ideas, representations, and the material world entails various technologies that mediate their relationships. Numerous books and articles have examined the concepts of "media" and "environment," and recently, there has been a proliferation of publications that explore the relationship between these two ideas in ways that go beyond early media theorists' formulations of *media environments* or *media ecology* as developed in the 1960s.[9] One of the criticisms of the limitations of these initial conceptions is that environment and ecology were treated metaphorically rather than materially; that is, they referred only to the relationships between humans and technology *as* environment and to ecology as the complex interactions between human cognition and media technologies—especially "mass media"—without paying attention to the material reality through which all technologies are made and in which they are embedded.[10]

Our approach to the relationship between these two terms is very much in line with that of Adam Wickberg and Johan Gärdebo's in *Environing Media* (2023), which was published while *Media Matters* was in progress. The editors define environing media as those that explicitly focus on shaping the human–earth relationship and describe activities, such as how data are collected and acted upon, as the middle ground of environment *as* media.[11] As Sverker Sörlin states in his contribution to their collection, "Environing consists of processes whereby environments appear as

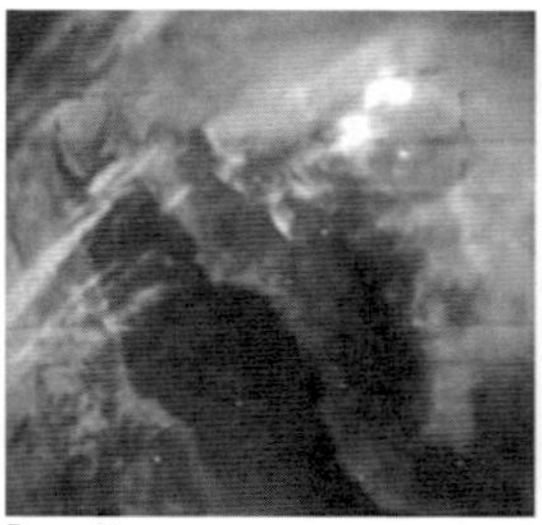
Frame 01

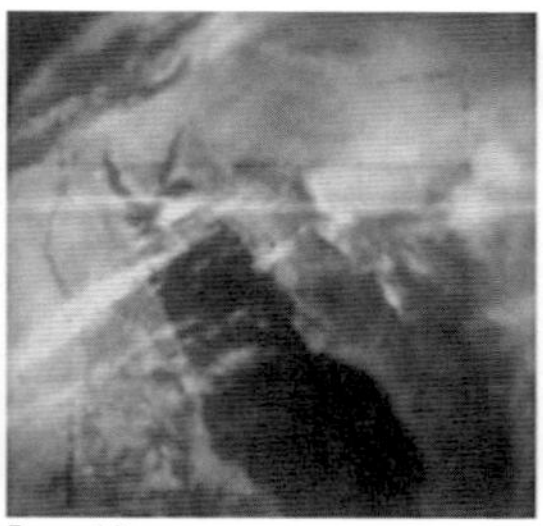
Frame 02

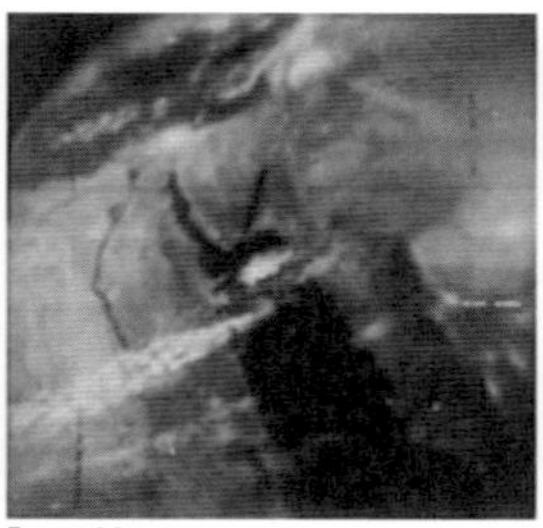
Frame 03

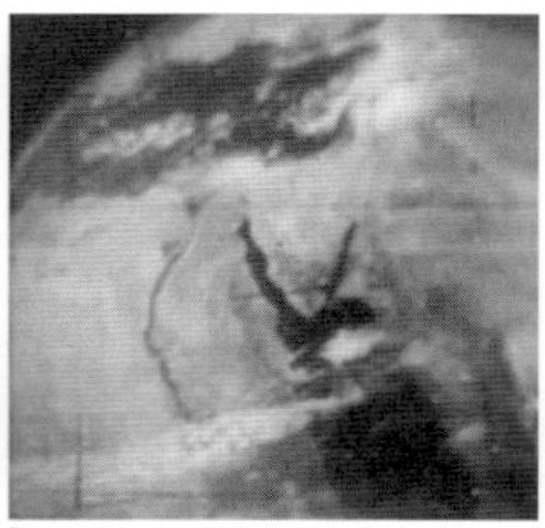
Frame 04

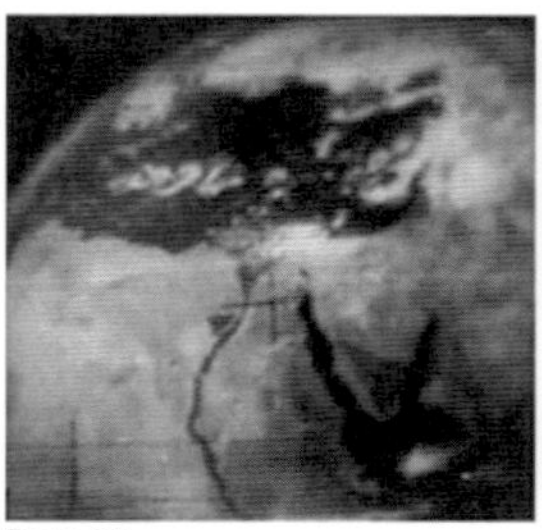
Frame 05

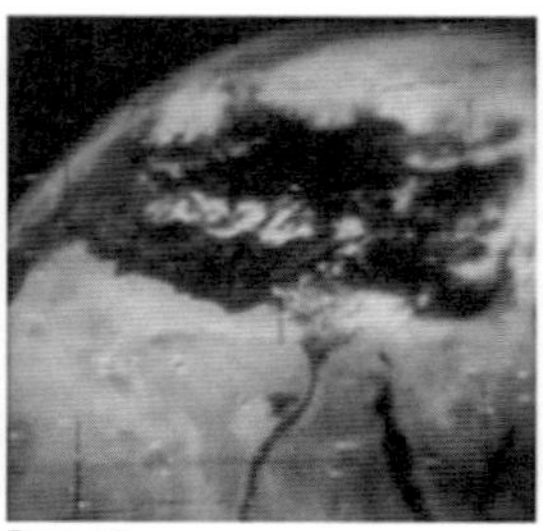
Frame 06

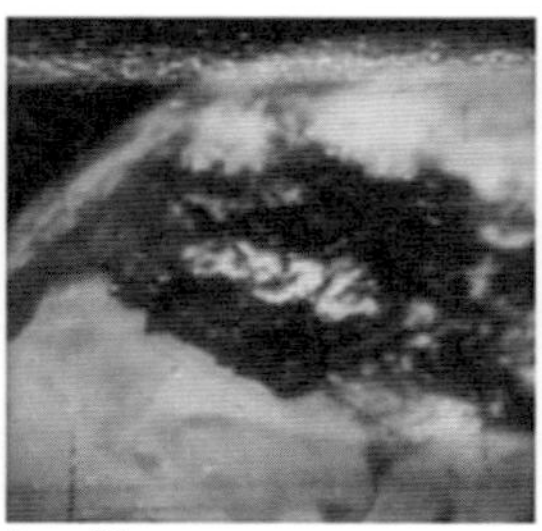
Frame 07

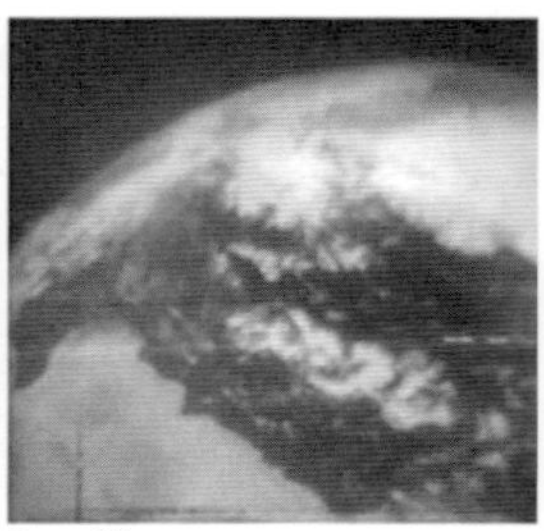
Frame 08

The first photo of Earth, captured by the TIROS-1 weather satellite on April 1, 1960.

historical products, and technologies and media as the tools required for the environing to take place."[12] Thus, as media change—and approaches to their study evolve—so do conceptions of "environment," and vice versa. Accordingly, it is essential to consider recent significant shifts in the operational aspects of images and models, especially those that mediate between landscapes—which are localized or regional and primarily terrestrial places—and environments that have a broader scope, encompassing the "ephemera" that affect local landscapes, as well as those that span across scales and include global environmental change.

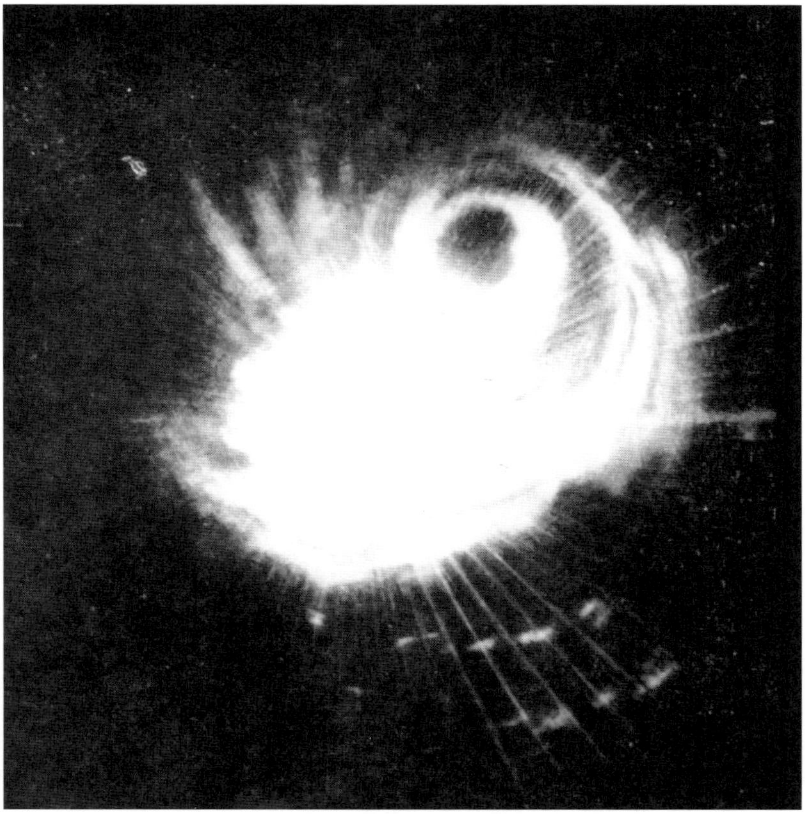

Time series of a typhoon captured by a US Navy ship's radar, 1944. This storm was the first tropical storm to be observed on radar.

In its early usage, the term "environment" referred to the immediate surroundings; at the scale of the landscape, it would therefore be considered coterminous with it.[13] Although efforts to modulate environments to create particular landscape characteristics through attempts at climate modification are not new—such as afforestation to generate moisture and fertile

Image comparison using two different formulas for calculating moisture levels in multispectral satellite imagery. Dark green depicts areas with the highest moisture levels, while dark brown represents areas with the lowest.

land—these effects have not been considered on a global scale until recently.[14] Similarly, since the late 19th and early 20th centuries, scientists have understood that global climate patterns such as atmospheric and oceanic circulation (the jet stream, El Niño, etc.) cause different weather patterns in different parts of the world. However, the concept that the environment itself is "global" is much more recent and would have made little sense before World War II and the development of nuclear technology. Subsequent developments in atmospheric sensing, Earth observation technologies, and the development of climate models have furthered this understanding.[15]

In his book *Surroundings*, historian Etienne Benson suggests that the relational aspect between an entity and what surrounds it is inherent in the meaning of environment, or "a relationship in which each party not only influences the other but also in some fundamental way

determines what the other is."[16] This quote is similar to the epigraphs of this introduction. If the entities to be considered are the landscape and the media used to elaborate aspects of that landscape, then it becomes clear why the nature of environmental media matters to landscape architecture. As Benson observes, "Each attempt to adapt the concept of environment to new circumstances and aims has been accompanied by changes in the understanding of the entities that are surrounded."[17] Indeed, it is impossible to think about the practice of landscape architecture without thinking of environment in this expansive sense, that is, in a global climate context, even though the impacts on landscapes—and the people, plants, and animals that live in them—are more localized and therefore highly variable. One of the key challenges for practitioners is the apparently unbridgeable gap between what we know about global environmental change and the local impacts of that change on landscapes.

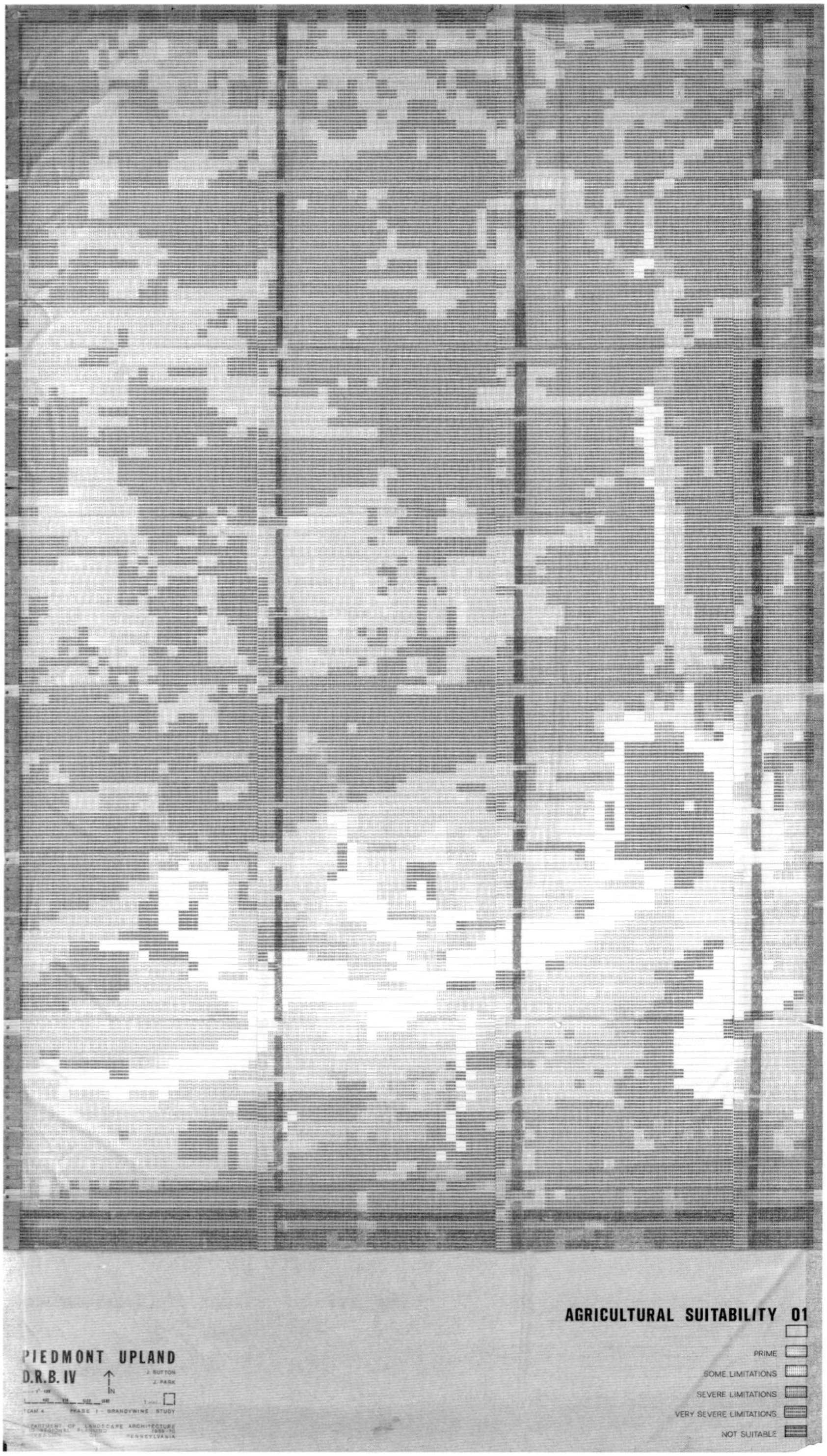

Computer plot of agriculture suitability map, c. 1970. Ian McHarg, *Delaware River Basin IV, Piedmont Upland Study, 1969–70.*

While landscapes and environments are materially and conceptually intermingled, they are also kept apart by the various media that underlie their creation. As Corner notes in the essay from which the above quotes are taken, images have always been *operational* for landscape architects.[18] They are the intermediaries through which concepts and designs are formed. Therefore, the divide between how we name, map, and model things that are "environmental"—so-called ephemera such as rain, mist, fog, tides, and clouds—and things that are "landscape" (e.g., lakes, rivers, etc.) significantly shapes the built environment.[19] For instance, the hard infrastructure of shorelines may be constructed of concrete, metal, and stone, but as several of the chapters emphasize, data collection, measurements, and subsequent delineation of "normal" environmental conditions help produce concepts such as floodplains and sea level, which are the basis upon which these hard infrastructures are designed and built. As Science, Technology, and Society Studies (STS) scholar Sara Pritchard writes in "Toward an Environmental History of Technology":

> Surveys, nails, drills, wells, radioactive tracers, traps, steamships, deep-sea dredging, and radio transmitters helped foresters calculate average tree size, engineers estimate rivers' flows, ecologists develop the notion of food webs, naturalists describe the deep ocean, and wildlife biologists track animals... New technologies, and new uses of established technologies, produced not only new forms of natural knowledge, but also new conceptions of 'the environment' itself.[20]

As mentioned, what applies to technologies that directly intervene in landscapes and environments also applies to media technologies that shape our understanding of them. This idea, now taken for granted, is further enriched by the wealth of exciting work by landscape historians, environmental historians, STS and media scholars, and historians and philosophers of science, some of whom are contributors to this book and to whom we are deeply indebted. Scholarship on the role of media in shaping perceptions, which in turn shape landscapes and vice versa, is, of course, not new. There has been considerable historical work on how landscape painting and photography have influenced perceptions.[21] However, the emphasis tended to be on the visible and visual elements—what the images represent or symbolize—rather than on the constellation of technologies, practices, and institutions through which images operate.[22]

The 1980s, however, marked a significant period for scholarly work on visual culture, including how cultural influences shape vision itself.[23] Discussions during this period often centered on landscape and representation, and maps as a form of media were central to this work. Grounded in critical theory and poststructuralism, and partly in response to the rise of GIS, critical cartography challenged claims of cartographic objectivity, focusing instead on the social aspects of maps and questions of whose interests were or were not served by these representations.[24] Given the prevalence of map use and mapping practice in landscape architecture, this work has had a significant impact on the discipline.[25] Yet, it is also acknowledged that mapping practices are far more varied and messy than some of these critiques have assumed.[26] Historian and cartographer William Rankin argues that these critiques solidified a view that was already widespread among practitioners.[27]

Lidar scan of a forest in Front Royal, VA.

Perhaps not surprisingly, many of the chapters in this book deal with surveying, sensing, and mapping and/or are written by practitioners. Rather than focusing solely on the media end products that result from these practices, some authors describe the measurement and data collection practices behind their creation. These include models and images that are not pictorial or representational and, in many cases, are seen only by those who make and use them. The non-picturable characteristics of these media are relevant here. Jussi Parikka, in his book *Operational Images*, calls this the "invisual" (not to be confused with invisible) aspects of data: "We should look at the operative transformations of the image as it pertains to the multiple materials and their abstractions, and abstractions coming back to transform the materials."[28] Parikka shows how photography and computer imagery are connected through techniques such as photogrammetry. Maps, he says, are the "link to the operational aspect of predigital instrumental images."[29] Just as Corner asserts that aerial representation is significant for its "instrumental utility in the modernization of the earth's surface" rather than for its scenographic perspective, Parikka argues that the Earth itself is made into an image through other images, such as photogrammetry, which has been rapidly advanced by digital imaging, even though it existed before digital technology.[30]

Following Parikka, it is important to emphasize that while digital technologies have significantly transformed our landscapes, environments, and design methods, we are not claiming that these technologies always represent a radical break, as some others have argued. For example, drawing attention to the ontological difference between photographs and digital images, architect John May quips, "No one has ever produced a digital photograph."[31] May says that we are deluding ourselves if we do not consider that the shift from photographs (light and chemicals) to images (electrical signals) is changing us profoundly, since each technical system has a specific conception of time that is "inseparable from the forms of thought and imagination that system makes possible or impossible."[32]

In contrast, W. J. T. Mitchell insists the distinction between an analog or digital "photograph" is, in itself, not relevant because the content is not inherent in the medium.[33] Using the example of a family photograph, Mitchell maintains that such a distinction "isolates the 'being' of photography from the social world in which it operates, and reifies a single aspect of its technical processes."[34] While we clearly agree with May's point that

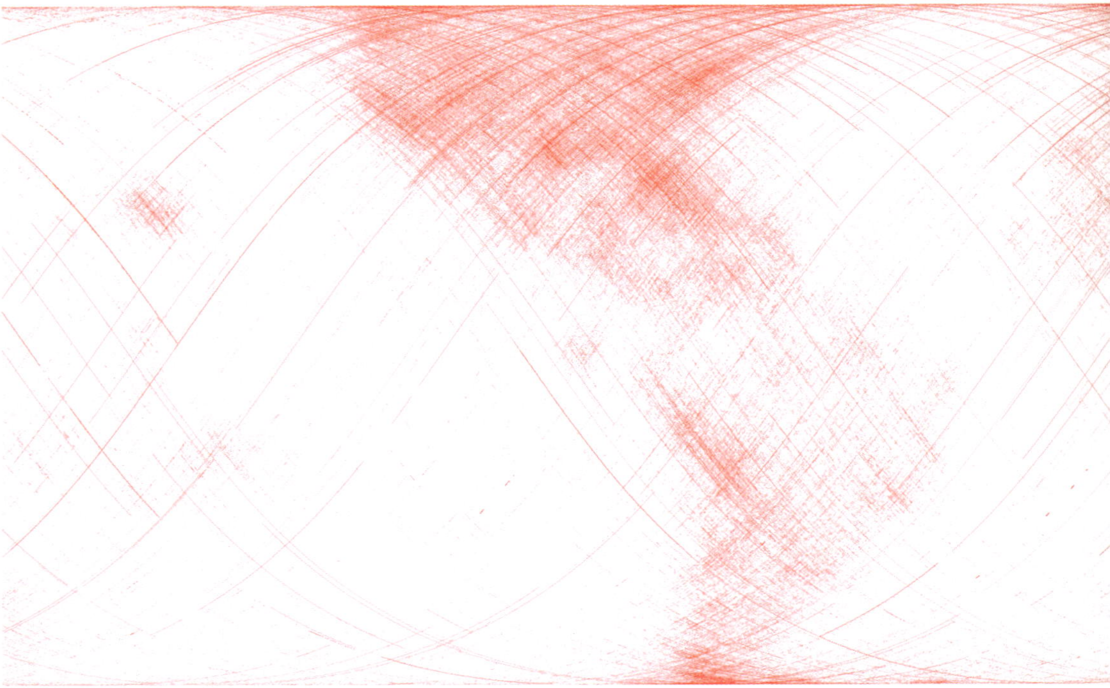

Image location of every photo of Earth taken from the International Space Station (2013).

the *medium matters*, the shift from analog to digital does not always constitute a fundamental change. In some cases, as in Mitchell's example of a family photograph, the medium is not critical to the image's function; the image itself is not infrastructural or operational in the sense described here. However, there are many instances where the distinction does matter, where the "technical process" *is* the content and *the medium is the message*.[35] This is undoubtedly true for images that embed spatial data for the express purpose of quantifying, mapping, and modeling environmental and landscape change. As Pritchard aptly states, "environmental knowledge cannot be isolated from environmental knowledge-making."[36]

Media Matters goes behind the scenes to consider how media technologies that have emerged in recent decades are reshaping the practices of artists, designers, and scientists. The media infrastructure of climate science and Earth remote sensing, coupled with the increased availability of spatial information and modeling software, provide the context for many of the chapters that follow. Many of the practices and projects are geospatial in nature, where the media and methods employed are designed to capture phenomena that are not directly visible to human perception and where

there is a high degree of uncertainty or changeability due to dynamic material conditions. What has become increasingly apparent is that the pace of climate change is faster than models predicted two decades ago, and with that comes the recognition that uncertainty and variability (which have always been there) cannot be tamed. As Durham Peters notes, "Media capture and fail to capture time, whose fleetingness is the most beautiful and difficult of all natural facts."[37] This has been a primary challenge for our discipline.

Contributors

In keeping with the interdisciplinary nature of practice and the aims of this book, we have invited contributions from a range of disciplines, including landscape architecture, ecology, civil engineering, art history, environmental history, STS, and media studies. The projects focus heavily on the US context, partly because of our familiarity with the practical context, but also because the data infrastructure and technology that underpin much of the media discussed originated in the United States. Many have pointed out the problematic military origins of these technologies. At the same time, the United States has the most open, freely accessible geospatial and Earth observation data. What Libby Robin calls "NASA bias" should not be downplayed, as it permeates how we environ globally, but this ongoing and much-needed critique is not the focus of this book. Instead, many of the chapters explore ways to move beyond the limitations of existing datasets, and the authors are not quite ready to abandon the "positivist" aspects of data mapping, even as they acknowledge the contingency of such information.

The crises of rapid climate change and biodiversity loss underlie a third of the chapters. Others, while not explicitly addressing climate change, deal with related shifts in the push for increased data collection, where environmental quantification comes at the expense of qualitative and "non-expert" ways of knowing. This includes attending to the root causes of the climate crisis in fossil fuel extraction as well as historical and ongoing racial injustices. Rather than abandoning data collection and mapping altogether, some projects use them to tell different stories using diverse kinds of information in order to complicate single, overarching narratives.

There would have been any number of ways to categorize the chapters by specific media, such as by Earth and aerial sensing technologies (drones, satellites) or environmental sensing technologies (*in situ* sensors for moisture, temperature, etc.), by techniques of data collection and measurement (such as grids, plane surveying, and photogrammetry), or by media products (such as maps or atlases). To do so oversimplifies the promiscuity of practice due to the aggregate media used to accomplish the work described. However, because common themes run through the book that connect some chapters more closely than others, we have clustered them below and organized the chapters accordingly.

Several chapters focus on data interpolation over vast spatial scales, which is achieved by translating measurements of ephemeral or highly variable conditions collected at local sites, such as stream gauges and weather stations. These measurements are then used to generate averages and probabilities about these ephemera, which subsequently inform decisions about landscape design and management. In other words, the media of grids and datums both *presume* and *produce* a stable view of the environment, resulting in landscapes of probability and risk. Although probabilistic knowledge emerged in the 18th century and was institutionalized in the 19th century, risk management did not emerge until the 20th century.[38]

In "Measuring the Sky from the Curve of the Earth," Jeffrey Moro provides a brief history of weather stations, tracing their emergence from the 18th and 19th centuries to the present. Moro describes the challenges of siting stations due to the variability of landscapes and the efforts to standardize data collection across different locations. As he demonstrates, weather stations do not simply "observe" conditions; they actively participate in constructing weather data. Wilko Graf von Hardenberg's chapter, "Levels of Lakes: Between Baselines and Research Objects," discusses the prominent role of lakes in the history of geodesy, particularly in the early 19th century. During this period, lake levels served as a zero datum for measuring the topographic elevations of nearby mountains before the mean sea level was established for that purpose. Although such measurements appeared to aim for scientific precision, early reference levels reflected individual measurements that did not capture natural variability. Nevertheless, these data-gathering processes affected lake management in different parts of the world. This example is an important precursor to recent debates about sea levels.

Attempts to link local measurements of ephemera to predictions of patterns over large regions are also crucial aspects of our chapter. We provide a brief overview of how probabilistic methods used by hydrologists in the early 20th century to measure rainfall frequency, volume, and downstream effects led to the creation of floodplains as risk objects. We focus on the maps produced by the Federal Emergency Management Agency (FEMA) for the US National Flood Insurance Program. FEMA's recent attempts to update the maps to be more accurate run up against the deep uncertainties involved in mapping such phenomena, especially as the agency attempts to incorporate climate change into its assessments.

In contrast to the projects described above, where data are collected to understand and produce norms for forecasting, Brian D. Harris and Justin Shawler, Matthew Jull and Leena Cho, and Ilmar Hurkxkens describe their work as part of ongoing experiments. While natural fluxes are inherent in landscapes and environments, global heating is exacerbating the frequency and intensity of these dynamics, revealing the inadequacy of old models based on stability and control. Many media are used to understand this accelerated change: material collection (e.g., soil borings), *in situ* sensors (e.g., for moisture and temperature), sensor array geometry (i.e., grids), and the various models into which these data are fed. Unstable sediment is inherent in these projects. Although surveying and core sampling of soils have always been part of landscape architectural practice, and the (re)making of landscapes has always required the addition and augmentation of living media, the projects highlighted in these chapters take uncertainty as their starting point, so that not all design decisions are made up front but are integrated into ongoing cyclical monitoring and assessment.

Harris and Shawler discuss incorporating adaptive management through field monitoring and feedback into the models for their work on coastal wetland restoration, the long-term success of which is highly uncertain. Unpredictable rates of sea level rise make modeling beyond the very short term impossible. Similarly, Jull and Cho report on a project in Utqiaġvik, Alaska, an area that is warming the fastest on Earth. Working with an interdisciplinary team of designers, scientists, and local leaders, the authors describe efforts to understand permafrost dynamics using a sensing approach that differs from traditional environmental monitoring, which aims to exclude local effects or "outliers"—the measurements that don't fit the norm.

Just as Harris and Shawler point out that it is impossible to know in advance the quality and quantity of material needed to elevate wetlands to keep pace with sea level rise, Ilmar Hurkxkens' chapter explores how adapting landscapes through continuous surveying and robotic construction could substantially change the typical working process of landscape architects and engineers. The emphasis is on designing formative processes rather than final forms, as well as adapting to changing material conditions on site over multiple time scales.

Similar to how Hurkxkens describes adaptive construction methods using autonomous sensing and robotics, Christopher Streb and David Blersch's chapter on "regenerative techno-ecosystems" imagines a future in which sensing and monitoring technologies will enable ecosystems to regulate themselves with the help of human technology. In Streb and Blersch's chapter, however, technology becomes imperceptible—that is, it becomes "environmental"—taking media ecology literally and in a direction its early proponents could not have foreseen.[39] Ubiquitous computing has been a goal of tech developers for over half a century. The question is what kind of environmental relationships might emerge beyond personal convenience, entertainment, or ever-more "intelligent" optimization that benefits technology companies above all else. Jennifer Gabrys's chapter illustrates one such approach through "The Smart Forests Atlas." This online, collaborative, and emergent atlas includes information gathered through multiple media forms—logbooks, a radio, stories, and a map—in ways that operate beyond the environmental management approaches of Big Tech and expert science. Gabrys's concept of "vegetalizing" digital technologies asks us to consider forests as a model for how we might view our media technologies as sites of "reciprocity and mutual flourishing" rather than limiting them to optimization.

In an example of an entirely virtual landscape, Paolo Patelli and Jussi Parikka's chapter describes different models and model types nested together to simulate ecological interactions and environmental changes across scales. "Model ecologies" are synthetic "ecosystems" created by separating the landscape into various model components (e.g., hydrology, geomorphology, etc.) and then reassembling these components to develop a comprehensive model for running simulations aimed at gaining insights into the natural world. The information gleaned from these simulations can be used to make decisions about how to manage the landscape itself. As Patelli and Parikka argue, models are not just representations; they are already interventions.

The remaining chapters focus on the promises and limitations of the view from above, made possible by increasingly sophisticated and widely available data and technology. The use of environmental data derived from aerial and satellite imagery is not new in our field—quite the opposite. Landscape architects were early adopters of computers and have been instrumental in developing and experimenting with geographic information systems (GIS). This work was, and still is, often focused on land and water conservation planning and developing scenarios to consider the impact of different settlement patterns on natural systems.

As Corner remarked in 1996, the synoptic view made possible by satellite and global sensing technologies has become increasingly sophisticated: "It is a view that affects not only the cultural imagination but also the actions that human societies take, especially with regard to new policies and practices aimed toward regional and global ecology."[40] The amount of data available to do this work and the sophistication of the hardware and software used to do it have grown by leaps and bounds over the last five decades. However, as a field, we still lack sufficient knowledge about the procedures and practices for collecting and organizing environmental and spatial data. We often rely on information collected and classified by others, which is then fed into models created by others.

The availability of drones for low-altitude surveying, discussed in Iryna Dronova's and Karl Kullmann's chapters, has the potential to change certain aspects of practice. Still, they, too, have their limitations—what Dronova refers to as the trade-off between "reach" (satellite data) and "richness" (UAV data). Dronova describes significant changes in landscape research and practice enabled by remote sensing and Earth observation technologies, particularly the use of UAVs and the ability of researchers to produce their own spatial data specific to the project at hand. Nevertheless, she points out that the integration of remote sensing into policy and decision-making is lagging behind. Karl Kullmann makes a similar argument about the slow adoption of drone technology in landscape architecture. In his chapter "The Seeing Machine," Kullmann argues for the potential of using drones to draw on *chorography,* a 15th-century predecessor, to depict landscapes in ways that combine aerial views with hyper-detailed ground views, an approach he believes should be groundbreaking for our field.

In a similar vein, the final three chapters consider how satellite and other disembodied views are layered with data, information, and stories collected on the ground and by other means to create a more situated or layered perspective. Here, mapping is partial and combined with other media. In a close reading of two books, Heather Houser contrasts Victoria Marshall et al.'s *Patch Atlas: Integrating Design Practices and Ecological Knowledge for Cities as Complex Systems* (2019) and Anuradha Mathur and Dilip da Cunha's *Mississippi Floods: Designing a Shifting Landscape* (2001). Houser explores how they each encode the temporality of landscapes in different ways and, in contrast to many of the other chapters and projects in this book that foreground the functionality of data and images, how they complicate the notion of utility.

In "Data, Relationships, and Action," Samantha Jo Fried discusses the relationality and scalability of Earth remote sensing data while also highlighting its limitations for on-the-ground decision-making, even when those decisions are intended to address inequities. Using data on impervious surface land cover and the associated heat island effect in Worcester, MA, Fried highlights the challenges for data users who are not data creators and, like Dronova, reminds us to be attentive to the gap between "expert" and layperson in structuring environmental narratives. As Gabrys has argued in this book and elsewhere, digital technologies play a formative role in crafting environmental narratives, and it remains critical to ask who can and cannot participate in their creation.

Continuing the exploration of multimedia works that recontextualize environmental data to situate them within the contexts of their production, Lila Lee-Morrison's chapter, "The Environmental Gaze: Visual Perspectives on Monitoring Landscapes of Ecological Devastation," compares the work of Forensic Architecture and artist Imani Jacqueline Brown to Louisiana's Coastwide Reference Monitoring System (CRMS), a project also referenced by Harris and Shawler. CRMS tracks land loss in coastal wetlands, while Forensic Architecture tracks air by cross-referencing data sources to show toxic pollution affecting communities along Cancer Alley. Imani Jacqueline Brown's projects also offer alternative ways of seeing ecological devastation, juxtaposing on-the-ground perspectives with aerial views and incorporating the stories of her ancestors. According to Lee-Morrison, these situated approaches combine partial views and contexts beyond the visual field to address the gaps and limitations of standard environmental monitoring.

Not only have media changed rapidly in recent decades, but so has the field of media studies, along with the growth and influence of STS and the history of science. All of these situate media–environment relations within a constellation of "actors"—human, nonhuman, and technological—rather than one-way communications or representations. Although many of the contributors examine specific places and landscapes, the implications of environmental media extend beyond any particular site to point to broader questions about the role of data collection, modeling, and image interpretation in how we come to know about our world. We are grateful to each author for illuminating the intertwined nature of landscapes and media and demonstrating how practices and knowledge coevolve in diverse ways.[41]

Notes

1. Raymond Williams, *Keywords: A Vocabulary of Culture and Society* rev. ed. (Oxford University Press, 1985), 205.
2. John Durham Peters, "What is Not a Medium?" *communication +1* 9, no. 1 (2022), openpublishing.library.umass.edu/cpo/article/78/galley/78/view/.
3. We expanded on this in our essay on standardization and land cover. See Karen M'Closkey & Keith VanDerSys, "Behind the Scenes: Multispectral Imagery and Land Cover Classification," *Journal of Landscape Architecture* 17, no. 1 (2022): 22–37.
4. Academic Dictionaries and Encyclopedias, "Latin-English Dictionary – medium," https://latin_english.en-academic.com/9731/medium (accessed July 20, 2024).
5. John Durham Peters, *The Marvelous Clouds: Toward a Philosophy of Elemental Media* (University of Chicago Press, 2015), 33.
6. Numerous publications address this critical aspect of digital media. See, e.g., Jennifer Gabrys, *Digital Rubbish: A Natural History of Electronics* (University of Michigan Press, 2011); Richard Maxwell, Jon Raundalen & Nina Lager Vestberg (eds), *Media and the Ecological Crisis* (Routledge, 2015); Lisa Parks & Nicole Starosielski (eds), *Signal Traffic: Critical Studies of Media Infrastructures* (University of Illinois Press, 2015); Sean Cubitt, *Finite Media: Environmental Implications of Digital Technologies* (Duke University Press, 2017); and Lisa Parks, Julia Velkova & Sadner De Ridder (eds), *Media Backends: Digital Infrastructures & Socialtechnical Relations* (University of Illinois Press, 2023).
7. James Corner, "Eidetic Operations and New Landscapes," in James Corner (ed.), *Recovering Landscape: Essays in Contemporary Landscape Architecture* (Princeton Architectural Press, 1999), 153. Italics in original.
8. Ibid., 168. Italics in original.
9. See the work of Marshall McLuhan and Neil Postman here, among others. See also notes 10 and 39.
10. The sources are too numerous to cite. Several that critique or expand on Marshall McLuhan include Ursula K. Heise, "Unnatural Ecologies: The Metaphor of the Environment in Media Theory," *Configurations* 10, no. 1 (2002); Lance Strate, *Media Ecology: An Approach to Understanding the Human Condition* (Peter Lang, 2017); Sarah Sharma & Rianka Singh (eds), *Re-Understanding Media: Feminist Extensions of Marshall McLuhan* (Duke University Press, 2022).
11. Adam Wickberg & Johan Gärdebo (eds), *Environing Media* (Routledge, 2023), 3. The phrase "as the middle ground of environmental media" is a direct quote. Similarly, Sverker Sörlin and Nina Wormbs describe *environing technologies* as "loosely or tightly coupled, assemblages of technologies and practices. Either way, environment is their product." Sverker Sörlin & Nina Wormbs, "Environing Technologies: A Theory of Making Environment," *History and Technology* 24, no. 2 (2018): 106.
12. Sverker Sörlin, "Environing and the Human-Earth Relationship: Synchronizing Geo-Anthropology," in Wickberg & Gärdebo, *Environing Media*, 44.
13. For a history of the concept of "environment" and its relationship to terms that preceded it or paralleled it in other languages, see Etienne S. Benson, *Surroundings: A History of Environments and Environmentalisms* (University of Chicago Press, 2020). Benson notes that the word did not come into widespread use in its modern sense until the second half of the 19th century. Benson, *Surroundings*, 9–10.
14. Global climate modification through solar geoengineering (stratospheric aerosol injection) has been discussed since the late 1960s, but the recognition of environmental modification through human action has been understood and used for much longer. See, e.g., George Perkins Marsh, *The Earth as Modified by Human Action* (1874), and more recent scholarship such as Yuriko Furuhata, *Climatic Media: Transpacific Experiments in Atmospheric Control* (Duke University Press, 2022), and Philipp Lehmann, *Desert Edens: Colonial Climate Engineering in the Age of Anxiety* (Princeton University Press, 2022). On modification through tree planting for environmental and political control, see, e.g., Irus Braverman, *Planted Flags: Trees, Land, and Law in Israel/Palestine* (Cambridge University Press, 2014), and Rosetta Elkin, *Plant Life: The Entangled Politics of Afforestation* (University of Minnesota Press, 2022).
15. As Sörlin and Wormbs state, "The environing technology of computerized climate science brought into being a global climate that hitherto had not existed." Sörlin & Wormbs, "Environing Technologies," 113.
16. Benson, *Surroundings*, 12. Emphasis added. See also Paul Warde, Libby Robin & Sverker Sörlin, *The Environment: A History of the Idea* (Johns Hopkins University Press, 2018).
17. Benson, *Surroundings*, 13.
18. Corner also addresses this issue in the following: "Like other instruments and methods of representation, the aerial view reflects *and* constructs the world; it has enormous landscape agency, in real and imaginary ways," in "Aerial Representation and the Making of Landscape," in James Corner & Alex MacLean, *Taking Measures Across the American Landscape* (Yale University Press, 1996), 16, 18. For an excellent study of the mutual formation of aerial views and physical landscapes, including the design of airports, see Sonja Dümpelmann, *Flights of Imagination: Aviation, Landscape, Design* (University of Virginia Press, 2014).
19. As Anuradha Mathur and Dilip da Cunha observe, "Water is everywhere before it is somewhere." For critical and compelling explorations about the divide between land and water, see their body of work, including *Mississippi Floods* (Yale University Press, 2001), *SOAK: Mumbai in an Estuary* (Rupa & Co., 2009), and *Design in the Terrain of Water* (Applied Research and Design, 2014). The quote is from the preface to *Design in the Terrain of Water.*
20. Sara B. Pritchard, "Toward an Environmental History of Technology,"

in Andrew C. Isenberg (ed.), *The Oxford Handbook of Environmental History* (Oxford University Press, 2018), 236–37. Pritchard notes that the convergence of environmental history and the history of technology began in the late 1990s.

21. On the relationship to landscape architecture, see, e.g., Dianne Harris & D. Fairchild Ruggles, *Sites Unseen: Landscape and Vision* (University of Pittsburgh Press, 2007); Vittoria Di Palma, "Is Landscape Painting?"; and Robin Kelsey, "Is Landscape Photography?" in Gareth Doherty & Charles Waldheim (eds), *Is Landscape...?: Essays on the Identity of Landscape* (Routledge, 2016).
22. Though media ecology, as its name implies, considered this larger context of technologies and communication, its focus tended to be on electronic mass media.
23. See, e.g., Jonathan Crary, *Techniques of the Observer: On Vision and Modernity in the Nineteenth Century* (MIT Press, 1990).
24. For some of the critiques coming from geography, see, e.g., J. B. Harley, "Deconstructing the Map," *Cartographica* 26, no. 2 (1989): 1–20; Jeremy W. Crampton & John Krygier, "An Introduction to Critical Cartography," *ACME: An International E-Journal for Critical Geographies* 4, no. 1 (2006): 11–33; and the work of Denis Cosgrove, Denis Wood, and Mark Monmonier, among others.
25. On the creative potential of mapping, see James Corner, "The Agency of Mapping: Speculation, Critique and Invention," in Denis Cosgrove (ed.), *Mappings* (Reaktion Books, 1999).
26. As Matthew H. Edney contends, cartography is an *ideal* that underlies all critiques of mapping, but it has no bearing on practice. See Edney, *Cartography: The Ideal and Its History* (University of Chicago Press, 2019).
27. See "In Conversation with William Rankin," in Karen M'Closkey & Keith VanDerSys (eds), *LA+ Interdisciplinary Journal of Landscape Architecture* 12 (2020): 27. As Corner suggests in "The Agency of Mapping," mapping is not only a means of projecting power-knowledge, but it also "unfolds potential," 213. See also Leah A. Lievrouw, "Materiality and Media in Communication and Technology Studies: An Unfinished Project," in T. Gillespie, P. J. Boczkowski & K. A. Foot (eds), *Media Technologies: Essays on Communication, Materiality, and Society* (MIT Press, 2014).
28. Jussi Parikka, *Operational Images: From the Visual to the Invisual* (University of Minnesota Press, 2023), 9.
29. Ibid., 99.
30. Corner, "Aerial Representation," 15; Parikka, *Operational Images*, 98.
31. John May, *Signal. Image. Architecture.* (Columbia University Press, 2019), 52.
32. Ibid., 39.
33. W. J. T. Mitchell, *Image Science: Iconology, Visual Culture, and Media Aesthetics* (University of Chicago Press, 2015). Mitchell is not arguing that digitalization makes no difference, only that this shift occurred within a constellation of other social, cultural, and technological changes and cannot be reduced to an analog-digital binary, which we agree with.
34. Mitchell, *Image Science*, 51.
35. This oft-quoted phrase is probably Marshall McLuhan's most famous. For a brief essay, see Lance Strate, "Understanding 'Medium' in the Media Ecology Tradition," in Jeremy Swartz & Janet Wasko (eds), *Media: A Transdisciplinary Inquiry* (Intellect, Ltd., 2021), 87–98.
36. The italics are a quote from Pritchard, "Toward an Environmental History of Technology," 236.
37. Peters, *Marvelous Clouds*, 11–12.
38. Paraphrased from Bishnupriya Ghosh & Bhaskar Sarkar (eds), "Media and Risk: An Introduction," in *The Routledge Companion to Media and Risk* (Routledge, 2020), 3. The editors note that "Risk mobilizes media technologies and infrastructures." Ibid., 4.
39. On the relationship between media and environment, Lance Strate indicates that when something becomes routine, "it will recede into the background, fade from our awareness, move out of our field of selective attention and perception, and become effectively invisible, essentially imperceptible and therefore environmental." Lance Strate, *Media Ecology: An Approach to Understanding the Human Condition* (Peter Lang, 2017), 112. For "media ecology" beyond its use as a metaphor for the human relationship to information and communications technologies and instead referring to technologies that gather information about environments, including their use in ecology for habitat monitoring, see Heise, "Unnatural Ecologies," 165. On the potential of embedded technologies in landscape architecture, see project examples in Bradley Cantrell & Justine Holzman, *Responsive Landscapes: Strategies for Responsive Technologies in Landscape Architecture* (Routledge, 2015).
40. Corner, "Aerial Representation," 16.
41. Sörlin, "Environing and the Human-Earth Relationship," 44.

Measuring the Sky from the Curve of the Earth

Jeffrey Moro

World map of weather stations. The red plus symbol highlights the Fogo Island station.

Weather stations are physical structures comprising diverse scientific instruments that measure meteorological phenomena. Some are building-sized facilities, while others are small enough to hold in your hand. They are located on land or at sea, or even—through weather balloons launched from such sites—reach high into the atmosphere. Larger weather stations often have staff who collect data and maintain the instruments; others, particularly those in remote geographic locations, are at least partially or even completely automated. It's difficult to fix a hard number to how many weather stations are operating across the planet right now—the global network for the World Meteorological Organization (WMO), an agency of the United Nations tasked with "promoting international cooperation on atmospheric science," comprises over 10,0000 national-level

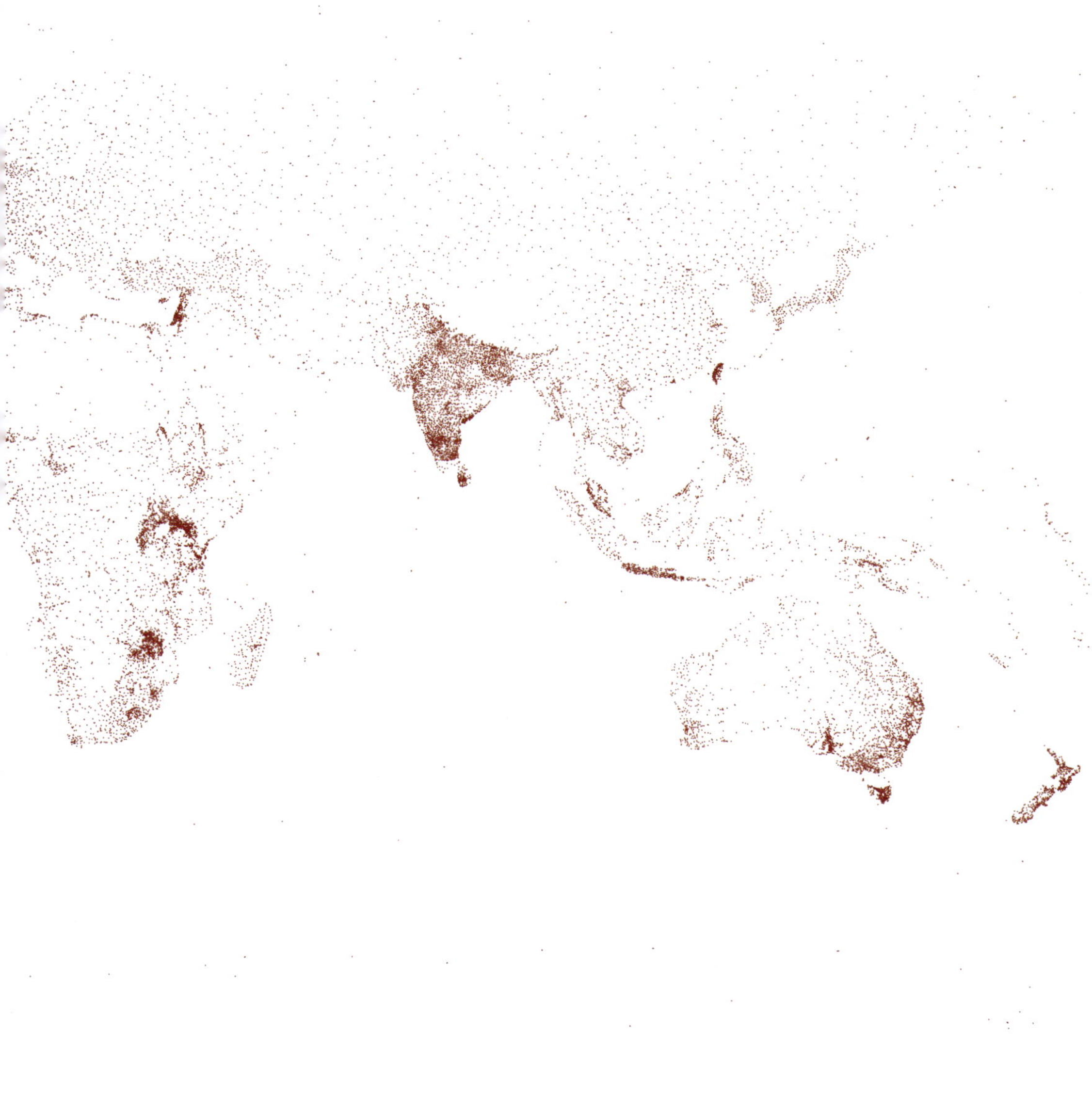

stations.[1] Smaller weather stations run by local jurisdictions, research scientists, private forecasting companies, and amateur weather enthusiasts add another zero to that number. The data weather stations collect serve a range of scientific and industrial functions, from the short-term data that power weather forecasting, to the regular monitoring of atmospheric conditions, to the long-term record-keeping essential to climate modeling. Taken together, weather stations serve as the front lines of the forecast. They are a globally distributed sensory apparatus continuously mediating environmental phenomena into meteorological data. As such, weather stations are windows into the meteorological landscapes of specific places, both in the moment of such data's collection as well as over climatological history.

While individuals have maintained weather records throughout written civilization, weather stations emerge in a recognizably contemporary form in the late 18th and early 19th centuries.[2] They arose in part due to two historical and scientific tendencies: first, the invention of scientific instruments capable of measuring such qualities as temperature (the thermometer), humidity (the hygrometer), and wind speed (the anemometer); and second, a political drive to establish territorial control over newly expanding empires.[3] In the United States, for instance, the first weather station networks were volunteer organizations that submitted observations in a tabular format to a central office run by the Smithsonian.[4] In 1870, President Ulysses S. Grant signed a joint congressional resolution creating the Weather Bureau, the ancestor of today's National Weather Service. Under the auspices of the Secretary of War, a testament to how weather data were considered complex and vital enough only to be entrusted to the armed forces, the Weather Bureau was tasked with "[taking] meteorological observations at the military stations in the interior of the continent."[5] Nevertheless, as historian of science Philipp Lehmann notes, the early stages of meteorological development were marked by a disjuncture between "the global vision" of data standardization and the messy physical realities of meteorology in practice: broken instruments and untrained observers alike stymied attempts to collect useful and consistent data.[6] With the development of computational weather prediction in the 20th century, weather stations became increasingly sophisticated nodes in a digital network. New kinds of sensing technologies alongside their concomitant miniaturization further multiplied weather stations and made their operations possible in more challenging environments, from far-flung islands to inner cities. However, the distribution of weather stations is still imperfect, leading to elisions in the data they collect. Furthermore, their operation is contingent on proper geographic siting, to say nothing of mitigating

Liam Gillick, "A Variability Quantifier (The Fogo Island Red Weather Station)," 2022.

signal interference from both human-made and natural causes. As media technologies, weather stations are thus in continuous conversation with the landscapes in which they operate, not simply as observers of conditions, but as active participants in the construction of meaningful weather data.

This chapter explores the formal relationship between weather stations and the landscapes they mediate. In it, I argue that weather stations as media technologies themselves are key to a meteorological project of distinction—that is, distinguishing between those environmental phenomena that will produce meaningful data and those that are statistical noise or interference. Articulating these distinctions entails a range of media techniques for the calibration of landscapes, from site selection to ongoing landscape management, which in turn influence a station's capacity to collect "good" data. Furthermore, just as technical instruments mediate landscapes, so too do landscapes leave their traces on instruments themselves, wearing them down over time and leaving friction and gaps in the meteorological record.

I pursue this argument in two moves. First, I explore weather stations as media technologies in and of themselves, asking how they collect their data and what impacts landscapes have in turn on such collection. Drawing on official governmental meteorological best practices and analysis of sensing technologies, I show how weather stations must respond dynamically to their changing environment, and how such shifts leave traces in stations' records. In particular, I also read landscape management in and around weather stations as a media technique that enables the construction of the social-scientific idea of "good"

Visualizations of four seasonal monthly weather averages from the Fogo Island weather station. The lines result from repeated daily temperature and wind direction samples plotted over one month.

weather data, which is to say data that are consistent, legible, and standardized. Second, I explore how media artists refract these technical and environmental questions through work that takes weather stations as points of aesthetic and formal departure. Specifically, I take up British artist Liam Gillick's 2022 work, "A Variability Quantifier (The Fogo Island Red Weather Station)," a fully operational weather station on Fogo Island off the coast of Newfoundland. "Quantifier" blurs distinctions between art object and scientific instrument in the service of a critique of how meteorological data get constructed and which communities can participate in global meteorological networks. Furthermore, it prompts questions about subjectivity in relation to weather stations: how the putatively dispassionate gaze of automatic sensor equipment, while useful from the perspective of scientific inquiry, elides other ways of sensing weather in place, particularly for remote landscapes like that of Fogo Island.

Grounding the Weather Station

Since 1954, the World Meteorological Organization has published the *Guide to Meteorological Instruments and Methods of Observation*, a volume of best practices for the operation, siting, and maintenance of weather stations. Now in its seventh edition, the *Guide* runs nearly 700 pages in length, detailing proper procedures not only for the measurement of familiar quantities like temperature and humidity, but also ones less known to casual viewers of the daily forecast, such as soil moisture, ozone, and cloud observation. Each of these data points requires distinct meteorological instruments, the operating conditions for which must be carefully balanced against each other. A schematic drawing from the *Guide* shows the proper site of such instruments, with minimum distances between them to limit interference. The requirements are complex. Finding a proper site that satisfies all of the best practices is, by the *Guide*'s own admission, a challenging first step. Weather station sites should be level patches of ground "preferably no smaller than 25m x 25m…covered with short grass or a surface representative of the locality."[7] Trees, buildings, and steep slopes are weather stations' enemies, as they can cast shadows and form disruptive microclimates. However, some instruments, such as rain gauges, dislike fully open air and require some dimension of enclosure. In a moment of candor, the *Guide* acknowledges that "it is obvious that some of the above considerations [for instrument siting] are somewhat contradictory and require compromise solutions."[8] The work of recording "good" weather data, which is to say data that are useful for the particular forecasting ends of a given station, begins with the ground itself.

The consequences of landscape on the operation and efficacy of weather stations are particularly evident in the case of climate data, even more so than weather data. Historian of science Paul N. Edwards characterizes the distinction between these categories as core to a quiet war within the atmospheric sciences. On the one hand, meteorologists who make forecasts need rapid returns on short-term, localized weather data; whereas climate scientists, on the other hand, need standardized consistency across multiple temporal and spatial scales.[9] This process, which Edwards terms the work of "making data global," entails attending to—and making sense out of—the necessarily variegated material reality of what data capture looks like on the ground. For example, as climate science concretized as a field in the 20th century, its practitioners began to take a harder look at previous decades of weather data. There, they found numerous interferences that made the data less meaningful for the durational time scales of climatology. One such interference, for example, is the "urban heat island effect," whereby urban landscapes record significantly higher average temperatures than rural ones, due to population concentration and heat-absorbing building materials such as asphalt. Even originally rural stations could be subsumed by expanding suburbanization, leaving traces in the record. Urban environments, where most weather stations are sited due to population proximity, also pose challenges to the basic collection of such data as temperature. Shadows from nearby buildings are enough to introduce "local peculiarities" to weather data, according to the *Guide*. Those looking to avoid interference by siting weather stations atop buildings will be similarly thwarted, as "[such measurements] are of doubtful significance and use because of the variable vertical temperature gradient and the effect of the building itself on the temperature distribution."[10] While meteorologists and climate scientists can employ sophisticated error-checking and normalizing mechanisms to account for inconsistencies in local data, where and how a station is sited—to say nothing of how these factors change over time—substantially influences the construction of weather data.

I say the "construction" of weather data here rather than the "collection" of weather data to draw attention to the processes of environmental mediation in which weather stations participate. Weather data, as

Image of the weather station in the context of the Fogo Island landscape, 2022.

the example of the urban heat island effect demonstrates, are not latent in the environment, waiting to be discovered by the correct instruments at the right time. Now, this is a basic truism of physics - even the most putatively "stable" climates demonstrate great variation over space and time. However, it points to how determining *how* one measures an environment is as much a social as a technical problem. Writing on temperature, media theorist Nicole Starosielski observes that systems of scientific measurement are ones of social distinction as much as reflections of physical phenomena. Temperature "offers a relational system, a means of sorting, separating, and orienting... The fact that many people believe temperature is an objective measurement system makes these [relational] descriptions even more powerful metaphors."[11] For weather stations, one of the most consequential distinctions they draw is between signal and noise. Which environmental phenomena are considered meaningful and which constitute pesky interference is a problem the *Guide* takes up at length, even going so far as to offer a crash course in information theory for weather station operators:

> Any measurement can be regarded as made up of two parts: the signal and the noise. The signal constitutes the quantity which is to be determined, and the noise is the part which is irrelevant. The noise may arise in several ways: from observational error [or] because *the observation is not made at the right time and place.*[12]

The "right time and place" are thus crucial for the construction of weather data. From the perspective of mediation, they are as load-bearing as the instruments themselves, conditions that must be calibrated in order to produce meaningful data. Land *matters* to weather data in the sense that it has material impacts for which scientists must account. Weather station siting and land management are media techniques, systems of enculturated practice repeated and developed over time, which in turn make possible technology's operation. Interventions upon the land—even in something as simple as choosing where to site a station, how to clear away brush, whether to move a station when trees grow taller or get cut down, and how to account for all these shifts in a station's record—are crucial meteorological work.

Weather at the World's Edge

Fogo Island, a rocky outcrop of low-lying forests buffeted by the North Atlantic's currents, lies two dozen miles off the coast of Newfoundland. Its name comes from the Portuguese word for "fire," a memory of the 16th-century fishing crews who used the island as a base, although Fogo is itself the ancestral home of the Mi'kmaq and Beothuk First Nations tribes.[13] The sea around Fogo is colloquially known as "Iceberg Alley," for as the spring thaws into summer, chunks of Arctic ice drift down and past the island. Iceberg watching, a Fogo pastime, has even become a cornerstone of the island's burgeoning tourism industry. On Fogo's northern side, off a forested walking trail, lies a curious sight that stands out from the island's brown and green turf: the bright red form of a hut, roughly two and a half meters high, with a matching red pier extending out before it, albeit onto the land rather than the nearby sea. Perched on the rear of the hut is a small collection of scientific instruments: a wind vane, an anemometer, and a rain gauge, among others. "A Variability Quantifier (The Fogo Island Red Weather Station)" was installed in October of 2022 by British artist Liam Gillick, whose work spans a range of media but often occupies the terrain of architectural and installation art. True to its name, "Quantifier" belongs simultaneously to the worlds of art and science, with the instruments atop the hut operating as a functional weather station, broadcasting data online.[14] Here then, at the edge of the world, lies one of our most curious weather stations.[15]

In an era of climate crisis, media artists across disciplines have turned to meteorology and climate science as both methodological and aesthetic inspiration for their work. As critic and artist Janine Randerson observes, "the difference between creative and scientific means of meteorological representation has diminished; artists use the same tools and meteorological data streams as scientists to gather digital weather media for their practice."[16] Weather stations, as Gillick's work demonstrates, are no exception. "Quantifier" remediates two architectural forms, that of the fishing pier and that of the weather station. The former is a common sight across Fogo, which long relied on cod—and now, with the depletion of its fishery, lobster—as an economic staple. The latter, by contrast, is new to the island, which had no weather station before Gillick's installation. Rather, Fogo Island has relied on "triangulated data" from weather stations on the mainland to provide what local Fogo arts organization Shorefast, which sponsored in part Gillick's piece, calls a "'best guess' on the day's weather events."[17] "Quantifier's" technology has received relatively little attention in the various press releases and articles written about the work, especially compared to the rest of the structure itself. Based on photographs, the station appears to be a Davis Vantage Pro2, a commercially available weather station popular among amateur weather enthusiasts. Davis is a well-known name in meteorology for their technology's reliability, accuracy, and ability to withstand punishing weather conditions such as those found on Fogo. Its compactness has the advantage of grafting easily onto the rest of "Quantifier's" structure, even as it does disrupt, in its plasticene protrusion, the architectural flow of the rest of the piece—a concession, perhaps, to the requirements of science.

"Quantifier" is part of a broader environmental arts initiative exploring weather stations as conceptual and aesthetic sites called the *World Weather Network*. The *Network*, launched in 2022 by a coalition of 28 arts organizations across the world, including the Fogo Island Arts council, positions itself as an "invitation to look, listen, learn, and act" on the global effects of climate change through art.[18] Each "station" in the network is keyed to a specific geography and offers periodic "reports," which are textual and visual missives from the project to the network more generally. For most of the projects, weather stations act as conceptual metaphors more than technical infrastructures. For example, one such project in the *Network*, "Other Scores of Water" by Luz María Bedoya, produces short films and sound pieces exploring aspects of water in various parts of Peru, including the coasts, mountains, and rainforests. In "Other Scores of Water," the sensing apparatus of its metaphorical weather station is the artist herself, along with local communities and collaborators, whose interpretations of the weather become core to the "reports." Other projects frame landscapes themselves as environmental sensors. "Spiral Jetty," land artist Robert Smithson's landmark 1970 sculpture in the Great Salt Lake, appears in the *Network* recast by the Holt/Smithson Foundation as an index of climate change's effects on Utah. The disappearance and reappearance of "Jetty" due to water level rise and fall, alongside the weathering of the structure more generally, transform the sculpture into a station sensing its own eventual destruction.

Gillick's piece is thus unique among projects in the *Network* for engaging meteorological sensing technologies directly, thereby removing human interpretation from its mediating circuit. That it is an automatic weather station is in line with similar practices for siting stations in remote and rugged locations such as Fogo, which make staffed stations impractical. It also imbues the artwork itself with a kind of meteorological-interpretive power, the station itself "speaking" to its online portal day and night without rest. However, Gillick's decision to append prefabricated equipment to the rest of the structure, like an appendix of sorts, while eminently practical and indeed scientifically valuable, has the effect of drawing perhaps too sharp a line between those parts of this piece that belong to the realm of art and those to the realm of science. Were the rest of "Quantifier" to vanish, save for the Davis equipment, the data it collects would no doubt read the same. Nevertheless, like "Spiral Jetty," the hut part of "Quantifier" will inevitably function as a weather station of sorts, as the wind, rain, and snow of Fogo wear it down over time. In this way, it is precisely in this tension between the quantitative operations of the Davis equipment and the hut structure as a decaying qualitative record of weathering that "Quantifier" speaks most meaningfully to the challenges of meteorological data collection. This is particularly salient to a place like Fogo, which while long excluded from global meteorological infrastructures, is nevertheless one of the places on the planet where one can most easily index the impacts of climate change.

Where Weather Happens

In the course of researching and writing this chapter, I decided the best way to understand the relationship between weather stations and the places they measure was to build a station of my own. Using a miniature computer called a Raspberry Pi and various off-the-shelf components, I attempted to assemble one for the Maryland Institute for Technology in the Humanities (MITH), the research institute at which I work at the University of Maryland. While the technology worked well enough, I quickly ran into a bigger obstacle to my dreams of a weather station of my own—I had nowhere suitable to site it. A handy PowerPoint from the National Weather Service only confirmed my suspicions that no building, courtyard, or side alley on my university's campus would yield good data. I had to avoid both asphalt and concrete, get the station at least 1.2 m off the ground (the anemometer should be ideally 10 meters up, an impossible task), to say nothing of ensuring adequate power and internet connection. My campus weather station, it seems, was doomed to be little more than a technical curiosity. Of course, unlike Fogo Island, the Washington, DC, metro area where I live and work is densely thicketed with weather stations. One more would be superfluous. Nevertheless, my failed experiment points to a paradox that has run through this chapter, namely that landscapes can easily overwhelm the sensory capacities of weather stations, especially in urban environments. A place like Fogo is perfectly suited for a weather station yet didn't have one until a well-funded and internationally renowned artist chose it as an installation site. Nor will it have one for long, as "Quantifier" is only committed to display on the island until 2026.

Since the emergence of atmospheric science *as* a science in the late 19th century, meteorologists have sought to negotiate a tension between the dream of truly global data and the messy realities of data collection on the ground. These tensions grow only more frayed in the face of climate change, whose global effects trouble received notions of what "good" meteorological data even constitute. Distinctions between environmental signal and environmental noise have begun to fray. It may very well be that the *World Weather Network*'s culturally specific data collection practices, while differing widely from those of the atmospheric sciences, nevertheless chart new (or indeed, quite old) methods for making climate change legible, especially on those landscapes otherwise neglected by the meteorological community. Weather stations are media technologies that reflect these conceptual and material tensions—tensions between the global and the local, between that which is coded as scientific and that which is coded as cultural, and between that which is coded as environmental and that which is coded as human. As climate change collapses these distinctions, scientists and scholars of media alike must collaborate on new models for the collection of weather data that consider such data's social and material contingency.

Notes

1. World Meteorological Organization, "Observations—Data—Modelling," https://web.archive.org/web/20230724110934/https://public.wmo.int/en/our-mandate/what-we-do/observations (accessed July 12, 2023).
2. However, the historical honor of the "first" weather station far precedes these dates. It traditionally belongs to a Roman building in Athens called the Horologion of Andronikos Kyrrhestes, dating from 50 to 200 BCE. The Horologion, also known as the Tower of the Winds, is an octagonal building into which were installed various weather vanes, sundials, and water clocks that could tell the time and the wind's direction. See UNESCO, "Tower of the Winds, Greece," https://www3.astronomicalheritage.net/index.php/show-entity?identity=90&idsubentity=1 (accessed July 10, 2023).
3. What media historian Caren Kaplan has termed the "view from above" afforded by aerial surveying technologies in the late 19th and early 20th centuries. See Caren Kaplan, *Aerial Aftermaths: Wartime from Above* (Duke University Press, 2018), 52–53.
4. Sara J. Grossman, "Archiving Weather Data," *Process: A Blog for American History* (May 4, 2017), https://www.processhistory.org/archiving-weather-data/ (accessed July 12, 2023).
5. NOAA US Department of Commerce, "History of the National Weather Service," https://www.weather.gov/timeline (accessed July 12, 2023).
6. Philipp Lehmann, "Average Rainfall and the Play of Colors: Colonial Experience and Global Climate Data," *Studies in History and Philosophy of Science* 70 (2018): 47.
7. World Meteorological Organization, *Guide to Meteorological Instruments and Methods of Observation* (World Meteorological Organization, 2008), ch. 1, I.1–4.
8. Ibid., ch. 1, I.1-5.
9. Paul N. Edwards, *A Vast Machine: Computer Models, Climate Data, and the Politics of Global Warming* (The MIT Press, 2010), 287–88.
10. World Meteorological Organization, *Guide to Meteorological Instruments and Methods of Observation* (World Meteorological Organization, 2008), ch. 2, I.2–3.
11. Nicole Starosielski, *Media Hot and Cold* (Duke University Press, 2021), 11.
12. World Meteorological Organization, *Guide to Meteorological Instruments and Methods of Observation* (World Meteorological Organization, 2008), ch. 1, I.1–15, italics mine.
13. Fogo Island Inn, "Indigenous Peoples and Fogo Island," https://fogoislandinn.ca/indigenous-peoples-and-fogo-island (accessed July 12, 2023).
14. The data can be accessed here: https://www.fogoislandweatherstation.com/.
15. The Flat Earth Society, a pseudoscientific organization promulgating theories that the Earth is, in fact, flat, considers Fogo Island to be one of the mythical "four corners" of the planet. In the service of tourism, Fogo has run with this perhaps dubious distinction, even hosting the Museum of the Flat Earth, dedicated to the history of the Flat Earth movement in Canada. See https://web.archive.org/web/20231207133859/http://www.museumoftheflatearth.ca/ (accessed January 15, 2025).
16. Janine Randerson, *Weather as Medium: Toward a Meteorological Art* (The MIT Press, 2018), 43.
17. Shorefast, "Liam Gillick to Unveil a Weather Station on Fogo Island," https://fogoislandinn.ca/liam-gillick-to-unveil-a-weather-station-on-fogo-island/ (accessed July 12, 2023).
18. World Weather Network, "World Weather Network – About," https://worldweathernetwork.org/about/ (accessed July 12, 2023).

The Levels of Lakes: Between Baselines and Research Objects

Wilko Graf von Hardenberg

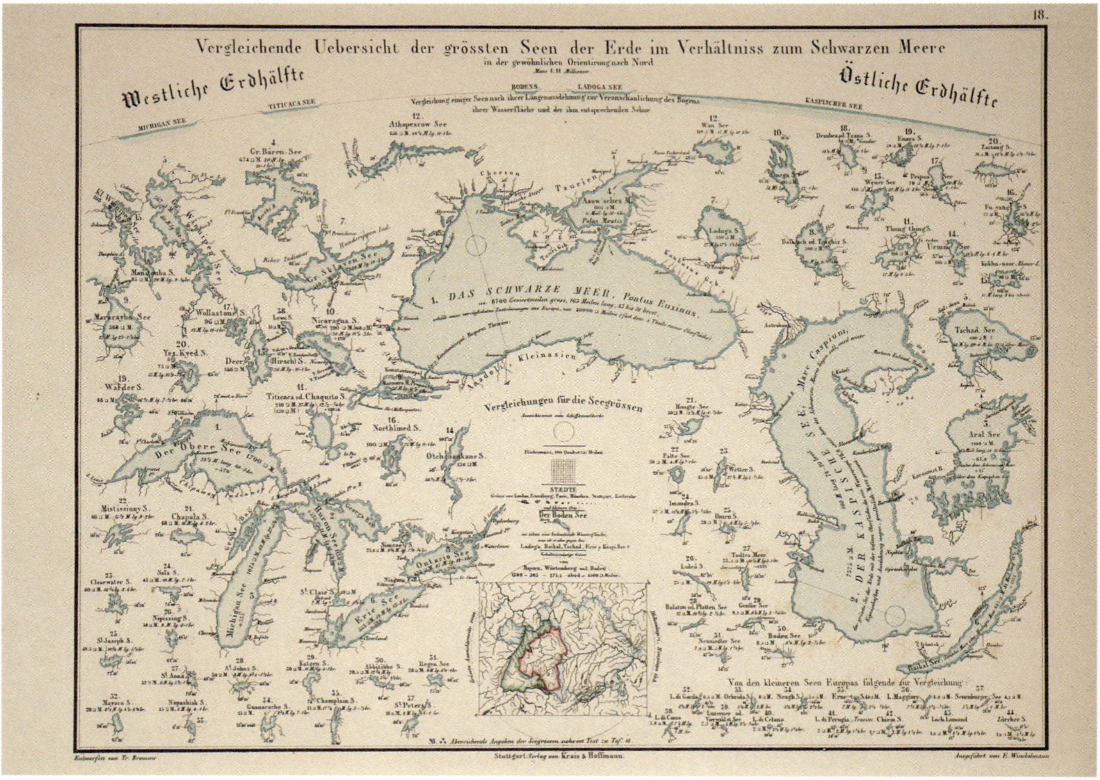

Drawing comparing Earth's largest lakes to the Black Sea, 1851.

Lakes and their levels are embedded in the history of geodesy both as reference points for local measurements and as objects of scientific inquiry. Before mean sea level was chosen, through a rather lengthy process, as the standard reference point for elevations, the level of a nearby lake was frequently used as the zero from which to measure the altitude of mountains.[1] In 1787, the Swiss physicist Horace Bénédict de Saussure, for instance, used the level of Lake Geneva as the primary baseline for his assessment of the elevation of Mont Blanc. By the end of the 19th century, geodesists around the world had settled upon mean sea level, but this did not immediately become a national standard in the United States. Around the turn of the 20th century, each county, municipality, and railway company still adopted its own particular vertical datum that could refer to virtually anything, from an arbitrarily chosen benchmark to a lake. For example, some municipalities in the region adjoining the Duluth & Iron Range railroad line in Minnesota were still using the mean low water of Lake Superior as their datum of reference, while the city of Duluth itself adopted the lake's mean level.[2]

However, the levels of lakes and inland seas were also objects of scientific inquiry on their own. In 1829, the German polymath Alexander von Humboldt initiated, during his expedition through Russia, a scientific quest for the level of the Caspian Sea and its elevation with respect to the open seas. Between 1837 and 1848, the Jordan Depression, at whose bottom lies the Dead Sea, was visited by no less than five expeditions to determine how much lower than the Mediterranean it lies. In the United States, changes in the levels of the Great Lakes have been recorded continuously since 1860. Accordingly, multiple inquiries have been started on how to control them.

In this essay, I address the place of lakes and inland seas in geodesy and geography in the long 19th century, how gathering data about lake levels directly affected their use and management in different parts of the world, and how this history speaks to current debates about the role of humans and capital in changing the geographical and geological context in which we live. Changes in the height of water surfaces, which also directly affect the extension of the lakes, involve several factors—meteorological, hydrographical, physiographical, geological, and anthropic. Thus, lakes offer a complex palette of reasons for their variability with respect to the oceans. Considering this, I am interested in highlighting how lake levels, as both baselines

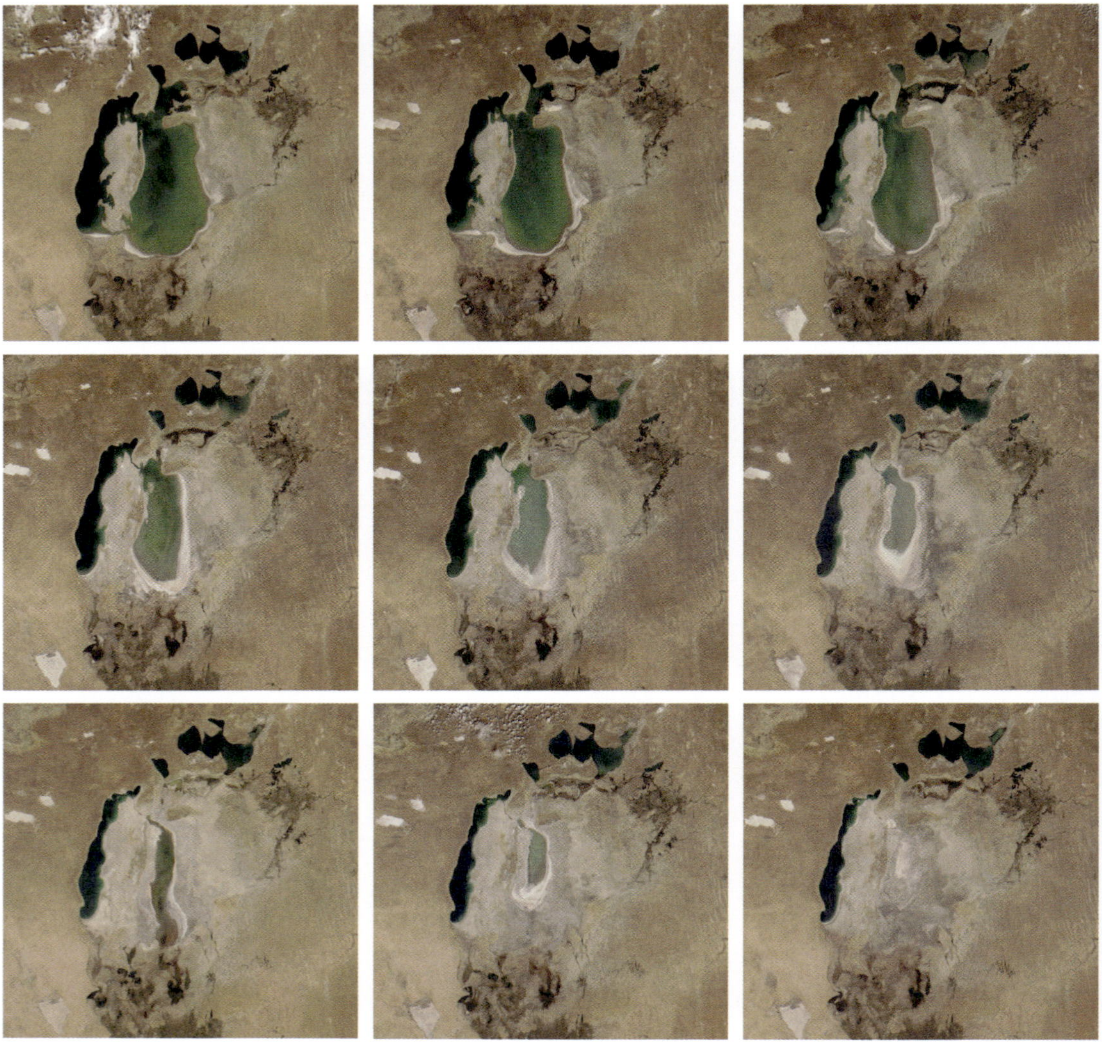

Array of satellite images showing water level reduction of the Aral Sea between 2000–2018.

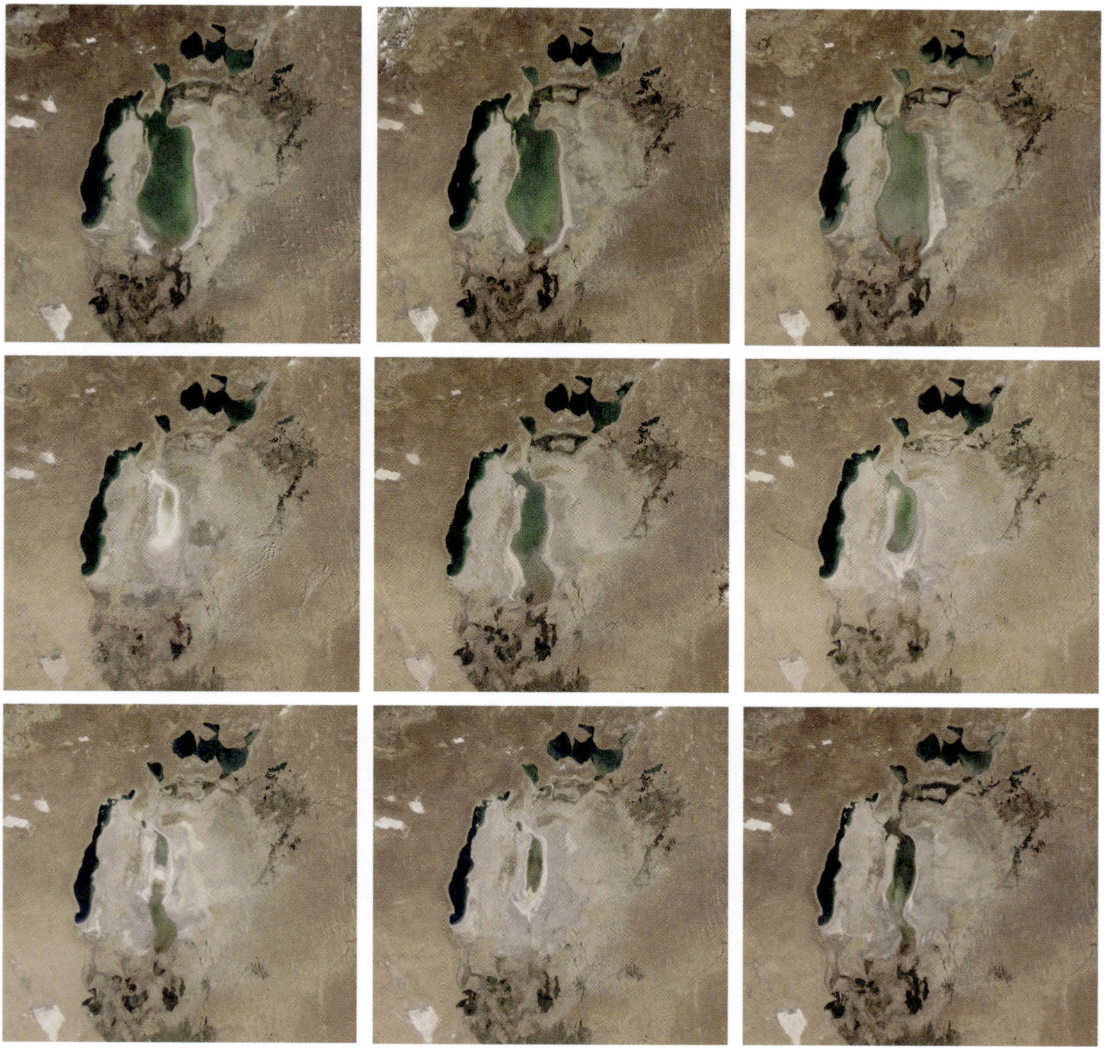

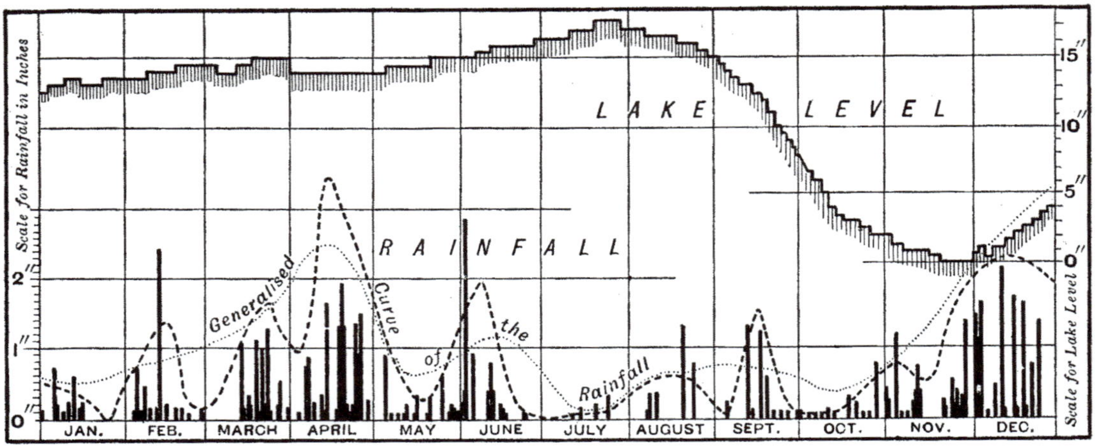

Diagram illustrating the fluctuations in the level of the Victoria Nyanza, at Ntebe, in 1900, compared with the rainfall.

and objects of scientific inquiry, can be read as environmental media, embedded in a relationship of reciprocal environing with their surroundings. In other words, lakes materially make coastal environments through their variations in level, while the social and economic activities along the coasts of lakes have a central and often immediate role in determining lake levels.[3]

This immediacy makes historical debates about lake level variations forebears of more recent debates about global sea level change. Anthropic causes were, for instance, acknowledged as possible factors in the variability of lake levels earlier than in the case of the sea. Similarly, the role of climate and weather in determining water levels in lakes and inland seas was an object of contention in the scientific literature from early on. In both cases, the analysis of lake level data contributed to shaping how water levels were managed by various actors. Level data were, thus, intermediaries in the definition of technical knowledge about lakes and inland seas. Such parallelisms show the transposability of environmental media, hinting at the usefulness of historical research in contextualizing human representations of the environment throughout time.

As the Caspian Sea is the world's largest inland water body, its level and vertical position relative to the oceans have been major objects of inquiry throughout the modern age. According to a letter sent by Wilhelm von Struve, the director of the Tartu observatory, to Humboldt in 1837, the height of its water had by then already been assessed with a certain degree of accuracy. A preliminary survey estimated the Caspian Sea to be between 29 and 32.5 meters (101.2±5 Russian feet) below the Black Sea.[4] Final results reported a few years later by Humboldt affirmed that the depression was about 25 meters below the level of the sea. However, in neither case was it specified how the level of the Caspian or Black Sea had been determined. Before the 1830s, repeated attempts had already been made to determine the extent of the Caspian depression barometrically. The results oscillated wildly between 25 and 118 meters, and they also referred, in this case, to a multiplicity of reference points.[5]

To explain the formation of such a vast depression as the Aralo-Caspian, Humboldt makes an example of what would happen to the Mediterranean if the Strait of Gibraltar were closed. The sea would turn into a lake, and evaporation would cause a reduction in its size, bringing vast parts of the seabed to the surface. A depression would, therefore, come into place in the area, he claims, essentially due to meteorological causes. In this respect, Humboldt asserted also that the Dead Sea "offers the closest analogy with the isolated basin of the Caspian Sea."[6]

Toward the end of the 1830s, multiple European and American scholars affirmed independently that the Dead Sea lies significantly lower than the Mediterranean. While this might have been known to the local population for centuries, the geodesists' work was the first recorded attempt to determine how low the lake lies. Between 1837 and 1838, at least five groups traveled in the region with barometers to survey the levels of the Jordan depression. However, certainty in this regard was only reached about a decade later through trigonometric leveling. After repeated attempts, a precise assessment of the level of the Dead Sea was finally provided in 1848 by the expedition led by the American Navy officer William Francis Lynch.[7]

Historical variations of the Great Lakes were another major issue of debate in scientific circles throughout the 19th and early 20th centuries. The lakes formed due to the retreat of glaciers at the end of the last ice age. By 1888, the lakes appeared to have been stable for many centuries after millennia of post-glacial oscillations that had radically modified their aspect and shape. The fact that most changes to the vast expanse of connected inland waters occurred on a geological timescale led scholars and practitioners to consider their levels as permanent for all practical purposes. Variations were, at this point, attributed to seasonal changes in rainfall that did not significantly affect their long-term average level. Adopting this view, the lakes appeared good candidates to become local reference points for elevations, as the sea had just become on a global scale.[8]

However, not all were convinced by the stability of the lakes' levels. The issue of their impact on the lakes' navigability, and thus more generally on the region's economy, remained a permanent matter of discussion. In particular, some late 19th-century scholars noticed a "constant tendency of the water to decline."[9] Consequently, river passages and channels were becoming ever shallower, allegedly making navigation more difficult. Work undertaken to counteract these tendencies, for instance, by excavating deeper channels, seemed useless in the long term: in the face of a perceived continuous loss of water, other more radical solutions needed to be broached.

The ways in which this problem was discussed are reminiscent of the alarm raised in recent decades about the drying out of the Aral Sea in Central Asia. This sea was virtually unmapped until the mid-19th century, but by the late 20th century, its level had dropped by 26 meters. Over the same time, its surface and volume diminished by more than 90%. This was the consequence of a veritable ecological collapse of the whole water basin caused by human interference, in particular by the diversion of some of its tributaries by the authorities of the Soviet Union to foster the transformation of the region into a cotton monoculture.[10]

Variations in level are in the nature of lakes. They can follow regular seasonal cycles and more irregular long-term variations. For Lake Erie, the transitory impact of wind on local lake levels has historically been recorded as on par with oscillations in the open sea. The measurement of lakes' levels and depths may easily be affected by the season in which it is performed or even by the time of day. Reference, or "datum," planes were thus introduced to compare depth soundings over time. These are crucial in enabling the planning and mapping of navigation channels through lakes. To ensure that these datum planes always indicate the minimum possible amount of water in each channel, the plane has customarily been set at low water. For some, however, such as property owners, other planes, like mean high water, may be of greater importance as they can be used to demarcate the area within which structures can (mostly) be safely built.[11]

Each of the Great Lakes—except Lakes Michigan and Huron, which are considered a single lake—has its own datum. As has long been the case for sea level measurements, early datum planes were determined from one single measurement, thus making a still picture of a single moment in time into a standard. It is clear that such planes did not reflect the natural variability of the lakes or ensure that they represented an average. The earliest adopted plane of reference was the highest level reached in 1838, when unusually high water was registered. Like the tsunami stones deployed in Japan since the ninth century, this reference plane was oriented toward the land rather than the water: it marked an extreme, telling more of a cautionary tale than giving a history of variations over time.[12]

The problem with using such a plane as a reference for construction works along the lakes' shores and in their harbors was that it was too high. Too many measurements would have involved the use of negative numbers, complicating planning and increasing the chance of errors. From 1876 onwards, reflecting global developments in the definition of sea level as a datum, the primary datum plane used for lake surveys became mean lake level as recorded between 1860 and 1875. However, just like the high water level of 1838 a couple of decades earlier, mean lake level soon proved too high in most cases for effective charting. Until 1933, different levels were used as reference planes for charting and improvement works. Only then were they unified as the low water datum for each individual lake. Subsequently, in 1955, as a means to make the lake levels recorded across the US-Canadian border more comparable, a new joint reference plane was selected: the International Great Lakes Datum, defined, however, not as a low water level, but again as mean water level at a single location: Pointe-au-Pére, Quebec.[13]

Balancing the needs of navigation with those of agriculture, the availability of fresh water and the production of hydropower is central to lake management as part of regional governance. To prevent hydropower, in particular, from significantly changing the level of Lake Superior, an allowed range of acceptable variability was established in the early 20th century. This was, strangely, lower than the recorded natural variability of the lake, and thus it was a limit that was probably impossible to maintain. Further rules were defined about what to do when the levels moved above or below the stated limits. In particular, if the level sank below 183.5 meters (602.1 feet) above mean tide in New York City on average over a month, the allowed outflow should not exceed the "natural" level, that is, the one recorded before any obstruction was set in place in 1887. This reflected an idea of the system's overall stability; however, it did not consider the possibility of mid- to long-term variations in the level of the lake itself. It was the implementation of conservative policies based on the assumption that lake levels are geologically permanent.[14]

Worries about a steady and uncontrollable decline in the levels of the Great Lakes were kindled in 1910 by the completion of a project started by the City of Chicago in 1886 to divert water from Lake Michigan to the Illinois River as a means to preserve its water supply. A major controversy began at this point, mainly about the canal's impact on the lake's overall level and how it might influence navigation. In 1926, the geologist Herman L. Fairchild, an expert in post-glacial landscapes, recorded a particularly low level of the Great Lakes, marked by a steady increase in the rate of decline over the previous six years. He noted how human interference adds new layers of complexity to existing geological processes, already characterized by the absence of clear multiannual cycles and essentially unpredictable.[15]

Due to a combination of climate conditions and soil absorption rates, the supply of water to each individual lake varies, both over the course of one year and from one year to the next. Considering the extension of the lakes' basins, conditions affecting one lake may be radically different from those affecting the others. In addition, as the Great Lakes are connected, each lake downstream is also affected by the levels of its tributaries. These highly variable "natural" conditions are then further affected by human activities such as deforestation, cultivation, and damming. According to Fairchild: "The total effect of human occupation of the basin of the Great Lakes has been a permanent lowering of the lakes."[16] In general, he noted, lakes are evanescent features, doomed to disappear on a geological time scale: "Lakes are extinguished by the downcutting of their outlets and by the filling of their basins." As proof of this, he noted how Lake Superior, which was substantially independent of the other lakes and unaffected by the Chicago diversion, was also experiencing a continuous fall in level at the time. He assumed that the leading cause of the recorded changes in the previous years was related to the weather. In addition, even if he stressed the potential role of human interference in the variability of the level of the Great Lakes, he thought that the actual impact of the diversion on the level of Lakes Michigan and Huron was minimal. Since water would have been extracted continuously, practitioners recognized that there was, however, the possibility of the lowering of the level of the lake becoming more significant in the long term.[17]

As a reaction to the excavation of the Chicago diversion, the State of Wisconsin and others sued the Sanitary District of Chicago and the State of Illinois. Wisconsin state representatives wanted an injunction to restrain the City of Chicago from permanently extracting water from the lake. Their main concern was that the Chicago diversion could significantly reduce water levels and disrupt their rights to use the lake for navigation. They estimated that the canal had the potential to lower the level of the lake by six inches. As we have seen, this claim was not unanimously supported by the scientific community. This was evidently a case of confusion between correlation and causation. While the reduction in level had, indeed, "a substantial and injurious effect upon the carrying capacity of vessels," as claimed in the report presented by the Republican politician Charles Evans Hughes (former governor of New York and Secretary of State) to the

Lake Nyasa/Malawi circa 1860.

Supreme Court in 1926, it was not unequivocal that the diversion was its cause.[18]

Some reactions to the perceived risks posed by the Chicago diversion were more outlandish than just requests for it to be shut. In a move that reminds us of recent debates about the need to use so-called geoengineering to respond to climate changes, in the mid-1920s, the fear that a steady reduction in the Great Lakes' levels might significantly affect the region's economy led C. Lorne Campbell, a Canadian railway engineer, to propose the excavation of a new lake north of Lake Nipigon, the main tributary of Lake Superior. The lake, planned to be about the size of Lake Ontario, would have been created by damming a number of streams in the region between Lake Superior and Hudson Bay, and it was supposed to act as a reserve basin for the Great Lakes. No mention was made of how such massive flooding might have affected the region and its inhabitants.[19]

The turn from the 19th to the 20th century seems to have been the golden age of lake level measurements. European efforts to explore the colonies geodetically connected an increasing number of places worldwide. British colonial officers worked to measure the relative levels of different lakes in their possessions. A campaign for measuring the level of Lake Victoria/Nyanza between current Kenya, Uganda, and Tanzania was started in 1896 with the selection of multiple gauges. Daily measurements were taken and mean levels were computed. A rather significant variability was recorded over the years, with a steady decrease in level in the years prior to 1900. Even anecdotal data provided by Catholic missionaries, who recorded that the lake level had fallen by eight feet since 1881, were listed. Variations were claimed to depend mainly on rainfall cycles: allegedly, the available rainfall data for the period between 1881 and 1901 seemed to confirm this supposition. This conclusion is hard to sustain, as the recorded data do not seem to support it.[20]

Similar care was put into measuring the level of Lake Nyasa/Malawi, between current Malawi, Tanzania, and Mozambique. The level of the lake had been first measured barometrically with respect to sea level by the British in 1859. By the early 20th century, measurements seemed to indicate that the lake level had steadily fallen over the previous decades despite a short-term surge at the turn of the century. Also, in this case, anecdotal data were presented to suggest that the lake's level had been reducing since well before 1887. The navigability of the rivers flowing out of the lake appeared to be at risk: "The best of channels is of little use if there is no water to fill it," claimed Alfred Sharpe, the first governor of then Nyasaland. Once in the 1920s measurements seemed to show that Lake Nyasa was subject to cyclical variations, scholars such as the meteorologist Charles E. P. Brooks and the geologist Frank Dixey proposed that they might be linked to sunspot cycles. This was, however, only an impression due to the specific timeframe chosen for analysis. Later measurements completely disproved such a connection. This debate is reminiscent of the recurrent attacks based on carefully cherry-picked data made by climate skeptics to attempt to disprove the widely accepted anthropogenic nature of global climate change.[21]

While located in a completely different geopolitical context, Lake Nicaragua also played an important role in the global scientific debate at the turn of the 20th century. The area is crossed by one of the routes proposed as an alternative to the Panama Canal to connect the Gulf of Mexico and the Pacific Ocean. It remained relevant even after the completion of the Panama Canal. In the 1960s, the area was proposed as a possible route for US plans to excavate a sea level canal using nuclear explosives. More recently, in 2014, the Nicaraguan government started works, with Chinese funding, to create a second canal crossing the Mesoamerican land bridge. All these projects put at risk not only the area's ecosystems, but also the region's social structures and overall livability, as the lake is Central America's largest freshwater reservoir. Early attempts to survey a route for such a canal encountered a troubling issue with the lake itself: its level appeared to vary over time at a much greater rate than expected. This caused surprise and incredulity among the canal's supporters, as fluctuations were thought to be due exclusively to seasonal variations. As was the case for the African lakes, in the absence of long-term data, surveyors used anecdotal data to support their measurements and conclusions. Considering that rainfall in the area is subject to major variability over time and space, the American geologist Angelo Heilprin, founder of the Geographical Society of Philadelphia, suggested that it would be best for the planners to consider the possibility that the measurements indicating a steady decrease in the lake's level were correct. The possibility of greater long-term variability in the level of the lake forced the proponents of an interoceanic canal passing through Lake Nicaragua to reconsider the feasibility of their plans.[22]

Beyond presenting lake levels as environmental media, this overview of cases in which geodesy affected coastal and lacustrine environments is part of a broader project on the environmental history of science. By this I mean a history of science that takes up the "lived realities of the Anthropocene" and historicizes them in an attempt to contribute to a better understanding of their place in shaping science(s) over time.[23] In doing so, this essay contributes to the analysis of how science interacts bidirectionally with the world. On the one hand, scientific work not only explains the world, but also contributes to making it. Measuring and categorizing lake levels produces particular forms of interaction between lakes and shores and shapes the way societies see and manage these littoral zones. On the other hand, both the way science is done in a particular time and place and its conclusions are not only the products of theories penned at the desks of Ivy League universities, but also of the practicalities of the environments encountered while doing research and of the socioeconomic conditions within which it is produced. In other words, modern science is—as shown in the discussed examples regarding its importance for improving commerce, navigation, and energy production—a product of what has been termed "capitalist world-ecologies," that is, the system of intricate relations between nature and societies governed by global capitalism. As shown, the choice of a certain lake level as a baseline and reference point depended mostly on its usefulness for the growth of capital, rather than any ideal of scientific precision.[24]

Notes

1. On the process by which mean sea level was selected as the *de facto* global standard reference point for elevations, see Wilko Graf von Hardenberg, *Sea Level: A History* (University of Chicago Press, 2024).
2. E. Lester Jones, *Use of Mean Sea Level as the Datum for Elevations*, Special Publications 41 (Government Printing Office, 1917), 5–6, 13.
3. Sverker Sörlin & Nina Wormbs, "Environing Technologies: A Theory of Making Environment," *History and Technology* 34, no. 2 (2018): 101–25.
4. "Our Weekly Gossip," *The Athenaeum*, no. 530 (1837): 929–30. Contemporary measurements indicate that the Caspian Sea is 28 meters below the level of the Black Sea. These refer, however, most probably to the level of the sea at Kronstadt on the Baltic Sea, the main vertical datum used in Russia.
5. Alexander von Humboldt, "On the Comparative Level of Lakes and Seas, as the Caspian, Lake Aral, Black Sea, Red Sea, Mediterranean, Lake Tiberias, Dead Sea, Atlantic, Pacific, &c," *The Edinburgh New Philosophical Journal* 35 (1843): 323–35.
6. Humboldt, "On the Comparative Level of Lakes and Seas," 330.
7. Haim Goren, "How Low Is the Lowest Point on Earth? The Story of Determining the Level of the Dead Sea," *Horizons in Geography/אופקים בגאוגרפיה*, no. 60/61 (2004): 150, 154–56.
8. "Formation of the Great Lakes and Their Changes of Level," *Scientific American* 59, no. 7 (1888): 102.
9. John Chamberlin, "Raising the Water Level of the Great Lakes," *Scientific American* 74, no. 19 (1896): 294.
10. Alexey Butakoff, "Survey of the Sea of Aral," *Journal of the Royal Geographical Society of London* 23 (1853): 93; G. S. Burr, et al., "A History of the Modern Aral Sea (Central Asia) Since the Late Pleistocene," *Quaternary Science Reviews* 206 (2019): 141–49; Maya K. Peterson, *Pipe Dreams: Water and Empire in Central Asia's Aral Sea Basin* (Cambridge University Press, 2019).
11. C. F. B., "Wind Effects on Lake Erie's Water Levels," *Bulletin of the American Meteorological Society* 15, no. 12 (1934): 309; Frank A. Blust, "History and Theory of Datum Planes of the Great Lakes," *International Hydrographic Review* XLIX, no. 1 (1972): 109.
12. Hardenberg, *Sea Level: A History*, 9–10, 48; Blust, "History and Theory of Datum Planes of the Great Lakes," 111. On tsunami stones see Elise Hunchuck, *An Incomplete Atlas of Stones*, 2017, https://cargocollective.com/elisehunchuck/An-Incomplete-Atlas-of-Stones-1 (accessed Oct. 25, 2023).
13. Blust, "History and Theory of Datum Planes of the Great Lakes," 111–14.
14. L. C. Sabin, "Regulation of the Level of Lake Superior and the Development of Water Power at Its Outlet," *The Military Engineer* 12, no. 65 (1920): 405. Mean sea level as measured at Sandy Hook, NJ, by New York was used throughout the Northeast and Midwest as a regional datum by the US Coast and Geodetic Survey. See Jones, *Use of Mean Sea Level as the Datum for Elevations.*
15. Herman L. Fairchild, "Changing Levels of the Great Lakes," *The Scientific Monthly* 22, no. 3 (1926): 193–99.
16. Ibid. 195.
17. Ibid.
18. Abel Wolman, "The Hughes Report on the Great Lakes Levels Controversy," *Journal of the American Water Works Association* 9, no. 1 (1928): 39.
19. "Plan to Solve Great Lakes Problem," *Winnipeg Evening Tribune* (November 6, 1925).
20. E. G. Ravenstein, "The Lake-Level of the Victoria Nyanza," *The Geographical Journal* 18, no. 4 (1901): 403–06.
21. John Kirk, "Notes on the Gradient of the Zambesi, on the Level of Lake Nyassa, on the Murchison Rapids, and on Lake Shirwa," *The Journal of the Royal Geographical Society of London* 35 (1865): 167–69; Alfred Sharpe, "Fall in Level of Central African Lakes: Lake Nyasa," *The Geographical Journal* 29, no. 4 (1907): 467; D. B., "Variations in the Level of Lake Nyasa in Relation to Sunspot Frequency," *The Geographical Journal* 65, no. 5 (1925): 437–39; Francis E. Kanthack, "The Fluctuations of Lake Nyasa," *The Geographical Journal* 98, no. 1 (1941): 23.
22. Christine Keiner, "The Panatomic Canal and the US Environmental-Management State, 1964–78," *Environmental History* 21, no. 2 (2016): 278–87; Angelo Heilprin, "An Assumed Inconstancy in the Level of Lake Nicaragua; a Question of Permanency of the Nicaragua Canal," *Scientific American* 82, no. 8 (1900): 115.
23. Bram Büscher & Robert Fletcher, *The Conservation Revolution: Radical Ideas for Saving Nature Beyond the Anthropocene* (Verso, 2020), 120.
24. Jason W. Moore, "World-Ecology: A Global Conversation," *Sociologia Urbana e Rurale*, no. 120 (October 2019): 10.

"Additional complications have emerged"

Karen M'Closkey and Keith VanDerSys

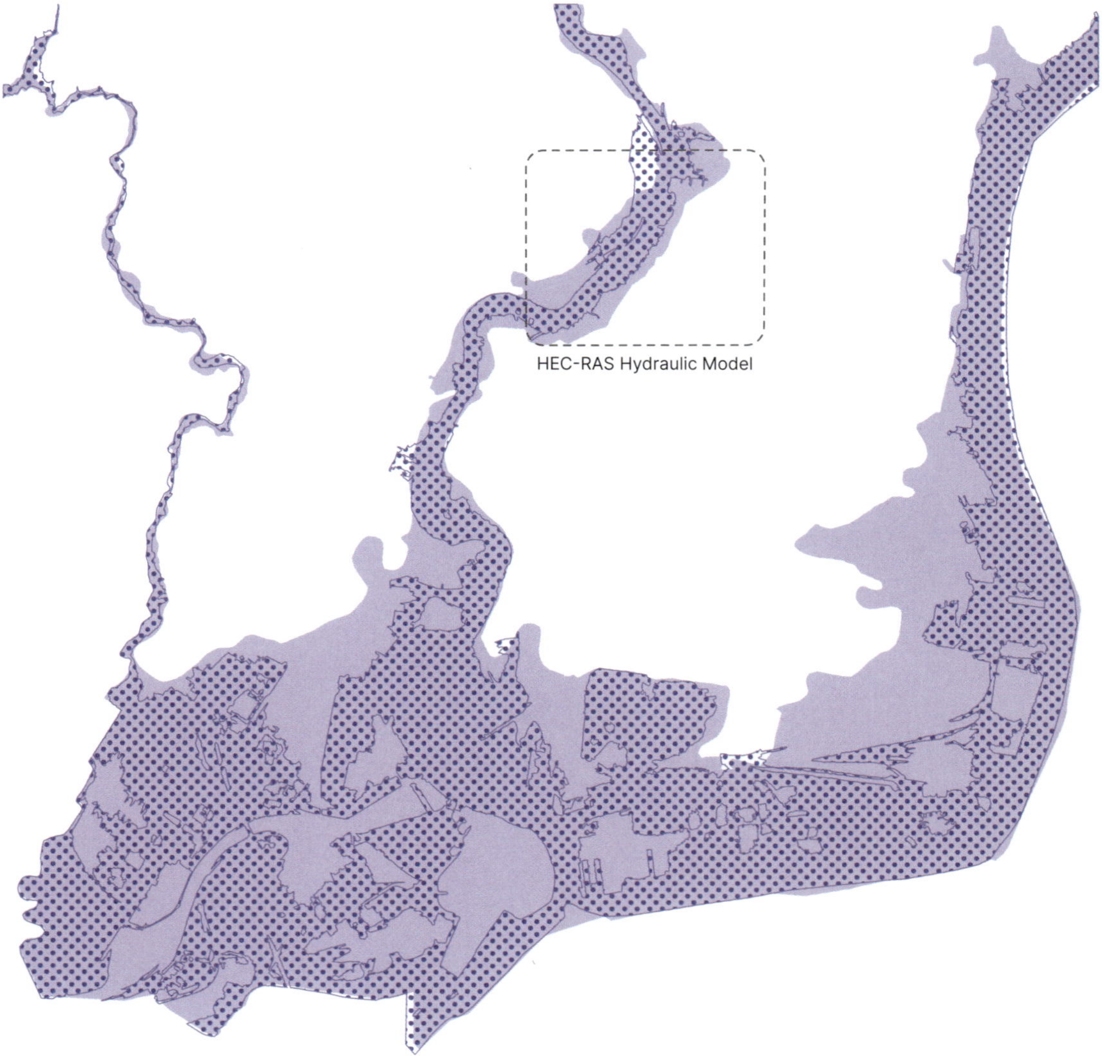

An overlay of Philadelphia's FEMA maps from 1979 and 2015 (purple dot pattern) shows a 14% reduction in the 100 year floodplain area (light purple tone) despite the population in the combined area increasing by more than 5%. Structures included in the 1979 map are no longer covered by the current 2015 FEMA zones, even though the risk of flooding has grown due to increased storm volatility.

On July 4, 2023, as Americans celebrated Independence Day with barbecues and fireworks, the Earth recorded its hottest day in over 120,000 years, a figure that will likely be surpassed by the time of this publication.[1] While this fact confirms the alarming trends projected by climate models, global averages cannot capture how the increasingly severe and unpredictable weather caused by a rapidly heating planet will affect specific places. In *The Great Displacement: Climate Change and the Next American Migration*, journalist Jack Bittle paints a vivid portrait of domestic climate migrants whose intimate stories portend what many millions more Americans will face in the not-too-distant future. Bittle's stories include people ranging from low-wage workers to the ultra-rich; those displaced by headline-grabbing "event" disasters such as hurricanes, floods, and wildfires; and those experiencing slow-moving, or less visible, disasters caused by drought, the creep of high tides, or heat.[2]

Although development in coastal areas and deserts is unfortunately still increasing, this trend will likely reverse as land subsidence and sea level rise push people away from coasts, and lack of water and extreme heat drive them away from deserts. As Bittle makes clear, this displacement will be "unpredictable, chaotic, and life-changing."[3] Not only is the United States, as a nation, ill-equipped to deal with the increasing numbers of people who will need assistance after experiencing loss from a disaster, but it is also woefully unprepared to prevent the same calamities from occurring in areas that are being developed in response to climate-induced migration.[4] This is especially true in the case of floods.

This chapter considers environmental media in relation to the concept of floods as "risk objects" and the *creation* of floodplains as a spatial result of this concept.[5] These media include hydrologic and hydraulic models that incorporate rainfall, water flow rate, and topographic data; flood maps that delineate the location and extent of floodplains based on the outputs of those models; and the physical and statistical apparatus that underlies the measurement of dynamic media—rain, wind, and tides—that the models and maps seek to represent. We use the word "creation" rather than "mapping" because, as discussed below, flood maps are not simply the media through which a hazard is documented. Rather, flood maps yield specific material and social conditions around which a particular understanding of "floodplain" emerges. This understanding conditions how and where we build and thus shapes the practice of landscape architecture. This phenomenon is not unique to the United States; however, we focus our attention on the United States because of the differences in floodplain definitions and regulations between countries.[6]

Floodplains

> [Flood mapping] demonstrates a collective faith in both the value of flood insurance and the need to regulate coastal development—how else to explain public acceptance of a statistical fantasy defined by a hypothetical flood with a recurrence interval of a hundred years?[7]
> —Mark Monmonier, *Coast Lines*

Geographer Mark Monmonier describes the emergence of what he calls the third and fourth coastlines in the second half of the 20th century. The first two coastlines—high and low water lines—can be observed visually and have long been represented on maps. The third and fourth coastlines—floodplains and sea level rise, respectively—are determined statistically using historical records and predictive models. While many map users understand that the variability in fourth coastline projections is due to myriad uncertain factors related to climate change—and that the variability of those factors can be "tested" with online interactive maps of sea level rise—it is easy to forget that this level of variability also applies to the delineation of floodplains, whether they are mapped for riverine flooding or coastal storm surges.

A floodplain depicted on a map does not represent a physical entity; it depicts a probability. It represents the likelihood that a certain amount of rainfall (depth) will occur over a certain period of time (duration) at a certain frequency (the recurrence interval), expected to submerge the land to a certain level (the base flood elevation). In other words, little is natural about these floodplains. They result from an agreed-upon set of practices and standards designed to signal risk and are used to set infrastructure design guidelines and insurance premiums.

Flood maps—officially known as Flood Insurance Rate Maps—are created for the National Flood Insurance Program (NFIP), which is administered by the Federal Emergency Management Agency (FEMA). The NFIP was developed in 1968 in response to increasing development along coasts and rivers, and the creation of our nation's flood maps began in the 1970s.[8] The NFIP was designed to help people who suffered losses due to floods, which it has for some. It was assumed that insurance pricing based on "accurate" flood risk assessments would deter people from moving into floodplains (as defined on the maps), which it has not; population growth in floodplains has outpaced growth in other areas. FEMA and other federal agencies, including the United States Geological Survey (USGS), the United States Army Corps of Engineers (USACE), and the National Oceanic and Atmospheric Association (NOAA), are earnest in their attempts to create better models and maps to reduce the extent of flood damage to people and property. However, the development of national standards for floodplain delineation in the 1960s—standards still in use—have also contributed to the creation of floods because of how floodplains are conceptualized for the purpose of their demarcation on maps.

There are numerous zones delineated on flood maps; however, the areas that are considered at high risk are based on the misleadingly

PDS-based point precipitation frequency estimates with 90% confidence intervals (inches)										
Duration	Average recurrence interval (years)									
	1	2	5	10	25	50	100	200	500	1000
5-min	0.347 (0.31-0.37)	0.414 (0.38-0.45)	0.486 (0.44-0.52)	0.537 (0.49-0.58)	0.599 (0.54-0.65)	0.641 (0.58-0.70)	0.683 (0.62-0.76)	0.720 (0.64-0.79)	0.763 (0.67-0.84)	0.795 (0.69-0.88)
10-min	0.555 (0.51-0.61)	0.661 (0.60-0.72)	0.779 (0.71-0.84)	0.859 (0.78-0.93)	0.955 (0.868-1.04)	1.02 (0.970-1.71)	1.08 (0.97-1.19)	1.14 (1.02-1.25)	1.21 (1.07-1.33)	1.25 (1.10-1.39)
20-min	0.693 (0.63-0.75)	0.831 (0.76-0.90)	0.985 (0.90-1.07)	1.09 (0.94-1.18)	1.21 (1.10-1.32)	1.29 (1.17-1.41)	1.37 (1.24-1.50)	1.44 (1.29-1.58)	1.52 (1.34-1.67)	1.57 (1.38-1.74)
30-min	0.950 (0.87-1.04)	1.15 (1.05-1.25)	1.40 (1.28-1.52)	1.57 (1.44-1.72)	1.79 (1.63-1.95)	1.95 (1.76-2.12)	2.10 (1.89-2.30)	2.24 (2.00-2.46)	2.42 (2.14-2.66)	2.54 (2.24-2.82)
60-min	1.18 (1.09-1.29)	1.44 (1.32-1.57)	1.79 (1.62-1.95)	2.05 (1.88-2.24)	2.39 (2.17-2.60)	2.64 (2.39-2.88)	2.89 (2.61-3.16)	3.14 (2.81-3.45)	3.47 (3.07-3.82)	3.71 (3.26-4.11)
2-hr	1.42 (1.30-1.56)	1.73 (1.58-1.89)	2.16 (1.97-2.36)	2.49 (2.26-2.72)	2.93 (2.64-3.20)	3.27 (2.94-3.58)	3.62 (3.23-3.26)	3.96 (3.51-4.35)	4.43 (3.88-4.89)	4.97 (4.15-5.32)
3-hr	1.56 (1.42-1.71)	1.89 (1.72-2.07)	2.37 (2.16-2.60)	2.74 (2.49-3.00)	3.23 (2.92-3.54)	3.62 (3.25-3.96)	4.02 (3.58-4.41)	4.43 (3.91-4.87)	4.98 (4.33-5.50)	5.41 (4.66-6.00)
6-hr	1.94 (1.78-2.14)	2.35 (2.15-2.59)	2.93 (2.68-3.22)	3.41 (3.10-3.74)	4.07 (3.67-4.46)	4.61 (4.12-5.06)	5.18 (4.59-5.69)	5.78 (5.06-6.36)	6.62 (5.70-7.34)	7.31 (6.19-8.14)
12-hr	2.36 (2.17-2.61)	2.86 (2.62-3.15)	3.58 (3.28-3.95)	4.20 (3.81-4.62)	5.09 (4.57-5.59)	5.84 (5.20-6.42)	6.66 (5.85-7.34)	7.55 (6.54-8.35)	8.85 (7.49-9.84)	9.94 (8.26-11.1)
24-hr	2.72 (2.51-2.96)	3.28 (3.03-3.57)	4.12 (3.80-4.48)	4.83 (4.44-5.24)	5.85 (5.35-6.34)	6.72 (6.11-7.26)	7.65 (6.92-8.26)	8.66 (7.77-9.34)	10.1 (8.99-10.9)	11.4 (9.98-12.3)
2-day	3.14 (2.89-3.41)	3.79 (3.49-4.12)	4.77 (4.39-5.18)	5.58 (5.12-6.05)	6.72 (6.14-7.28)	7.67 (6.98-8.31)	8.69 (7.86-9.40)	9.77 (8.78-10.6)	11.3 (10.1-12.3)	12.6 (11.1-13.7)
3-day	3.31 (3.05-3.60)	3.99 (3.68-4.34)	5.01 (4.62-5.45)	5.84 (5.37-6.34)	7.02 (6.43-7.62)	8.00 (7.30-8.67)	9.04 (8.20-9.80)	10.2 (9.15-11.0)	11.7 (10.5-12.7)	13.0 (11.6-14.2)
4-day	3.48 (3.22-3.80)	4.20 (3.88-4.57)	5.25 (4.84-5.72)	6.11 (5.63-6.64)	7.33 (6.71-7.95)	8.34 (7.61-9.04)	9.40 (8.54-10.2)	10.5 (9.52-11.4)	12.2 (10.9-13.2)	13.5 (12.0-14.7)
7-day	4.07 (3.78-4.41)	4.88 (4.53-5.29)	6.04 (5.60-6.55)	6.99 (6.47-7.57)	8.35 (7.69-9.05)	9.48 (8.69-10.3)	10.7 (9.73-11.5)	11.9 (10.8-12.9)	13.8 (12.4-14.9)	15.2 (13.6-16.5)
10-day	4.62 (4.31-4.98)	5.52 (5.15-5.94)	6.74 (6.27-7.26)	7.72 (7.17-8.31)	9.08 (8.41-9.77)	10.2 (9.40-11.0)	11.3 (10.4-12.2)	12.5 (11.4-13.5)	14.2 (12.9-15.3)	15.6 (14.0-16.8)
20-day	6.24 (5.88-6.64)	7.41 (6.98-7.89)	8.84 (8.32-9.41)	9.97 (9.38-10.6)	11.5 (10.8-12.2)	12.7 (11.9-13.5)	13.9 (13.0-14.8)	15.1 (14.0-16.1)	16.8 (15.5-17.8)	18.0 (16.5-19.2)
30-day	7.78 (7.37-8.21)	9.17 (8.68-9.68)	10.7 (10.1-11.3)	11.9 (11.2-12.5)	13.5 (12.7-14.2)	14.6 (13.8-15.4)	15.8 (14.8-16.7)	17.0 (15.9-17.9)	18.5 (17.2-19.5)	19.6 (18.2-20.7)
45-day	9.89 (9.41-10.4)	11.6 (11.0-12.2)	13.4 (12.7-14.0)	14.7 (13.9-15.4)	16.4 (15.5-17.2)	17.6 (16.7-18.5)	18.8 (17.8-19.7)	19.9 (18.8-20.9)	21.3 (20.0-22.4)	22.3 (20.9-23.5)
60-day	11.8 (11.3-12.4)	13.9 (13.2-14.6)	15.8 (15.1-16.6)	17.3 (16.5-18.2)	19.1 (18.2-20.1)	20.5 (19.4-21.5)	21.7 (20.6-22.8)	22.9 (21.7-24.0)	24.3 (23.0-25.6)	25.3 (23.9-26.6)

Minor (11 ft) Flood Stage
(2 in/ 24hr = 43,600 cfs avg)

Moderate (13 ft) Flood Stage
(4 in/ 24hr = 69,800 cfs avg)

Major (15.5 ft) Flood Stage
(8 in/ 24hr = 101,400 cfs avg)

Peak (17 ft) Flood Stage
(9 in/ 24hr = 137,200 cfs)

Peak Future (23 ft) Flood Stage
(12 in/ 24hr = 174,400 cfs)

NOAA Atlas 14 precipitation frequency data chart for Pennsylvania. 100-year storm events are based on 24-hour precipitation quantities (highlighted in gray). Equivalent rainfall amounts may occur over shorter or longer periods but are not included as recorded storm events. The plans (below) depict flood elevations of the Schuylkill River based on rain gauge data from the watershed catchment.

named 100-year storm (coastal areas have additional designations due to storm surges, tides, and wind, which we will not address here). There has been ample criticism of this nomenclature; we will not repeat it except to remind readers that a 100-year floodplain is calculated based on a storm (rainfall depth and duration) that has a 1% chance of occurring in a given year (the frequency or recurrence interval); a 500-year storm has a 0.2% chance of occurring in a given year, and so on. However, each major storm changes the math. Today, 100-year storms occur as frequently as once every 25 years for one in five people living in the United States. By mid-century, a 100-year storm in some areas could have a recurrence interval of 1 in 11 years.[9]

Houston had three 500-year storms between 2014 and 2017, and, more recently, Hurricane Harvey dumped almost 52 inches of rain on Houston over eight days, a probability that has been called a 1,000-year storm by some and a 3,000- to 20,000-year storm by others, depending on the time frame in which rainfall data are calculated.[10] The size and frequency of such large storms—now part of the official record—lead to the redrawing of lines on flood maps. As the maps are updated, previous floodplain delineations are omitted. As Liz Koslov notes, this promotes an ahistorical understanding of flooding—the use of a single demarcation makes the floodplain appear to be "the natural attribute of a place rather than the result of human action and decisions made from afar."[11] In this way, floodplain mapping is retroactive, but floodplain designations are intended to be proactive—they are there to guide local planning decisions and trigger insurance purchases.

There is no specific reason why a 100-year frequency was chosen as the basis for defining floodplains, other than that rainfall of that depth and duration was considered a major, albeit rare, event. FEMA argued that it was "a reasonable compromise" between saving lives and the economic benefits of floodplain development, while Monmonier quipped that if we had 12 fingers, we might be mapping 144-year recurrence intervals instead.[12] In any case, the 100-year floodplain is *the* primary spatial indicator for assessing and communicating flood risk—anyone living within it is required to have flood insurance if they want a federally backed mortgage.[13] Its delineation is also intended to assist local governments in creating their own development restrictions.

While policymakers, mapmakers, and citizens alike may acknowledge that risk assessments are as social as they are technical—after all, they must circumscribe the risks people are willing to take (assuming they understand them)—such risks must be rendered statistically if they are to be usable for planning measures and insurance premiums. There were many occasions during the creation of floodplain designations when different decisions could have been made. In its initial conception, some provisions would have discouraged the rapid development of low-lying areas.[14] Geographer Gilbert White, often referred to as the father of floodplain management, warned of the potential for adverse outcomes if the NFIP did not include restrictions on development and use insurance pricing that reflected "true" risk rather than being subsidized, as is currently the case.[15] However, even if the 100-year floodplain had been taken more seriously as a deterrent to development, it would not have prevented many of the flood disasters of the past five decades because so many of them have occurred outside that floodplain. It will not be easy to design our way out of

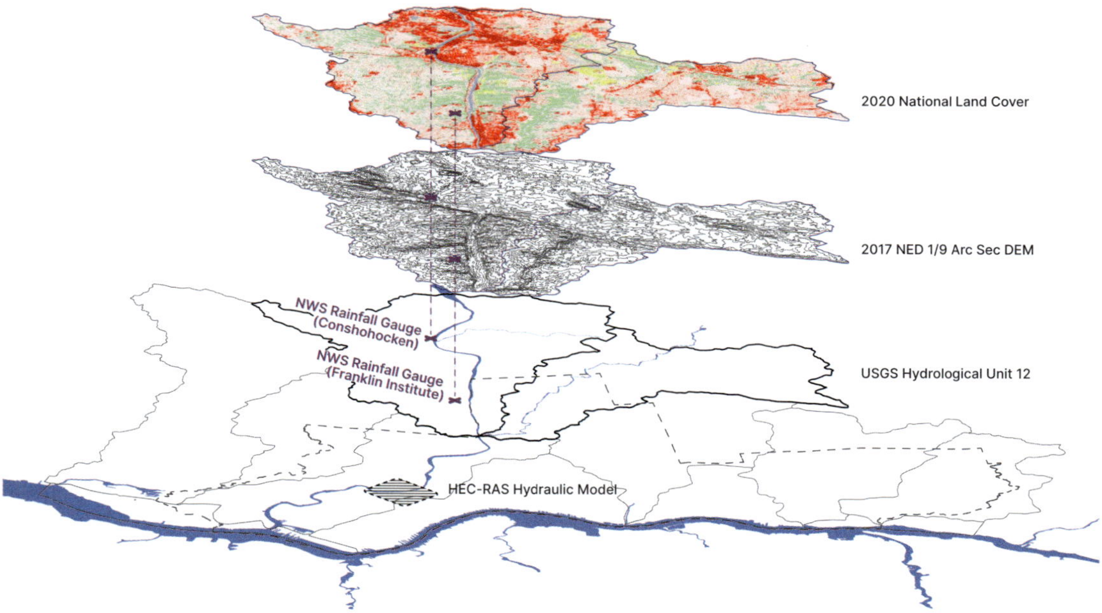

Illustration of the primary inputs (land cover, digital elevation model, and rain gauge data) needed to create a hydrology model (HEC-HMS) used to determine the discharge quantities necessary for a hydraulic model (HEC-RAS). Over 80% of tidal and nontidal riverine floodplains in the US are determined with HEC-HMS/HEC-RAS.

this situation precisely because of the way we have calculated our relationship with water.[16]

The inadequacy of the United States' approach to mapping flood hazards is becoming increasingly apparent as the Earth continues to heat up and the impacts of this rapid transformation become more unpredictable. Some have even argued that "rational planning in conditions of uncertainty is, by definition, impossible," which poses a challenge to designers and planners.[17]

The Creation of a Floodplain

Many types of estimates are used to determine floodplains, each with its own source of uncertainty or error. The most obvious uncertainty—and one not yet accounted for in US flood maps—is the impact of climate change on precipitation and sea level. Uncertainty, however, is not simply a product of the unknowability of the compounding effects of global heating; it is also inherent in assumptions about storms and errors in the measurements taken during storms, which are the data fed into flood models.

The models used to determine floodplains can produce widely divergent results, but each result can be supported by its corresponding technical information. It is estimated that between 13 million (according to FEMA) and 40 million people in the United States live within a 100-year floodplain.[18] The difference between these numbers is due to differences in data and models. Many more people live in coastal counties, some of whom live in designated flood zones and are therefore included in the floodplain population estimates above; the rest are not included, or not yet.[19] Sea level rise and increased storm intensity are shifting the lines on floodplain maps in both coastal and inland areas. Below, we describe some key factors used to forecast flooding along tidal and nontidal rivers.

Two types of models are used to delineate floodplains associated with riverine flooding: hydrologic and hydraulic. A hydrologic model is a *watershed model*. Its primary data are topography, land cover, and rainfall. These three factors are combined to produce the stream flow rate, measured in cubic feet per second, of a given storm at various points in the watershed model. The second type is a hydraulic model, which is a *river model*. Its primary data are topography, land cover, and the stream flow rate obtained from running a hydrologic model or from stream gauge records. Hydraulic models simulate a given stretch of a stream or river under flood conditions (e.g., a 100-year or 500-year storm), and cross sections are taken from the simulation to determine where the water level intersects the topography. Using a contour map or a digital elevation model, the areas between the cross sections are connected by following the contour elevation where the water surface meets the land, thus defining the extent and depth of the flood in a given area. This area is called the 100-year floodplain (i.e., the base flood elevation) or the 500-year floodplain, depending on the storm being modeled.

When it comes to modeling floods, topography is the only variable that can be made more accurate than previous maps and models because, although its accuracy depends on spatial resolution, its existence is not predictive or based on a probability of occurrence. In fact, this is why the National Research Council (NRC), in its 2007 recommendation to Congress for funding of FEMA's ongoing map upgrades, suggested focusing primarily on improving topographic accuracy through the use of lidar.[20] It argued that increased accuracy would enable better decision-making about floodplain development, stating that *accurate topographic data are the most important factor* in determining base flood elevations, which "overturns the conventional view that map accuracy is affected at least as much by the accuracy of the hydraulic model and hydraulic parameters as by the accuracy of the topographic data."[21] The NRC made its recommendation based on several case study areas where the use of more accurate topography *expanded* the number of structures included within the base flood elevation zone. However, in our comparison of six cities, where we overlaid older FEMA maps with those that had been updated with more accurate topographic data from lidar, we found that the floodplains shrank while the population increased in five of the six locations.[22]

Although FEMA's updated flood zones are based on more accurate topography, the presumption of stationarity—that variation occurs within *known* boundaries—is assumed for all other model inputs, from rainfall to stream flow to the landscape itself.[23] Land cover—such as whether something is forested or cleared, permeable or paved—changes too frequently to be kept up to date in models, and rainfall data are based on a 100-year storm event, which changes as new storms are added to the dataset. Even as recently as 2019, USGS guidelines for determining flood frequency did not account for changes in the watershed. Furthermore, FEMA maps ignore small streams—it is estimated that only 40% of streams have been mapped—and very few account for pluvial flooding, which is rainfall that stays in place, gets trapped in low-lying areas, and thus never makes it to those streams. It may surprise many to learn that until 2015, there was no recognition of pluvial flooding in floodplain delineation at the national level, yet over 85% of the population lives in areas that experience this type of flooding. Because it is difficult to model, accounting for pluvial flooding remains rare.[24] This is why so many flood losses—between 25% and 40%—occur outside officially designated floodplains, even in areas where maps have been recently updated.[25]

In its most recent reports, the Technical Mapping Advisory Council (TMAC), a federal advisory committee established in 2014 to make recommendations to FEMA on its flood mapping program, has made suggestions for changing the way US floodplains are represented. The recommendations include moving away from a single floodplain line—where structures are either "in" or "out" of the 100-year zone—to a gradient-based map that shows low to high risk, along with descriptions of the probabilities that correspond to those rankings. As of 2023, FEMA has implemented a method to address the inequities baked into the way flood insurance is priced by providing a risk rating based on the specifics of individual structures, such as how high above the base flood elevation a home sits.[26] The further granularization of our maps may help individuals pay a rate that more accurately reflects their insurance risk but it sends the wrong message about floodplains.

While clearer communication with the public, local governments, and decision-makers is needed, as many people are unaware of the significance of floodplain designations in relation to the likelihood and severity of flooding, the implicit assumption in the push for more accurate maps is that if we can better understand the hazards, then we can better communicate the risks. However, even maps produced with gradients based on different storm intensities and rainfall amounts will have uncertainties that cannot be accounted for, and these will only be exacerbated by changing precipitation due to climate change.

Because it appears much more detailed, the pixelated floodplain may give the (false) impression that it is a more *accurate* map. It may be, but only within a very limited time frame and only with respect to topography and building elevation. TMAC's recent reports summarize their findings with working groups comprised of various communities, including testimony from participants who support changing flood representations on maps from lines to gradients. However, participant quotes also indicate that people are looking for assurances that the gradient maps will be "correct" because of their increased accuracy. In other words, a mosaic floodplain is unlikely to lead to better decisions about development because homeowners and developers can build their structures on fill or stilts "out of the flood zone." Those who can afford to take more risks or build higher will do so, as is currently the case, and only the wealthy, the real estate industry, and developers will benefit. Furthermore, the roads and utilities that support these buildings—which are the areas that flood and where people get trapped—are paid for with taxpayer dollars.[27]

Given the variables and uncertainties involved in producing flood maps, it is not possible to provide the kind of assurance that people want. Even within the scientific and modeling communities, there is no consensus on how to account for climate change in understanding the effects of riverine or pluvial flooding, and little consensus on how to account for pluvial flooding even under stationary conditions.[28] As one hydrologist puts it, a "suitable successor" to stationarity has yet to be found.[29] The "great displacement" from the coasts will lead people to areas that do not have development restrictions to account for rain, and there is no easy way to define them, especially for the longer term. Even TMAC, which insists that the theory behind risk-based flood management is "well established and sound," acknowledges that with climate change, "additional complications have emerged."[30]

Lost in Translation: Rain, Flow, and Flood

Myriad sources of error occur "upstream" of a hydrologic model. There are data errors in the process of collecting rainfall and stream flow at points, such as broken equipment, limited record length, and record gaps. There are also method errors, such as interpolation, to fill in

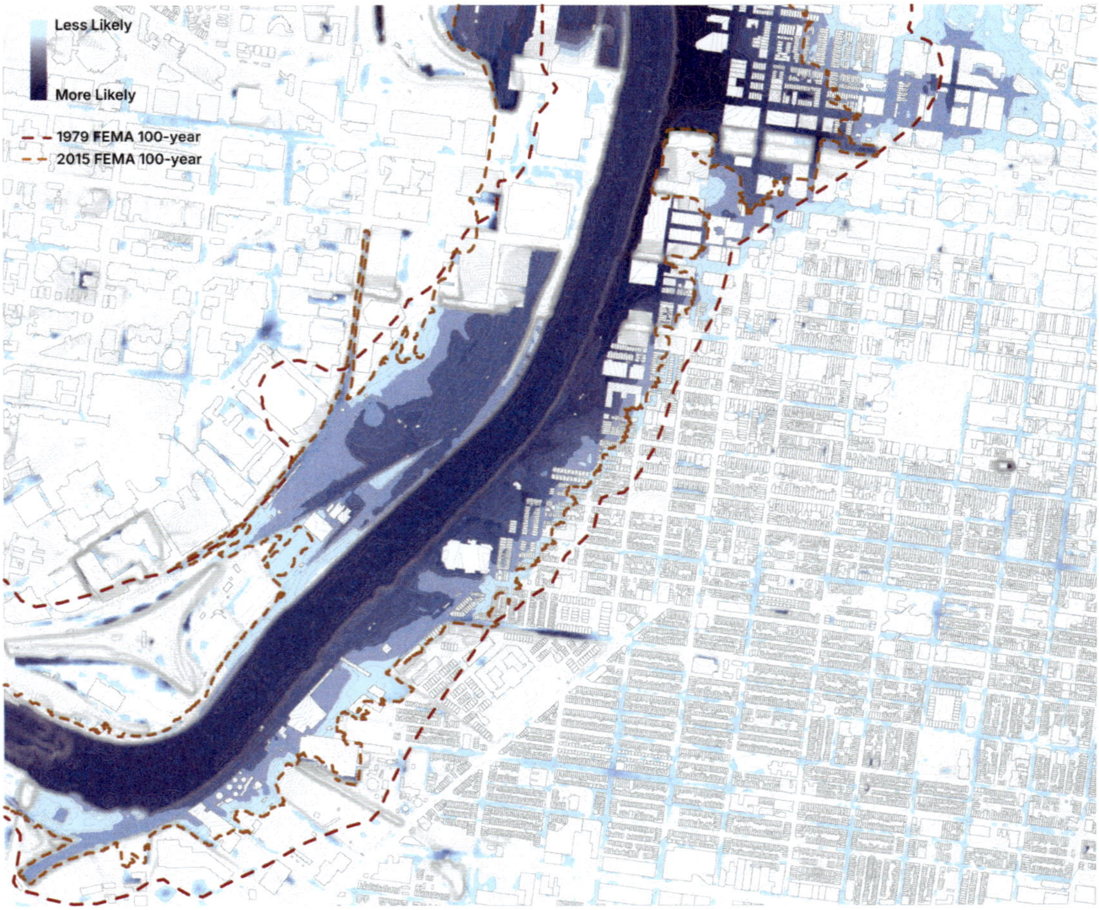

Extent of flood probabilities of combined fluvial and pluvial events with a projected rainfall increase of approximately 22% (a near-future increase estimated by the US Army Corp of Engineers, Philadelphia District, and New Jersey Dept of Environmental Protection). The 1979 floodplain more closely matches the projected flood extent compared to the 2015 map.

data gaps and translate the point collection to a watershed. The correlation between these measurements—rainfall, stream flow, and their downstream effects—is fraught with assumptions about averages and norms that occur in translating point data to spatial distribution and from one medium to another.[31] Even if rainfall and land cover data were kept up to date and the most accurate topographic data were used, the correlation between a storm and its associated floodplain is weak. This has always been the case, but the gap between the two will be exacerbated by climate change.

There are numerous reasons for the incongruence between storms and floodplains. For example, as storms have become more intense, the amount of rain that falls during certain storms has increased. Still, these changes have not been updated in NOAA's Rain Atlas, which serves as the data input into hydrologic models. Also, a 100-year storm does not necessarily result in a 100-year flood. If the ground is saturated before a storm, a much smaller event can cause flooding up to the 100-year base flood elevation. In contrast, rain gauges can register a 100-year storm without resulting in a 100-year flood, as measured by stream gauges. A study in Colorado, for instance, showed that rain gauges recorded precipitation levels that would constitute a 100-year rainstorm more than 150 times in one year, yet very few flood-level records appear from the stream gauge data. In addition, rainfall and stream flow data are also estimated, even though hydrologic models are supposed to be calibrated to actual rainfall.

A hydrologic model is calibrated to real-world conditions by comparing its flood volume outputs to a "known" 100-year storm based on measurements from stream gauge data collected during the storm. Some studies have found that stream gauge data are incorrect or unavailable 25% of the time due to gauge damage. In these cases, the flood volume—that is, the stream flow rate measured in cubic feet per second—entered into a hydrologic model *to calibrate the model to real conditions* is calibrated to an estimate, not to field measurements. This is called a rating curve estimation, and it is accomplished by taking the flow rate under normal conditions and estimating what the flow rate would be under a 100-year storm. In other words, in many instances, peak flood volumes are not measured so much as they are indirectly generated, but these estimated data are what go *on record* as the peak flow rate of a real storm. Researchers have found that using rating curves to calibrate hydrologic models often underestimates flood volumes by as much as half and, in many cases, by 100% in steeply sloped areas.[32] Because large storms are underrepresented in the data, these errors are compounded when they are fed into hydrologic models, resulting in lower peak stream flow rates that are then fed into hydraulic models used to delineate floodplains.

Finally, NOAA's atlas, which shows the "probable maximum precipitation" for a given storm, is based on a model that "intentionally eliminates major weather outliers in order to smooth its observations in an attempt to correct for gauge variability."[33] In other words, not all rain measurements make it into the official record. And because NOAA models rainfall events over 24-hour periods, they do not account for short bursts of heavy rain that are expected to increase as the planet heats up.[34] These "smaller," higher-frequency storms produce damaging floods that significantly impact people's lives and have triggered many federal emergency declarations. NOAA's rainfall data—which are used not only for floodplain delineation but also for massive infrastructure projects, including those funded by the Infrastructure Investment and Jobs Act (2021)—are 20 years old in some regions, and the next atlas will not be available until 2027 at the earliest.[35] Nearly half a billion dollars from the infrastructure bill are earmarked for NOAA's flood mapping and water modeling activities.[36] Until then, our nation's roads, bridges, utilities, and railways will be built to outdated standards.[37]

Given all the errors and uncertainties inherent in attempts to translate dynamic environmental media into fixed representations, it should come as no surprise that maps are contested when floodplain lines are changed. In *Underwater*, Rebecca Elliott explains how FEMA's flood maps of New York City after Hurricane Sandy expanded the 100-year flood zone, which *doubled* the number of structures considered in the zone. In response, the City of New York hired its own consultants to create models that used different inputs for wind velocity, tide ranges, and past storm events. The results of these models shrank the floodplain compared to FEMA's maps, and the city's floodplain delineation prevailed.[38] Although the city and FEMA ultimately agreed to a two-map solution—one based on current risk for flood insurance purposes and one for the city to plan for climate change—the only upside of a shrinking floodplain is that it keeps homes affordable for those who might otherwise default due to higher insurance premiums. The downside is that these businesses and homeowners stand to lose everything due to a lack of insurance—or underinsurance—when the next storm hits. As this example demonstrates, the move toward greater accuracy was not contested; what was controversial was how to go about getting the *most accurate* results from our models. This case study does not bode well for our floodplain futures.

Conclusion

> Floodplain futures are national futures.[39]
> —Rebecca Elliott, *Underwater*

Luna Leopold, a contemporary of Gilbert White, headed the USGS Water Resources Division from the late 1950s to the mid-1960s and was instrumental in developing statistics for water management. Over the course of his career, Leopold became increasingly convinced that it was impossible to account for all of the variability that contributes to flooding, noting that "the ability to measure may always exceed the ability to forecast or explain."[40] Now, we must also acknowledge that the ability to measure is equally problematic, given the gaps in space and time over which we collect measurements.

Our *modus operandi* has been to impose technical solutions, whether by trying to increase the accuracy of our models and maps or by providing physical protection in attempts to keep the water at bay. This increasing push for flood map detail for insurance purposes is at odds with the larger issues of floodplain delineation and development, which have brought us to the point where many people live in flood-prone areas, and many have no (economic) way out. Although TMAC acknowledges that floodplain insurance and floodplain regulation are two different things, they end up being conflated in our maps with the assumption that we can continue "confidently quantifying what we don't know."[41] Decision-making should be local and place-specific, but when it comes to floodplains, this further entrenches people in place and obscures the fact that we continue to build with total disregard for the inherent variability of our environment.

Furthermore, nonstationarity is a characteristic not only of the many environmental media we attempt to measure and represent but also of the socioeconomic changes that will occur in the time frame in which infrastructure is built, and cost-benefit analyses are conducted.[42] In *The Great Displacement*, Bittle says that while we cannot predict where people will move, and there is no haven from climate change, Rust Belt cities bordering the Great Lakes are among the likely recipients of climate migration.[43] Regardless of the region, people will increasingly move from low-lying coasts to inland areas that are not restricted from development due to our notions of floodplains. When there is no way to "foresee" certain types of flooding with our current methods, they may be considered an act of God, as happened recently when the Great Lakes Water Authority denied 24,000 claims for people in Detroit and surrounding areas who did not have flood insurance.[44] Those making decisions and designing at the local level are often unaware of how floodplains have come to be rationalized, and the pixelation of our floodplains through mapping gradients may reinforce the impression that there is a high degree of factuality in our flood maps.

Landscape architects work between public and private interests, as well as local, state, and federal regulations. Rather than treating uncertainty as something to be tamed, as continues to be the trend, landscape architects can treat it as something generative, bringing the assumptions behind best-laid plans to the forefront. There is no ideal way to do this; much depends on the participants or recipients of these media. Some have argued that creating ambiguity in maps—gradients, blurred boundaries, tones, and transparencies—rather than clear lines of distinction is the way forward for any kind of spatial information with a high degree of uncertainty.[45] However, FEMA plans to use gradients to represent *more* accuracy (for insurance assessments), not more ambiguity. Another study that conducted interviews and workshopping to understand flood maps with residents who had experienced a significant flood supported ambiguity by depicting multiple floodplains on maps.[46] In other cases, however, maps without clear distinctions have been shown to induce what is known as ambiguity aversion, leading participants to underestimate their risk.[47] Perhaps we should heed the advice of geographers Magali Reghezza-Zitt and Samuel Rufat, who argue that *uncertainty is irreducible to risk* and acknowledge the unprecedented nature of this challenge.[48]

Notes

1. Damien Gayle, "Tuesday Was World's Hottest Day on Record – Breaking Monday's Record," *The Guardian* (July 5, 2023), https://www.theguardian.com/environment/2023/jul/05/tuesday-was-worlds-hottest-day-on-record-breaking-mondays-record.
2. The United States does not consider heat-related deaths as disasters, and thus federal funding through FEMA is not available. For the devasting effects of heat, see Jeff Goodell, *The Heat Will Kill You First* (Little, Brown & Co., 2023).
3. Jack Bittle, *The Great Displacement: Climate Change and the Next American Migration* (Simon & Schuster, 2023), xvi.
4. For example, after Hurricane Harvey flooded Houston, the homeowners who received federal buyouts could move anywhere, including into another flood zone, and thousands of the flooded homes were sold to large investment firms and hedge funds. See Bittle, *The Great Displacement*, 153, 168. Also see Jon Gorey, "What Will Make Home Buyers Consider Climate Risk? What Happens Once They Do?" *Land Lines Magazine* (Spring/Summer 2024), https://www.lincolninst.edu/publications/

article/2023-11-homebuyers -climate-insurance-risk?

5. The phrase "risk object" is from Rebecca Elliott, *Underwater: Loss, Flood Insurance, and the Moral Economy of Climate Change in the United States* (Columbia University Press, 2021), 110.
6. See, for example, Rachelle Alterman & Cygal Pellach (eds), *Regulating Coastal Zones: International Perspective on Land Management Instruments* (Routledge, 2021).
7. Mark Monmonier, *Coast Lines: How Mapmakers Frame the World and Chart Environmental Change* (University of Chicago Press, 2008), 164.
8. NFIP was originally under HUD, but it was taken over by FEMA when FEMA was established in 1979. For a timeline of flood management, disaster relief, and insurance, see Elliott, *Underwater*, xiii–xvii.
9. First Street Foundation, "NOAA's 1-in-100 Year Flooding Can Now Be Expected Every 8 Years," https://firststreet.org/press/noaas-1-in-100-year-flooding-can-now-be-expected-every-8-years/ (accessed September 6, 2023).
10. See Harris County Flood Control District Memorandum (June 4, 2018), https://reduceflooding.com/wp-content/uploads/2018/06/Final-HCFCD-Harvey-Report.pdf (accessed September 6, 2023).
11. Liz Koslov, "How Maps Make Time: Temporal Conflicts of Life in the Flood Zone," *City* 23, no. 3–4 (2019): 662.
12. FEMA, "Answers to Questions About the NFIP," *FEMA F-084* (March 2011), 11; Monmonier, *Coastlines*, 117.
13. Paraphrased from Wesley E. Highfield, Sarah A. Norman & Samuel D. Brody, "Examining the 100-Year Floodplain as a Metric of Risk, Loss, and Household Adjustment," *Risk Analysis* 33, no. 2 (2013). Recently, there have been exceptions to this. For example, cities like Austin, TX, are not waiting around for updated maps and are using the 500-year floodplain as the regulatory 100-year floodplain.
14. For an excellent book on the federal subsidization of risky building, see Gilbert M. Gaul, *The Geography of Risk: Epic Storms, Rising Seas, and the Cost of America's Coasts* (Sarah Crichton Books, 2019).
15. For an excellent overview of NFIP, see Scott Gabriel Knowles & Howard C. Kunreuther, "Troubled Waters: The National Flood Insurance Program in Historical Perspective," *Journal of Policy History* 26, no. 3 (2014).
16. For example, between 2017 and 2019, 40% of NFIP claims were for properties outside official floodplains. "America Underwater," *The Washington Post* (December 6, 2022), https://www.washingtonpost.com/climate-environment/interactive/2022/fema-flood-risk-maps-failures/?itid=lk_interstitial_manual_24.
17. A. R. Siders & Andrea L. Pierce, "Deciding How to Make Climate Change Adaptation Decisions," *Current Opinion in Environmental Sustainability* 52 (2021): 2.
18. Oliver E. J. Wing, et al., "Estimates of Present and Future Flood Risk in the Conterminous United States," *Environmental Research Letters* 13 (2018).
19. Coastal zones are defined as counties bordering the Atlantic, Pacific, or Arctic Ocean, the Gulf of Mexico, Long Island Sound, or the Great Lakes. As of 2010, 39% of Americans lived in coastal zones, up 40% since 1970. See Knowles & Kunreuther, "Troubled Waters," 327.
20. FEMA began its Flood Map Modernization initiative in 2000 with the intent that flood maps would be updated every five years, which has not occurred.
21. National Research Council, *Mapping the Zone: Improving Flood Map Accuracy* (National Academies Press, 2009), 66.
22. The locations are Jacksonville, FL; Boston, MA; Charleston, NC; Philadelphia, PA; Virginia Beach, VA; and Trenton, NJ, the last of which did not significantly change.
23. Elliott describes this on p. 112. On stationarity, a foundational concept in water management, see P. C. D. Milly, et al., who state that stationarity "assumes that natural systems fluctuate within an unchanging envelope of variability." P. C. D. Milly, et al., "Stationarity is Dead: Whither Water Management?" *Science* 319 (February 2008): 573.
24. National Climate Task Force, *Federal Flood Risk Management Standard Climate-Informed Science Approach (CISA) State of the Science Report* (March 2023), 59, https://www.whitehouse.gov/wp-content/uploads/2023/03/Federal-Flood-Risk-Management-Standard-Climate-Informed-Science-Approach-CISA-State-of-the-Science-Report.pdf.
25. Highfield, et al., "Examining the 100-Year Floodplain," 189.
26. On the inequities embedded in floodplain regulations and insurance, see, for example, Elliott, *Underwater*; Gaul, *The Geography of Risk;* Koslov, "How Maps Make Time"; and Karen M'Closkey & Keith VanDerSys, "For Whom Do We Account in Climate Adaptation?" in Carolyn Kousky, Billy Fleming & Alan Berger (eds), *A Blueprint for Coastal Adaptation: Uniting Design, Economics, and Policy* (Island Press, 2021).
27. One study found that there are $1.32 of flood losses to public infrastructure for every $1.00 of flood losses to insured buildings. See National Research Council, *Mapping the Zone*, 84. Likewise, Jack Bittle states that, in the Florida Keys, one dollar of adaptation spending yields only 41 cents of future savings. Bittle, *The Great Displacement*, 28.
28. National Climate Task Force, *Federal Flood Risk Management*, 62.
29. Milly, et al., "Stationarity is Dead."
30. Technical Mapping Advisory Council, *Future Conditions Risk Assessment and Modeling* (December 2015), 5-2.
31. See, for example, Sandra Pavlovic, et al., "Intercomparison of Selected Fixed-Area Areal Reduction Factor Methods," *Journal of Hydrology* 537 (2016): 419–30.

32. USGS, *Guidelines for Determining Flood Flow Frequency Bulletin 17C*, Book 4 (USGS, 2019), 20.
33. Zack Colman, "Study Shows Federal Weather Model Underplays Flooding, Putting Infrastructure Spending at Risk," *Politico* (June 26, 2023), https://www.politico.com/news/2023/06/26/federal-weather-model-underplays-flooding-00102888.
34. NOAA's definition of a 24-hour, 100-year storm event in 1973 (Atlas 2), compared to the same frequency event in 2004 (Atlas 14), is 6.5 inches and 7.7 inches of rain, respectively, for 14 states in the Mid-Atlantic, South Atlantic, and Midwest regions. See *NOAA Atlas 14: Precipitation-Frequency Atlas of the United States* 2, version 3 (NOAA, 2006). The First Street Foundation argues that this is an underestimate. See First Street Foundation, "Highlights from 'The Precipitation Problem,'" (June 26, 2023), https://firststreet.org/research-lab/published-research/article-highlights-from-the-precipitation-problem/ (accessed September 13, 2023). Furthermore, there are different outcomes depending on how the rainfall data are analyzed. See Leslie Munoz, "Rainfall Duration Series: What's the Difference Between Annual Maximum and Partial Duration?" (October 12, 2017), Freese and Nichols, https://www.freese.com/rainfall-duration-series-what-s-the-difference-between-annual-maximum-and-partial-duration/.
35. The current data are from Atlas 14. Atlas 15 is underway. The National Academies website states that the academies are assessing how to define the spatial and temporal scales for decision-making, how to account for impacts of climate change on extreme precipitation into the probable maximum precipitation (PMP) estimates, and to "recommend a preferred approach for PMP estimation that incorporates the impacts of climate change and the characterization of uncertainty." National Academies, "Modernizing Probable Maximum Precipitation Estimation," https://www.nationalacademies.org/our-work/modernizing-probable-maximum-precipitation-estimation (accessed September 7, 2023).
36. Thomas Frank, "Climate Change Overtakes Archaic NOAA Rain Records," *E&E News by Politico* (January 7, 2022), https://www.eenews.net/articles/climate-change-overtakes-archaic-noaa-rain-records/.
37. Federal projects will be constructed using one of three metrics: the 100-year floodplain plus freeboard, which is a safety factor that adds two or three feet of elevation; the 500-year floodplain; or a "climate-informed science approach," which is a set of guidelines but none with specific metrics. It assumes a worst-case scenario *over the course of the project*, however defined. See the National Climate Task Force, *Federal Flood Risk Management Standard*.
38. Elliott, *Underwater*, 122–23.
39. Ibid., 175.
40. Environmental historian Etienne Benson describes Leopold's shift in thinking over a 20-year period during which he created hydraulic models. The quote is Leopold's, cited in Etienne S. Benson, "Random River: Luna Leopold and the Promise of Chance in Fluvial Geomorphology," *Journal of Historical Geography* 67 (2020): 21.
41. This phrase was used to describe the use of probabilistic modeling, which allows uncertainty to be quantified. Technical Mapping Advisory Council, *Annual Report* (2020), 27.
42. See, for example, B. Francois, et al., "Design Considerations for Riverine Floods in a Changing Climate – A Review," *Journal of Hydrology* 574 (2019).
43. Bittle, *The Great Displacement*, 274.
44. Corey Williams, "Detroit-Area Utility Denies Flooding Claims from 2021 Storm," *AP News* (July 19, 2022), https://apnews.com/article/floods-storms-michigan-detroit-a820d6cb89ff33578a48eb-0fb613334b.
45. Alan M. MacEachren, et al., "Visualizing Geospatial Information Uncertainty: What We Know and What We Need to Know," *Cartography and GIS* 32, no. 3 (2005): 139–60.
46. Robert Soden, "Modes of Uncertainty: Rethinking Flood Risk in Colorado," *Items: Insights from the Social Sciences* (July 30, 2019), https://items.ssrc.org/chancing-the-storm/modes-of-uncertainty-rethinking-flood-risk-in-colorado/.
47. For example, see David P. Retchless, "Sea Level Rise Maps: How Individual Differences Complicate the Cartographic Communication of an Uncertain Climate Change Hazard," *Cartographic Perspectives* 77 (2014); Sue Hope & Gary J. Hunter, "Testing the Effects of Thematic Uncertainty on Spatial Decision Making," *Cartography and GIS* 34, no. 3 (2007): 199–214.
48. Magali Reghezza-Zitt & Samuel Rufat, "Disentangling the Range of Responses to Threats, Hazards and Disasters. Vulnerability, Resilience and Adaptation in Question," *Cybergeo: European Journal of Geography* (2019): 11.

Elevating Coastal Wetland Restoration

Brian D. Harris and Justin Shawler

Composite map of measured (1996–2023) and projected (until 2073) land loss due to climate-induced sea level rise and subsidence along the Gulf of Mexico coastline, Louisiana.

Coastal wetlands are naturally dynamic environments, undergoing phases of expansion and deterioration driven by natural depositional cycles and changing environmental conditions. They are immensely beneficial ecosystems that provide habitat for a multitude of species, including migratory birds and fish; diminish the effects of coastal storms on inland areas; improve water quality; and sequester carbon and other nutrients.[1] These vital ecosystems support thousands of dollars per acre in economic value, including those associated with recreational activities such as bird watching, boating, and hiking, as well as recreational and commercial fisheries, which generate $238 billion in sales annually.[2] It is also estimated that coastal wetlands indirectly provide over $23 billion per year in storm protection services.[3] Unlike traditional hardened infrastructure, such as stone revetments and wooden bulkheads, wetlands can adapt to changing environmental conditions, promote the sustainability of critical habitats, and

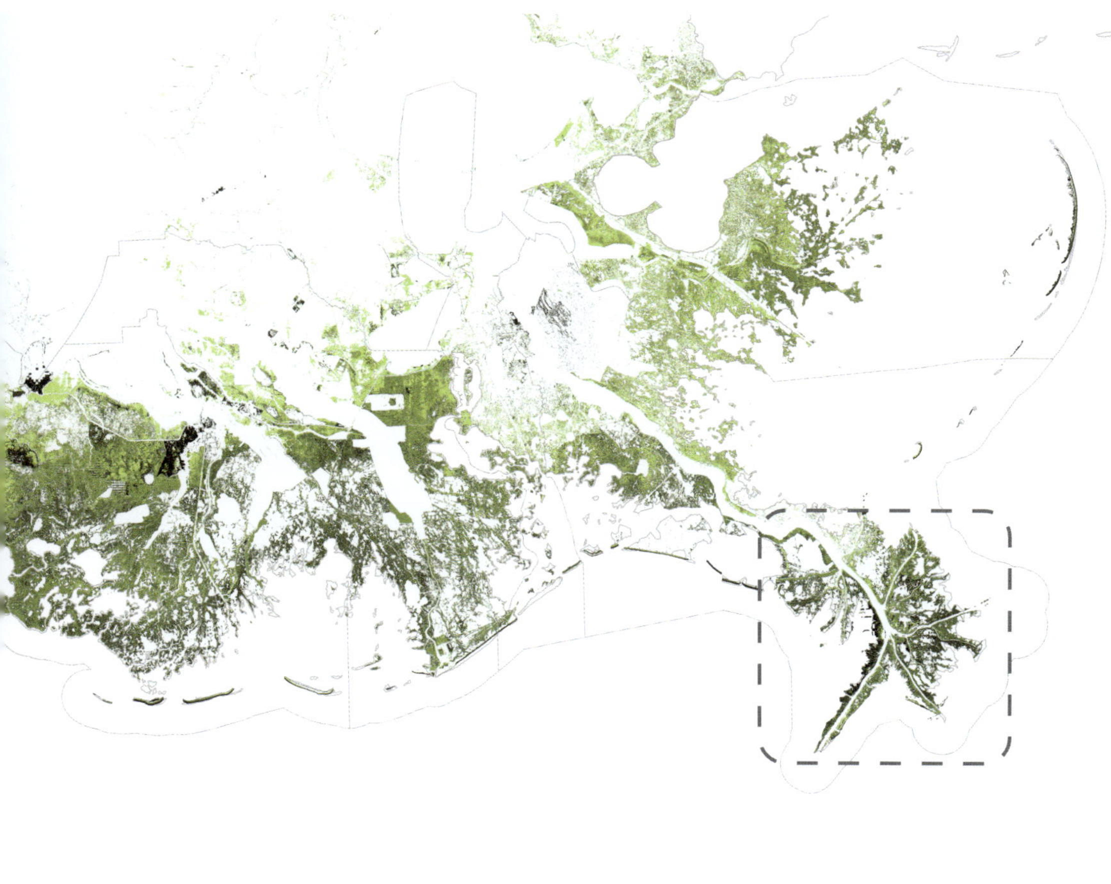

keep pace with sea level rise, while slowing chronic coastal erosion and dampening storm surge and wave-driven processes.[4] Despite the myriad benefits of wetlands, historical and modern anthropogenic disturbances threaten their long-term viability.

Wetlands are rapidly degrading due in large part to historic management practices. Historically, wetlands were viewed as areas of little importance and were either filled to dispose of refuse or create land, or "improved" to serve a more useful function. An example of improvement is ditching, which is a form of direct alteration that modifies site hydrology. This method was widely used across the New England states to reduce standing water to eliminate mosquito populations or to improve farming via irrigation and salinity reductions. In New England, mosquito ditches are present in over 90% of salt marshes; however, they were largely unsuccessful in reducing mosquito populations.[5] As for farming applications, these ditches paired with embankments could increase vegetation yields three to four times and allow farmers to move beyond subsistence farming.[6] Ultimately, this direct site alteration has led to prolific reductions in salt marshes as legacy impacts from agriculture and mosquito ditching continue to alter hydrology and stress vegetation.

Public consensus on wetland significance has vastly improved over the years, and, in response to the crisis of wetland loss, federal agencies such as the United States Army Corps of Engineers, United States Geological Survey (USGS), and United States Fish and Wildlife Service—in collaboration with state-level organizations like Louisiana's Coastal Protection and Restoration Authority (CPRA)—have been experimenting with wetland "nourishment," also known as the "beneficial use of dredged material (i.e., sediment)." This approach uses material extracted from waterways and ports—which need to be expanded periodically to accommodate larger vessels or to counteract natural sedimentation—and strategically deposits it in wetland areas. This form of direct nourishment is intended to supplement the ground elevation and to reconnect discontinuous wetlands, thereby expanding the wetland and reducing open water. These two benefits are essential to long-term wetland stability because elevation is the controlling factor of hydroperiod—i.e., flooding frequency and duration, which controls biological productivity—while the reduction in open water reduces the potential for wind-induced wave action to cause erosion of marsh edges. Despite the benefits of supplementing wetlands with dredged material, there is a high degree of uncertainty in how to design and monitor them.

This chapter focuses on the media used in geomorphic modeling and monitoring for the adaptive management of restored wetlands. Coastal wetland geomorphology—defined here as the elevation and extent of a wetland site—directly influences the function and productivity of an ecosystem, which in turn determines the benefits provided by a restored wetland. We offer examples of the geomorphological media used for wetland restoration site selection and post-construction monitoring. We emphasize the opportunities and limits of the media used (in terms of both data visualization and dredged sediment) and

Wetland Loss Composite

1996–2006

2006–2016

2023

+10 YEARS

+20 YEARS

+30 YEARS

+40 YEARS

+50 YEARS

Sequential maps of measured (1996–2023) and projected (until 2073) land loss due to climate-induced sea level rise and subsidence along the Gulf of Mexico coastline, Louisiana.

Sediment dredge pumping for the Spanish Pass wetland restoration project, Louisiana, November 2021.

how that may impact management decisions. In site selection, we discuss what media (e.g., maps and models) are used to select sites within the limitations of available dredged sediment. In particular, we emphasize that, given the tremendous threats to wetlands and the limits of available material, not all wetlands can be restored, and thus, managers must carefully consider which media to use to select restoration priorities. Similarly, when it comes to monitoring, we argue that restoration practitioners must carefully select from a suite of available tools and media to determine when to intervene to correct undesirable outcomes post-construction. Finally, we offer a path forward that focuses on best practices in adaptive management.

Uncertainty

Uncertainty about the long-term viability of wetland restoration projects is driven by three factors: soil properties, construction conditions, and future rates of sea level rise. Together, the first two factors contribute to the immediate post-construction geomorphology—elevation and extent—of a wetland. The soil properties of dredged material, along with its initial placement, determine how the sediment will disperse across the site and consolidate. To model this, soil samples taken from both the dredge site and the placement site are necessary; however, both areas are often large, making the collection of representative samples infeasible. For example, CPRA guidelines recommend one soil boring (typical sample diameter of three inches) for every 100 acres of the dredged material borrow area, and every 50 to 100 acres for the placement area.[7] Exacerbating the uncertainty about material conditions, due to insufficient samples, soft deltaic soils are highly susceptible to sample disturbance (i.e., artificial compaction) introduced during the collection, transportation, extrusion, and testing phases of sediment analyses, which produces flawed data when compared to undisturbed field conditions.[8] During construction, an operator has limited control over how the dredged material flows from the pipeline and disperses. While it is common to construct containment from earth or coir logs and to install drainage structures to remove excess water from the placed material, practitioners are ultimately trying to control a highly fluid material across a relatively flat area with an extremely porous containment system. The dredged material will follow a path of least resistance, scouring an ever-deepening channel that can undermine containment features. Both types of uncertainty propagate, leaving doubt about the restored wetland's short- to medium-term (sub-decadal) surface elevation, which controls ecosystem productivity. Over the long term (decades to centuries), uncertainty exists about sea level rise rates. While global sea level will certainly rise, the latest International Panel on Climate Change report and the literature therein define multiple potential rates based on global emissions scenarios.[9] Additionally, local rates of sea level rise can vary drastically from global rates due to subsidence and land uplift.[10] While those local factors and trajectories are often known within some range of error, they nonetheless increase uncertainty.

A technique to reduce this uncertainty is the application of adaptive management principles. Adaptive management is a structured, iterative process of incorporating new information to improve decision-making over time, and it is commonly used to refine regional-scale management.[11] However, adaptive management is equally useful at the project scale. For a wetland nourishment project, this would involve using all known data to develop a set of potential outcomes and adaptive measures to initiate if deviations from expected outcomes arise. Planners—which broadly refers to engineers, scientists, landscape architects, and managers associated with project design and implementation—can establish a simple monitoring system to determine if these corrective measures should be implemented to rectify any deviation from expected trajectories. For example, by monitoring parameters such as dredged material densities, surface elevations, or zones of accretion and erosion, planners can refine geomorphological models to develop more realistic outcomes and communicate with construction personnel to enact necessary alterations in dredged material discharge rates, volumes, or locations to achieve desired surface elevations better. Doing this systematically during and after initial construction can reduce the risk of suboptimal project outcomes induced by uncertainty.

Geomorphology

Wetland geomorphic monitoring and modeling focus on the (in)stability of wetland landforms and the resulting changes in elevation and area. Wetlands are complex, three-dimensional, natural features that change at their boundaries and interiors. Along shorelines, waves erode marsh edges; along upland zones, marshes can migrate into shallow slopes, but they are often impeded by steep slopes and infrastructure such as levees and seawalls.[12] Additionally, wetland geomorphic change occurs through the deposition of suspended sediment brought in by tides.[13] Vegetation dieback and resulting channelization further drive geomorphic change.[14] In their interiors, wetlands undergo geomorphic

Soil can store centuries' worth of the carbon absorbed by marsh plants. This core sample from Virginia's Goodwin Island reveals when drier land transitioned to marsh.

change in the form of ponding, which results in increased unvegetated areas and less stable sediments.[15] In addition to these surficial processes, shallow and deep subsidence can cause wetland elevations to decrease relative to local sea level.[16] In some areas with tectonic activity (e.g., earthquakes, post-glacial uplift) marsh elevations may actually increase relative to local sea level.

Wetland elevation plays a critical role in controlling wetland hydrodynamics, ecology, and sedimentation.[17] For tidal wetlands, a loss of elevation will eventually lead to a loss of function, ultimately resulting in a wholescale landscape transition to an unvegetated mudflat.[18] In particular, the *elevation capital* concept, wherein sediment deposited and retained during tidal wetland development establishes wetland height relative to the tidal frame, is especially important for understanding the overall trajectory of wetland health.[19] In a site with decreasing elevation capital, anthropogenic placement of sediment can increase overall wetland sustainability in the face of sea level rise.[20]

In addition to elevation, the vegetated extent of a wetland is an important indicator of stability.[21] Vegetation is essential as it attenuates waves and traps sediment, which in turn can increase marsh stability if sufficient sediment is in suspension in the water column.[22] Thus, there are feedbacks among wetland elevation, extent, biological function, and hydrodynamics. Specifically, the extent of wetlands can influence the flow of water and sediment in the adjacent landscape. Additionally, wetland area and geomorphology influence the type and quality of habitat available for fish and other wildlife.[23]

Site Selection and Modeling

The first step of a coastal wetland restoration project is to conduct a regional study to identify candidate sites. Initially, planners may conduct a review of historical geospatial and site monitoring data, such as existing maps, aerial and satellite imagery, and ecological health data from government, academic, and nonprofit groups. Specific to wetland geomorphology, planners should analyze spatial and temporal trends of erosion and deposition to identify areas of degradation and progradation using maps generated in geographic information systems. As more data become available from prior wetland monitoring, insights from past experiences can inform site selection of future sites from the same and similar regions.

Once planners identify and understand historical trends, they can make assumptions about the likelihood of change and determine at-risk areas most in need of attention. It is important to note that just because an area faces severe erosion, it does not mean it warrants restoration. For example, areas may be considered beyond saving within current financial, environmental, and design constraints. Furthermore, sites may be prioritized not just based on their environmental viability, but also for their potential benefits to coastal communities.

A growing number of publicly accessible maps and siting tools are emerging to aid planners and stakeholders in visualizing, selecting, and prioritizing sites for wetland restoration. As one example of the media used for geomorphic analysis, the USGS has developed downloadable and web-accessible land cover analyses of the ratio of unvegetated to vegetated coastal wetland areas for the coterminous United States from 2014 to 2018.[24] The unvegetated to vegetated ratio is a telling wetland health metric, with higher ratios associated with increased degradation and decreased health. For example, the Delaware Department of Natural Resources and Environmental Control used maps of historical natural conversions of vegetated wetlands to unvegetated ponded areas as one of many criteria to select the Muddy Neck Marsh Complex as a restoration site.[25] Additionally, tools such as the National Fish and Wildlife Foundation's Coastal Resilience Evaluation and Siting Tool (CREST) allow users to view web-accessible spatial data on community, wildlife, and physical factors that together can be used to select restoration sites for maximum beneficial impact.[26]

The exact maps used to select sites matter because they impact areas that get restored. For example, CPRA recently updated the maps of subsidence used in predictions of future geomorphic change.[27] Potential limitations and assumptions highlighted by CPRA are that subsidence rates are derived from point measurements, and that different interpolation methods between points may result in varying maps; and that if subsidence rates are averaged over too large an area or aggregated across an entire region, then site-specific variations in subsidence may be missed. As a result of these limitations, which are inherent in any data-based media such as maps and web viewers, one geographic area or community may receive coastal restoration benefits while other sites with critical needs for restoration are missed simply because the map averaged over their extreme need.

In addition to site selection, potential sediment sources must be identified. The costs to move sediment can account for over two-thirds of total project costs, so careful consideration of the sediment source is essential. Both the transport distance and sediment type must factor into these calculations. As described earlier, the sediment type impacts the future stability of the restoration, and the sediment must be suitable for the new environment by being sufficiently consistent with existing grain sizes and meet environmental standards related to contamination. As an additional consideration, sands will not consolidate, whereas fine-grained materials such as silts and clays will. The location, type, and amount of dredged material available means that not all coastal wetlands can be protected in the face of sea level rise.

Once a candidate site and sediment source are identified, geomorphologic models to predict surface elevation consolidation must be used to determine how high the dredged material must be placed. The volume of sediment drastically increases during the dredging process as water is entrained, and, once placed, it will undergo large deformations (i.e., consolidation). These models predict the soil surface elevation with time, which is a controlling factor of vegetation health and productivity.

Monitoring

No matter how much effort is devoted to modeling a wetland restoration accurately, uncertainty will always be present due to assumptions about soil properties and initial elevations. Additionally, there will likely be discrepancies between the construction plans and the actual construction. Thus, it is vital to monitor the progression of geomorphological phenomena, which, for the purpose of this chapter, is focused on ground elevation change. Most surface elevation changes occur in the months to years following the placement of dredged material. During this time, consolidation, erosion, and deposition are the driving forces behind the establishment of the wetland ecosystem. Biological processes and plant productivity begin to dominate only after consolidation has largely finished. Long-term (decadal scale) changes driven by these biological processes and sea level rise may occur more slowly but likewise alter the wetland surface and ecosystem. This rapid geomorphic change post-construction and the long-term change driven by biological processes and sea level rise make it essential to monitor the surface elevation.

Elevation monitoring may seem straightforward initially, but it poses many challenges. In fact, wetlands can be considered a worst-case scenario in terms of ease of monitoring for a number of reasons. The post-construction ground surface is commonly incredibly soft, inhibiting easy access for direct measurements or establishing ground control points for unoccupied aerial systems (UAS; i.e., drones); wetland surfaces can change rapidly post-construction, thus requiring more frequent and costly monitoring; sites are often expansive, which increases the time necessary to survey the entire site; wetlands are tidally inundated, limiting site access and surveying to specific time windows since photogrammetry and topographic lidar often can only monitor areas exposed above the water surface such as during low

Professor Emeritus Jim Morris from the University of South Carolina sets up a surface elevation table (SET) to measure wetland sediment elevation at the Baruch Center, Debidue, South Carolina. The SET provides a noninvasive way to collect precise measurements over long periods.

tide; and, finally, vegetation poses challenges for photogrammetry and lidar elevation data collection and post-processing, though this is not typically an issue for the first months to years following initial construction when vegetation has not re-established.

These difficulties in monitoring coastal wetland elevation post-restoration influence the media used to visualize elevation monitoring data, which in turn impacts our understanding of site conditions and restoration outcomes. Common approaches to measuring surface elevation changes include direct, UAS-based, airborne, and satellite-derived measurements. Direct measurements using on-ground survey equipment produce highly accurate point measurements that are often visualized as fixed transects with changing elevations through time. However, relying only on widely spaced elevation transects can miss locations that are failing, resulting in a lack of adaptive management to correct the undesirable outcome. For a more complete visualization of geomorphic change, UAS-based lidar and photogrammetry and piloted airborne lidar methods can be used to create highly detailed surfaces, which are often displayed as elevation change maps. The temporal resolution of these remotely sensed data can be influenced by project-specific budgets that dictate the frequency of contractual or in-house surveys. Furthermore, publicly available lidar is typically only collected every three or more years by various state and federal agencies. These resulting temporal gaps in the monitoring media can result in missed opportunities for early adaptive management. Once vegetation has established, photogrammetry and lidar data require extensive quality assurance and control and manual editing to isolate and remove points that are classified as vegetation. This often necessitates subjective decision-making about which points are truly the ground elevation; managers must consider carefully how these processing steps change the media they use to make adaptive management decisions. Satellite-based monitoring methods (e.g., synthetic aperture radar) offer exceptionally expansive, open-source datasets that can be updated as frequently as every two weeks (based on the return period of the satellite). Major advances are being made on this front, making it a more viable option each year; however, like ground-based measurements, satellite monitoring has large point spacing, and derivative media, such as maps, often have large cell sizes. Thus, a small area of negative outcomes may be missed. To overcome the drawbacks of each monitoring method and its associated media, the best adaptive management strategies should incorporate a variety of geomorphic monitoring approaches.

Path Forward

Despite major advancements in our ability to survey, model, and predict the progression of coastal wetland geomorphology, a significant gap between this work and the field persists. Dredging techniques have remained virtually unchanged throughout the last half century, and our elevation change models are largely unverified for this type of application. For many agencies, the funds allocated to the long-term management of nourished sites is a small percentage of the initial construction costs of a restoration. As a result, measurements to determine the accuracy of projections during the design phases and what is actually established are few and far between. This is especially important in areas of rapidly increasing sea levels and changing climate, where outdated methods that rely on stagnant projections and predictions will not suffice.

One path forward is for coastal managers to follow the lead of Louisiana's CPRA, an organization that has been pushing the envelope by incorporating adaptive management principles through the development of a master plan that includes adding elevation measurements to its wetland restoration monitoring stations. Using these and other data, CPRA produces visual media and reports to describe the progress to date and the anticipated future of Louisiana's coast. Field monitoring should be continuously fed back into our modeling efforts to ensure accuracy; these lessons can inform our future design guidance, and as guidance improves, we must monitor the impact in the field, which starts the cycle again. Lessons can and should be learned from each project, and monitoring results should inform future site selection and designs. This cycle would improve our ability to implement adaptive management across both individual projects and entire restoration programs. Given the myriad types of uncertainty in all forms of environmental media—from data collection to digital interpretation to soil composition—along with unpredictable rates of change from a rapidly warming planet, an adaptive management approach is the only way to proceed.

Notes

1. Stephen W. Broome, Ernest D. Seneca & William W. Woodhouse, Jr, "Tidal Salt Marsh Restoration," *Aquatic Botany* 32, no. 1–2 (1988): 1–22; William J. Mitsch & James G. Gosselink, *Wetlands*, 2nd ed. (Wiley, 1993); Robert Constanza, et al., "The Value of Ecosystem Services: Putting the Issues in Perspective," *Ecological Economics* 25, no. 1 (1998): 67–72; John W. Day, et al., "Consequences of Climate Change on the Ecogeomorphology of Coastal Wetlands," *Estuaries and Coasts* 31 (2008): 477–91; Edward B. Barbier, et al., "The Value of Estuarine and Coastal Ecosystem Services," *Ecological Monographs* 81, no. 2 (2011): 169–93; Brian D. Harris, et al., "Establishment of Soil Strength in a Nourished Wetland Using Thin Layer Placement of Dredged Sediment," *PLoS One* 16, no. 5 (2021): e0251420.
2. Edward B. Barbier, "The Value of Coastal Wetland Ecosystem Services," in Gerardo M. E. Perillo, et al., *Coastal Wetlands*, 2nd ed. (Elsevier, 2019), 947–64, https://www.sciencedirect.com/science/article/pii/B9780444638939000277#bib54; National Marine Fisheries Service, *Fisheries Economics of the United States 2020* (US Dept. of Commerce, NOAA Tech. Memo. NMFS-F/SPO-236A, 2023), 231.
3. Robert Costanza, et al., "The Value of Coastal Wetlands for Hurricane Protection," *AMBIO: A Journal of the Human Environment* 37, no. 4 (2008): 241–48.
4. Katie K. Arkema, et al., "Coastal Habitats Shield People and Property from Sea-Level Rise and Storms," *Nature Climate Change* 3, no. 10 (2013): 913–18; Siddharth Narayan, et al., "The Effectiveness, Costs and Coastal Protection Benefits of Natural and Nature-Based Defences," *PLoS One* 11, no. 5 (2016): e0154735.
5. Caitlin M. Crain, Keryn B. Gedan & Michele Dionne, "Tidal Restrictions and Mosquito Ditching in New England Marshes: Case Studies of the Biotic Evidence, Physical Extent, and Potential for Restoration of Altered Tidal Hydrology," in Brian R. Silliman, Edwin D. Grosholz & Mark D. Bertness (eds), *Human Impacts on Salt Marshes: A Global Perspective* (University of California Press, 2009), 149–70.
6. Susan C. Adamowicz, et al., "Farmers in the Marsh: Lessons from History and Case Studies for the Future," *Wetland Science & Practice* 37, no. 3 (July 2020): 183–95.
7. Jaskaran Singh & Russ Joffrion, "Geotechnical Standards for Marsh Creation and Coastal Restoration Projects," Louisiana Coastal Protection and Restoration Authority (2017), https://coastal.la.gov/wp-content/uploads/2015/07/Appendix-B-CPRA-Geotechnical-Standards_12.21.17.pdf.
8. Navid H. Jafari, et al., "Wetland Shear Strength with Emphasis on the Impact of Nutrients, Sediments, and Sea Level Rise," *Estuarine, Coastal and Shelf Science* 229 (2019), 106394, https://doi.org/10.1016/j.ecss.2019.106394; Brian D. Harris, et al., "Establishment of Soil Strength."
9. Michael Oppenheimer, et al., "Sea Level Rise and Implications for Low-Lying Islands, Coasts and Communities," in Hans-Otto Pörtner, et al. (eds), *IPCC Special Report on the Ocean and Cryosphere in a Changing Climate* (Cambridge University Press, 2019), 321–445, https://doi.org/10.1017/97810091579-64.006.
10. Alessio Rovere, Paolo Stocchi & Matteo Vacchi, "Eustatic and Relative Sea Level Changes," *Current Climate Change Reports* 2, no. 4 (December 2016): 221–31, https://doi.org/10.1007/s40641-016-0045-7.
11. Ann Hijuelos & Denise J. Reed, "Coastal Master Plan: Appendix F: Adaptive Management," *Coastal Protection and Restoration Authority Master Plan* (Louisiana Coastal Protection and Restoration Authority, 2017), 1–43, https://www.lacoast.gov/crms/crms_public_data/publications/Hijuelos%20_%20Reed%202017.pdf.
12. Xiaorong Li, Nicoletta Leonardi & Andrew J. Plater, "Wave-Driven Sediment Resuspension and Salt

Marsh Frontal Erosion Alter the Export of Sediments from Macro-Tidal Estuaries," *Geomorphology* 325 (2019): 17–28; Marco Marani, et al., "Understanding and Predicting Wave Erosion of Marsh Edges," *Geophysical Research Letters* 38, no. 21 (2011); Matthew L. Kirwan & Keryn B. Gedan, "Sea-Level Driven Land Conversion and the Formation of Ghost Forests," *Nature Climate Change* 9, no. 6 (2019): 450–57.

13. Denise J. Reed, et al., "Marsh Surface Sediment Deposition and the Role of Tidal Creeks: Implications for Created and Managed Coastal Marshes," *Journal of Coastal Conservation* 5 (1999): 81–90; T. Christiansen, P. L. Wiberg & T. G. Milligan, "Flow and Sediment Transport on a Tidal Salt Marsh Surface," *Estuarine, Coastal and Shelf Science* 50, no. 3 (2000): 315–31.
14. Zoe J. Hughes, et al., "Rapid Headward Erosion of Marsh Creeks in Response to Relative Sea Level Rise," *Geophysical Research Letters* 36, no. 3 (2009); C. A. Wilson, Z. J. Hughes & D. M. FitzGerald, "The Effects of Crab Bioturbation on Mid-Atlantic Saltmarsh Tidal Creek Extension: Geotechnical and Geochemical Changes," *Estuarine, Coastal and Shelf Science* 106 (2012): 33–44.
15. Joshua Himmelstein, et al., "Mechanisms of Pond Expansion in a Rapidly Submerging Marsh," *Frontiers in Marine Science* 8 (2021): 704768.
16. R. S. Hatton, R. D. DeLaune & W. H. Patrick, Jr, "Sedimentation, Accretion, and Subsidence in Marshes of Barataria Basin, Louisiana," *Limnology and Oceanography* 28, no. 3 (1983): 494–502; Donald R. Cahoon, Denise J. Reed & John W. Day, Jr, "Estimating Shallow Subsidence in Microtidal Salt Marshes of the Southeastern United States: Kaye and Barghoorn Revisited," *Marine Geology* 128, no. 1–2 (1995): 1–9; Torbjörn E. Törnqvist, et al., "Mississippi Delta Subsidence Primarily Caused by Compaction of Holocene Strata," *Nature Geoscience* 1, no. 3 (2008): 173–76.
17. Carl T. Friedrichs & James E. Perry, "Tidal Salt Marsh Morphodynamics: A Synthesis," *Journal of Coastal Research* 27 (2001): 7–37; Donald R. Cahoon, et al., "Coastal Wetland Vulnerability to Relative Sea-Level Rise: Wetland Elevation Trends and Process Controls," in Jos T. A. Verhoeven, et al. (eds), *Wetlands and Natural Resource Management* (Springer, 2006), 273–92.
18. For example, Richard Orson, William Panageotou & Stephen P. Leatherman, "Response of Tidal Salt Marshes of the US Atlantic and Gulf Coasts to Rising Sea Levels," *Journal of Coastal Research* 1, no. 1 (1985): 29–37; James T. Morris, et al., "Responses of Coastal Wetlands to Rising Sea Level," *Ecology* 83, no. 10 (2002): 2,869–77.
19. Donald R. Cahoon, et al., "Evaluating the Relationship Among Wetland Vertical Development, Elevation Capital, Sea-Level Rise, and Tidal Marsh Sustainability," *Estuaries and Coasts* 42, no. 1 (2019): 1–15.
20. Ibid.
21. Neil K. Ganju, et al., "Development and Application of Landsat-Based Wetland Vegetation Cover and Unvegetated-Vegetated Marsh Ratio (UVVR) for the Conterminous United States," *Estuaries and Coasts* 45, no. 7 (2022): 1,861–78.
22. Friedrichs & Perry, "Tidal Salt Marsh Morphodynamics," 7–37.
23. Benjamin C. Green, David J. Smith & Graham J. C. Underwood, "Habitat Connectivity and Spatial Complexity Differentially Affect Mangrove and Salt Marsh Fish Assemblages," *Marine Ecology Progress Series* 466 (2012): 177–92.
24. B. R. Couvillion, N. K. Ganju & Z. Defne, "An Unvegetated to Vegetated Ratio (UVVR) for Coastal Wetlands of the Conterminous United States (2014–2018)," *U.S. Geological Survey Data Release* (2021), https://doi.org/10.5066/P97DQXZP.
25. Delaware.gov, "White Creek and Assawoman Canal Dredging," https://dnrec.alpha.delaware.gov/watershed-stewardship/waterways/white-creek-dredging/ (accessed January 11, 2024).
26. National Fish and Wildlife Foundation, "Regional Coastal Resilience Assessments," https://www.nfwf.org/programs/national-coastal-resilience-fund/regional-coastal-resilience-assessments (accessed January 11, 2024).
27. Catherine Fitzpatrick, Krista L. Jankowski & Denise Reed, *2023 Coastal Master Plan: Determining Subsidence Rates for Use in Predictive Modeling* (Coastal Protection and Restoration Authority, 2021), 70, https://coastal.la.gov/wp-content/uploads/2021/03/Subsidence-Rates_Mar2021.pdf (accessed January 11, 2024).

Outside the Operating Envelope

Matthew Jull and Leena Cho

"Back up the truck a little farther!" Standing at the edge of Barrow Environmental Observatory a few miles southeast of Utqiaġvik, Alaska, Howie Epstein—tundra ecologist—was holding a large rotary hammer drill attached to a meter-long masonry bit.[1] "Just add another extension cord; we can't get the generator any closer!" A few hours earlier, the three of us had managed to borrow the largest drill available in town, along with a gas-powered portable generator and a pile of extension cords so that we could drill holes a meter into the ground to set up a control site for our research. "That's got it!" The sound of the drill rang out over the open expanse. With full weight bearing down, the drill was hammering through the microbiome of tundra vegetation and thawed active layer that sits atop frozen, concrete-like permafrost.[2] The drill labored as the bit went deeper, slowly bringing up a mixture of frozen silt, clay, rock, and ice, which had not been disturbed for thousands of years, before finally bottoming out. "Let's get the probe inserted and linked up to the logger." With that, we had installed one of 120 new measurement nodes into a new Utqiaġvik sensor array that monitors micrometeorological and ground conditions in the northernmost city in the United States.

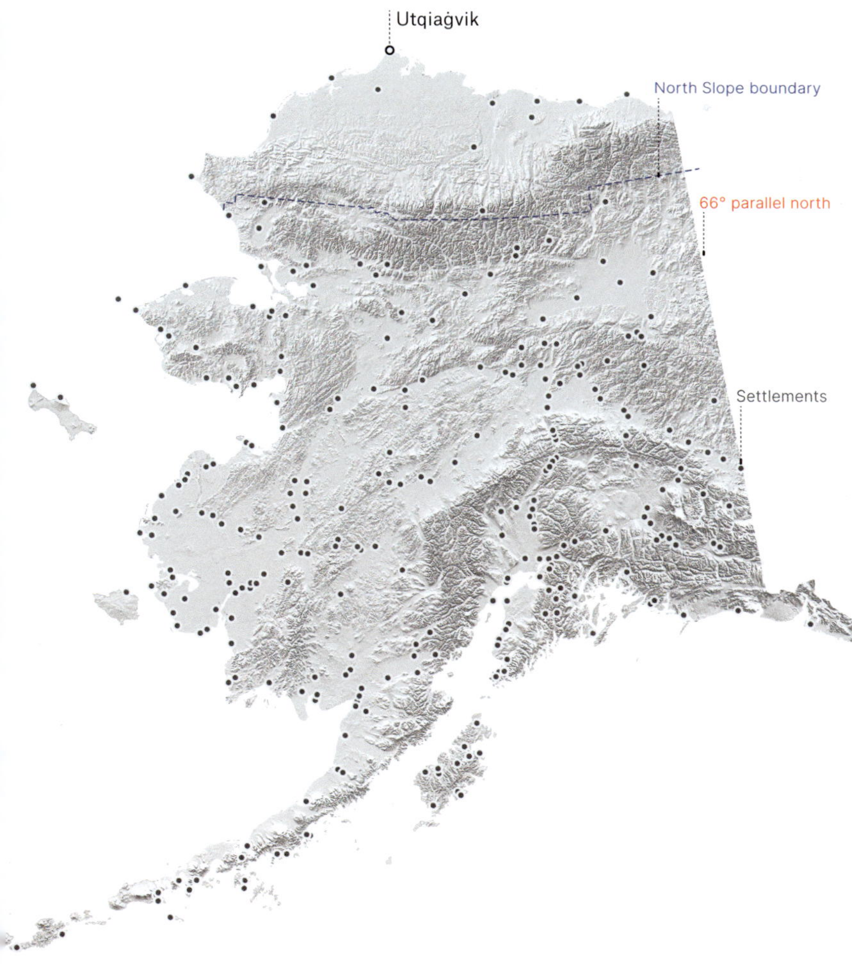

Location of Utqiaġvik, Alaska (71.2906° N, 156.7886° W). Utqiaġvik is the administrative center of North Slope Borough and a scientific and logistical hub for Arctic research.

Utqiaġvik, formerly known as Barrow, is the locus of our five-year study to develop design and planning approaches and tools that address changing built-natural environmental interactions.[3] The Arctic is warming faster than any other region on Earth; air temperatures have increased up to four times faster than the global average, leading to warmer ground conditions and thawing permafrost with major effects on the stability of the built environment and ways of living that depend on it.[4] The population has grown substantially from several hundred in the early 1900s to over 4,000 at time of publication. As a result, the city has expanded into new neighborhoods in a typical suburban morphology with detached houses in a gridded road and utility network. Since 1972, the North Slope Borough has built a host of community infrastructure in its administrative center of Utqiaġvik, including water and electrical utilities, roads, sanitation facilities, snow fences, and numerous single- and multi-story buildings. Nearly all structures are raised on wood or steel pilings driven into the underlying permafrost, permitting air flow in one meter-high crawl spaces to minimize the destabilizing effects of heat flow into the ground. However, with increasing permafrost degradation due to climate change, current ways of designing, constructing, and maintaining buildings and infrastructure in the city—and for so many more across the Arctic—face serious, if not existential, challenges that require significant multifaceted adaptations over time.

Our research team—composed of a diverse group of scientists, designers, engineers, anthropologists, and data scientists—working in

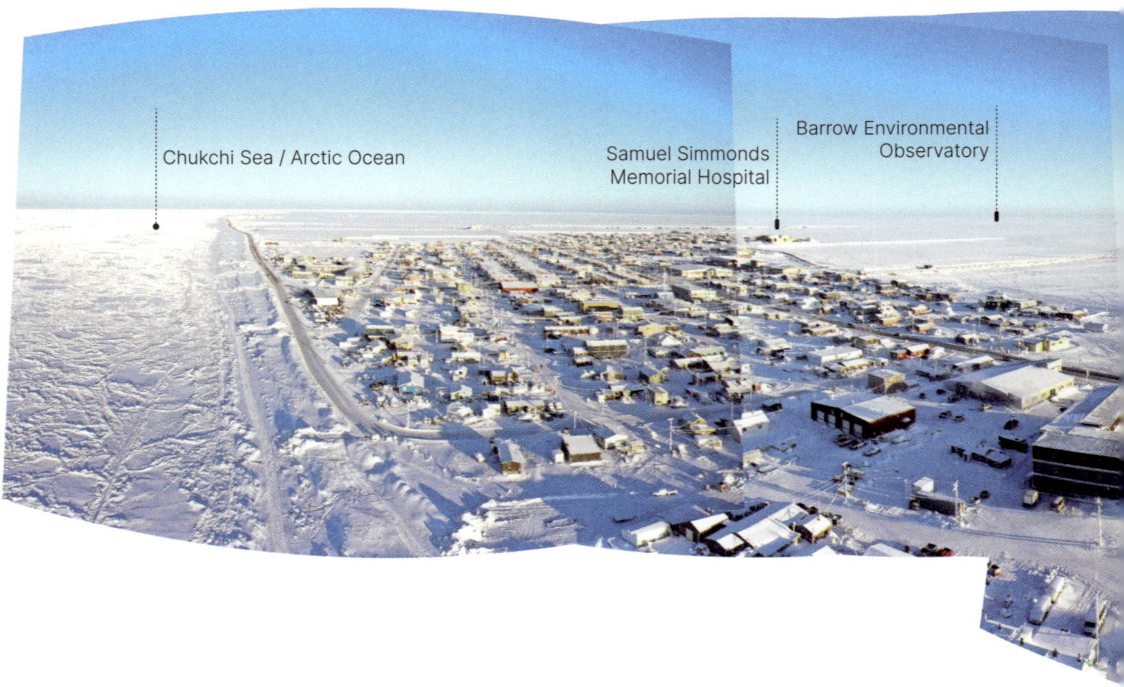

View of Utqiaġvik (pop. 4,927; 2020 US Census) from Chukchi Sea toward tundra in winter. Four sensor array sites (indicated by black rectangles) are distributed across Utqiaġvik. The image shows the sensors' locations relative to the Chukchi Sea and the Lower Isatkoak Lagoon, two significant waterbodies.

partnership with local, borough, and tribal organizations as well as federal research labs, arrived at the North Slope of Alaska in the early summer of 2022 for the first field season. The project, sponsored by the US National Science Foundation, has as its primary goal the measurement and characterization of environmental conditions in and around buildings and infrastructure built on permafrost by deploying environmental sensor arrays at several sites across Utqiaġvik. The result will be a multi-year high-resolution spatial and temporal dataset. This approach differs from most of the scientific research that has taken place on the North Slope due to the focus on the instrumentation of buildings, infrastructure, and adjacent ground instead of only focusing on the undeveloped tundra.[5]

The project consists of a coordinated array of environmental monitoring, with three independent networks of fixed sensor arrays within which geophysical surveys are conducted annually. In addition to a control site located on undisturbed tundra outside of the city limits at the Barrow Environmental Observatory, our instruments are located at sites with various land use designations and environmental gradients as well as on or near structures built during different time periods: Taġiuġmiullu Nunamiullu Housing Authority's "29 Plex" residential building (built in 1977); Barrow Utilities and Electric Cooperative's public utilities infrastructure complex (1983); and the regional Samuel Simmonds Memorial Hospital (2013). Many of these specific locations, as well as general study areas, were initially identified and suggested to us by our community partners. Within each site, the configuration

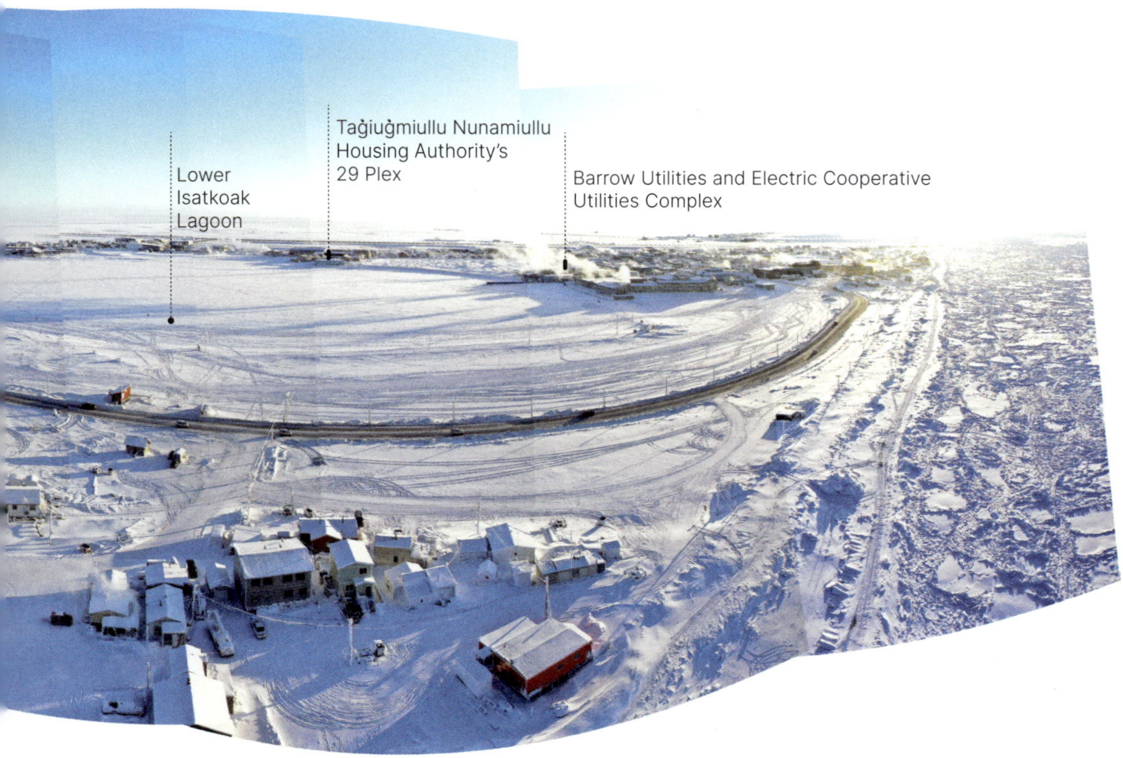

of the sensor array was based on observations of where the largest changes might occur around buildings and infrastructure. Each site consists of a primary base station—a tripod mounted with a data logger, communications modules, and solar panel—linked wirelessly to five or six satellite sensor stations located within each study site that relay data back to the base station at set intervals. Each site contains a combination of micrometeorological (e.g., wind speed, wind direction, atmospheric pressure, air temperature, relative humidity, solar radiation, precipitation, and snow depth) and ground-based sensors (e.g., soil moisture and temperature) that extend to depths of 90 cm into the ground with a sampling frequency of 15–30 minutes. Altogether, there are about 120 individual sensors measuring time-varying characteristics of the ground and near-surface air across the study sites, collecting 20,000 data points per day. Annual geophysical surveys conducted by our research partner (USACE's Cold Regions Research and Engineering Laboratory) at each of the three sites using ground penetrating radar, electrical resistivity tomography, and thaw probing provide a means of characterizing subsurface conditions of ground ice, water, active layer thickness, and ground composition via transects adjacent to the sensor stations.

The location, density, and sampling frequency of the sensors deployed for this project are unusual. For example, clusters of sensors, such as those measuring meteorological variables (e.g., air temperature, wind speed, and direction), are placed at the corners and edges of buildings and at variable heights extending above the ground surface, while other soil-specific sensors extend below. The placement of these sensors in "disturbed" locations is intentional. Historians of science James Fleming and Vladimir Jankovic have pointed out that in meteorology's development, this "zone of disturbance"—the boundary layer close to the ground—has intentionally been excluded from environmental analysis despite being most "entangled with human energy."[6] Weather instruments, they note, have been placed two meters above the ground since the late 19th century to standardize measurements and minimize outliers over large spatial and temporal extents. From this macroclimate perspective (which also tends to govern our modern sense of "climate"), near-surface data are considered "contaminated." But this zone of disturbance is essential in characterizing local conditions and energy balance—something environmental scientists have understood since the mid-20th century when the idea of a calculated "*N*-Factor" was introduced to represent the heat flux across this boundary layer, which is essentially derived from the difference between the ground and overlying air temperature.[7]

The micrometeorological data we are recording close to the ground and near buildings and structures is characterizing spatial and temporal variability and allows us to analyze the potential impact of these variations on the stability of the underlying permafrost. Sampling this zone of disturbance is sampling environmental events that matter the most, and most immediately, to the design and maintenance of buildings and infrastructure. We are also sampling environmental conditions at high temporal resolutions. This can prevent the problem of what microbiologist Michael Allen called "missed critical events," which are the immediate and highly relevant environmental shifts that are

A micrometeorological base station installation at the control site within the Barrow Environmental Observatory (BEO). BEO is exclusively zoned as a Science Research District and is where most of the area's funded research occurs.

Drilling to install ground sensors adjacent to one of the four micrometeorological satellite stations at the Taġiuġmiullu Nunamiullu Housing Authority's 29 Plex site. The building faces Lower Isatkoak Lagoon and has been experiencing subsidence.

not observed due to low sampling frequency.[8] Furthermore, high temporal resolution allows rates of change of environmental variables to be characterized fully. Weather in the Arctic can change drastically during the day and certainly within an hour, which annual, monthly, or even daily averages would not show. Rapid changes in wind speed and direction, for example, can quickly deposit or shift large amounts of snow. With its high albedo and insulating capacity, this can have significant effects on local thermal regimes on the ground. Short-duration events may not significantly affect permafrost, but if this were to occur repeatedly due to the inherent design or siting conditions of a building or structure, it could contribute to an acceleration of permafrost degradation, leading to the subsidence and destabilization of overlying structures.

The high spatial and temporal density of our dataset is also designed to match the high degree of environmental sensitivity, ephemerality, and unpredictability of the Arctic urban landscape. Understanding near-surface weather conditions at this granular scale is especially important in Utqiaġvik because of the direct and significant implications for the underlying permafrost, which is characterized by high ground-ice content (up to 80% on the North Slope) and an active layer at the surface of 30–90 cm that freezes and thaws annually.[9] The thermal stability of permafrost is a critical factor in the management of buildings and infrastructure as well as for locating future development. The foundations of most built structures in the North Slope including buildings, pipelines, and utility poles, for example, are drilled into the permafrost for stability, with the assumption that it will stay frozen. With a rapidly warming climate, this is no longer the case. "If 10 meters of permafrost thaws," geophysicist Vladimir Romanovsky explains, "9 meters of ice may melt and flow away, leaving only a meter of soil in its place."[10] Despite being built on this potentially highly unstable ground, communities in the North Slope do not have comprehensive surveys of the location of ground ice in large part due to the high cost of geotechnical surveys and mapping. Compounding this problem is the variable impact that heat-producing urban structures—such as buildings and utilities (both buried and above-grade)—can have on the thermal and physical stability of the permafrost.

The large temporal and spatial changes we are observing in the active layer and permafrost thermal conditions, coupled with data from subsurface geophysical studies, could be described as a type of "underground weather system." While the idea of weather extends deep into the soil and the measure of good data ultimately depends on its collective usefulness for the community, the process of siting, installing, and maintaining sensing technologies has also proved critical in the shaping of shared environmental knowledge. Sites of instrumentation reflect a spectrum of physical locations that have already been changing (e.g., subsidence, waterlogging) or likely will be in the future, warranting a focused, multi-year observation. These sites have been identified and agreed upon by various groups involved in the project, including researchers and community partners as well as permitting organizations, property owners, managers, and residents. Siting instruments is a commitment and requires consensus, a delineation of common objectives and discipline-specific inquiries that are interoperable and beneficial to the broader group, especially in a collaborative, multi-year urban and community-based project such as ours. As many geographers, including David Livingstone and Michael Bravo, have shown, science is a cultural and social practice deeply rooted in

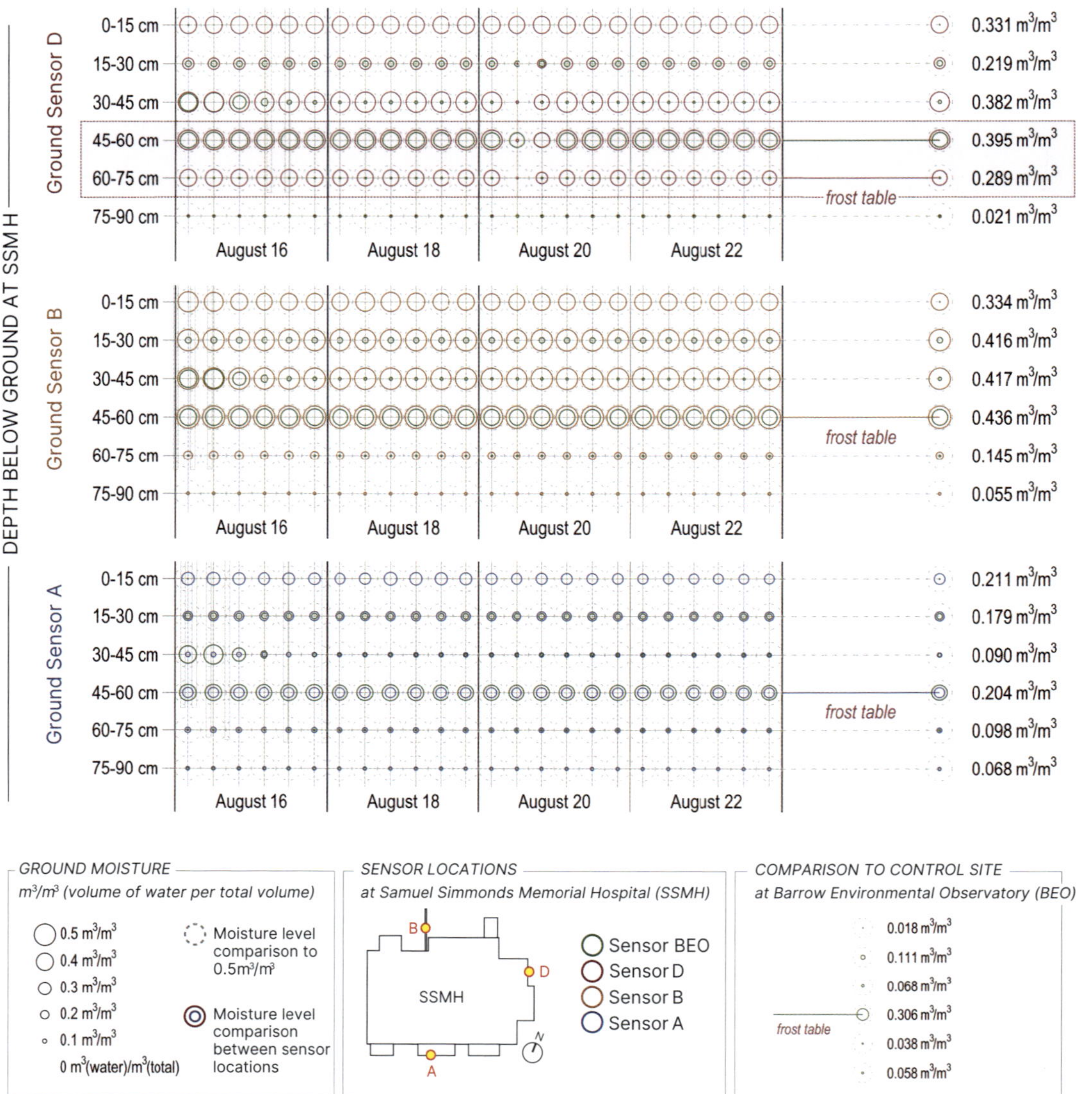

Diagrams showing comparative ground moisture data from three locations (A, B, and D) at the Samuel Simmonds Memorial Hospital. This data, collected on four days during the thaw-maximum month of August, measured the presence of liquid water in the soil at 15 cm intervals to a depth of 90 cm. The moisture levels at B and D are higher than at A, but all three levels are higher than at the undeveloped control site at BEO. Higher moisture content in the soil accelerates permafrost degradation.

"specific spaces" as well as "historical and geographical circumstances."[11] It is about discerning not only "what to sense," but also "where to sense" that can elicit meaningful information for the research and about the places of which the research is profoundly a part.

Delineating the geography of sensing technologies—the process of collectively figuring out where to place sensors, what these sites might indicate, and why they matter to many people in the first place—creates an opportunity to negotiate and form a mutual method for the production of environmental knowledge. Instrumented sites are not only sites of monitoring and measurement, but also of collective matters of concern and care materialized in places over time. These sites register environmental phenomena and a community of people mutually exchanging ideas and developing shared habits of environmental perception, or what microbiologist Ludwik Fleck described as "thought collectives."[12] Members of a thought collective, he explained, maintain a cognitive and intellectual interaction by adopting certain ways of perceiving and thinking; they also transform their own ways of "seeing" through shared activities in their interpersonal space that enable such exchange. In our project, placing and installing sensors has played a pivotal role in the formation of a thought collective, with sensing technologies acting as a critical medium for cognitive mediation. Working with tangible things in specific contexts as well as through equally specific installation protocols has not only brought together a group of people with different expertise, backgrounds, and even worldviews to perceive the landscape scientifically, technically, and collectively, but also accelerated the emergence of such collective perception. It has also exposed specific differences in the ways we perceive, prioritize, and problematize changes that are occurring in the Arctic urban landscape while allowing us to recognize that there are multiple, valuable, and equally critical ways of knowing that could be useful in the design and management of complex socioenvironmental systems.[13]

Furthermore, siting instruments reveals the influence of context—historical, legal, formal, social, political, infrastructural, and logistical—on the content of scientific knowledge and the design process.[14] Sensing stations, like other media technologies, are deeply enmeshed with the landscape in which they operate and actively participate in the emergence of (selective) environmental data instead of merely observing those conditions.[15] For example, the locations of all sensor stations in our study had to be inspected on site and approved by various local utilities and regulatory organizations prior to installation. During this process, one of the stations had to be moved closer to the city lagoon due to the unexpected presence of a buried gas pipeline at the original site. This relocation has likely shifted the results of the localized dataset (e.g., soil moisture) given the high resolution of data and subsequent analysis outcomes. Similarly, placing sensing technologies is not a neutral act shielded from external influences. In the case of our project, the resultant data are a byproduct of invisible regulatory and infrastructural realities of the measured landscape in addition to the environmental conditions they capture. Just as the "environments do not simply surround media but run through and enable them," the messy palimpsests of human and non-human actions fielding the site dynamically contribute to the construction of data and their continual mediation with the site as well as with sensing technologies.[16]

The processes of installing instruments and visiting them repeatedly over time for fine-tuning, troubleshooting, and tending—in myriad weather conditions and seasons, as well as in the accompaniment of various researchers, technicians, curious residents, and even other animals—catalyze a series of exchanges exposing previously unseen details, patterns, and stories emerging from the instrumentation sites. Moreover, the installation of new sensing equipment in an urban environment prompts new social and material actions around it and activates the landscape with novel encounters.[17] The sensor stations have become distinct geographic markers, meeting locations, and conversation topics for many residents. They are everyday sites and means of sociality mediated by the technologies. These stations also accumulate new materials (e.g., snow, trash) and previously uncommon interactions (e.g., encircling foot traffic, cleared snow around the stations), transforming the surrounding landscape itself in visible ways. As media theorist Jennifer Gabrys describes, sensing technologies articulate how "sites and subjects commingle" and actively inform what types of new sites, citizenships, and design might emerge in the process.[18] Likewise, the Arctic sensing stations have catalyzed new kinds of interactions and habits that lead to the emergence of new social and material landscapes.

The spatial and temporal geographies of data reflect the sensitivity, temporality, and unpredictability of the Arctic urban landscape while prompting novel socioenvironmental and sociotechnological relations. To that end, sites of sensing are not just reserved for science or for the performance of an operating envelope, where the technical equipment enacts only intended functions. They are the products of shared environmental perceptions and preconceptions that have evolved with time and that both stem from and influence how we see and experience the landscape.[19] They register *and* shape data and mediate the contents of scientific knowledge as well as its meaning and use for design. They can foster sociotechnological conviviality—"the heterogeneous company and messy business of *living together*"—especially in places where rapid environmental change and the densification of scientific fieldwork and technologies are becoming the new reality.[20] Tracing and understanding such geography of technical equipment reveals a fuller spectrum of its agency in the production of environmental knowledge and material landscape. Sometimes it may be what lies beyond the operating envelope of instruments that gives clear meaning and directions for design.

Acknowledgment

This study is funded by the US National Science Foundation (award #2022639).

Notes

1. Established in 1992 by the Ukpeaġvik Iñupiat Corporation, BEO is reputedly the only exclusively zoned Science Research District in the United States. It is 30 km2 in size, about nine times bigger than Central Park in New York City, and it exhibits a wide spectrum of environmental conditions that are high in scientific value.
2. Permafrost is ground that remains frozen continuously for at least two years. The active layer is the soil above the permafrost that freezes and thaws seasonally based on air temperature changes. Designated by the Global Climate Observing System, near-surface permafrost dynamics is also one of 55 "Essential Climate Variables (ECV)" that constitute Earth's climate and an effective indicator of climate change due to its thermal sensitivity.
3. The study has three interrelated objectives: (1) the deployment of micrometeorological and aquatic sensors and geophysical surveys to provide data on how urban infrastructure and buildings interact with the surrounding air, ground, and water; (2) the application of sensor and survey data to generate urban environmental analysis, design, and planning tools for the community to address current and future management of the city's

built environment; and (3) the study of how our research team and city's residents communicate across disciplines and cultures to co-produce knowledge. An extended summary of the project can be found on the US National Science Foundation (NSF) website: https://www.nsf.gov/awardsearch/showAward?AWD_ID=2022639&HistoricalAwards=false.

4. Mika Rantanen, et al., "The Arctic has Warmed Nearly Four Times Faster Than the Globe Since 1979," *Communications Earth & Environment* 3, no. 168 (2022): 2, https://doi.org/10.1038/s43247-022-00498-3.
5. The US National Science Foundation created the Navigating the New Arctic (NNA) program in 2017 to support "creative new directions for understanding and adapting to a rapidly changing Arctic." The authors' project discussed in this chapter is also funded through the NNA program. See National Science Foundation, *NSF 23-088 Dear Colleague Letter: Updates to the Navigating the New Arctic (NNA) Program*, April 17, 2023, https://www.nsf.gov/pubs/2023/nsf23088/nsf23088.jsp?org=NSF.
6. James R. Fleming & Vladimir Jankovic, "Introduction: Revisiting *Klima*," *Osiris* 26, no. 1 (2011): 4.
7. Anna E. Klene, et al., "The N-Factor in Natural Landscapes: Variability of Air and Soil-Surface Temperatures, Kuparuk River Basin, Alaska, U.S.A.," *Arctic, Antarctic, and Alpine Research* 33, no. 2 (2001): 140–48, https://doi.org/10.1080/15230430.2001.12003416.
8. Michael F. Allen, "If You Want to Understand Nature, Stick Your Head in the Sand!" *LA+ Interdisciplinary Journal of Landscape Architecture* 4 (Fall 2016): 16–21.
9. Min Liew, et al., "Understanding Effects of Permafrost Degradation and Coastal Erosion on Civil Infrastructure in Arctic Coastal Villages: A Community Survey and Knowledge Co-Production," *Journal of Marine Science and Engineering* 10, no. 3 (2022): 3, https://doi.org/10.3390/jmse10030422.
10. Alena Naiden, "Alaska Scientists Study Accelerating Land Subsidence Affecting Coastal North Slope Communities," *Anchorage Daily News* (January 16, 2022), https://www.adn.com/alaska-news/rural-alaska/2022/01/16/alaska-scientists-study-accelerating-land-subsidence-affecting-coastal-north-slope-communities/.
11. David N. Livingstone, *Putting Science in Its Place: Geographies of Scientific Knowledge* (University of Chicago Press, 2003), 180. See also Michael Bravo, "The Rhetoric of Scientific Practice in Nunavut," *Ecumene* 7, no. 4 (2000): 468–74.
12. Lorraine Daston, "On Scientific Observation," *Isis* 99, no. 1 (2008): 106; see also Ludwik Fleck, *Genesis and Development of a Scientific Fact*, trans. Fred Bradley & Thaddeus J. Trenn (University of Chicago Press, 1979).
13. Thaddeus Miller, et al., "Epistemological Pluralism: Reorganizing Interdisciplinary Research," *Ecology and Society* 13, no. 2 (2008): 46, https://www.jstor.org/stable/26268006.
14. Livingstone, *Putting Science in Its Place*, 86.
15. Jeffrey Moro, "Measuring the Sky from the Curve of the Earth," in this collection.
16. Jonathan Turnbull, et al., "Digital Ecologies: Materialities, Encounters, Governance," *Progress in Environmental Geography* 2, no. 1–2 (2023): 9, https://doi.org/10.1177/27539687221145698. See also Philipp Lehmann, "Average Rainfall and the Play of Colors: Colonial Experience and Global Climate Data," *Studies in History and Philosophy of Science* 70 (2018): 38–49, https://doi.org/10.1016/j.shpsa.2018.05.007.
17. Turnbull, et al., "Digital Ecologies," 11.
18. Jennifer Gabrys, "Ecological Observatories: Fluctuating Sites and Sensing Subjects," in Laura Beloff, Erich Berger & Terike Haapoja (eds), *Field_Notes: From Landscape to Laboratory—Maisemasta Laboratorioon* (Printon Printinghouse, 2013), 180.
19. Kristina Hill, "Shifting Sites," in Carol J. Burns & Andrea Kahn (eds), *Site Matters: Design Concepts, Histories, and Strategies* (Routledge, 2005), 132.
20. Steve Hinchliffe & Sarah Whatmore, "Living Cities: Towards a Politics of Conviviality," *Science as Culture* 15, no. 2 (June 2006): 134, original emphasis, https://doi.org/10.1080/09505430600707988.

Toward a Time-Critical Design Approach

Ilmar Hurkxkens

Everything has its own temporality, its own sequence of events, its own process. In nature, we can think of geological processes in the creation of mountain ranges that span millions of years or of the rapid hazard events, such as flash floods and debris flows that pass within minutes. Site-time dimensions of a natural event are how they unfold and how they take shape. As such, the form of the terrain is nothing but a frozen moment of a system in continuous motion. Similar to a photograph, when we use sensors such as lidar to capture its form, we capture a still frame.[1] It is like working with a topographic still image of a condition that has already passed. The recent advent of robotic construction equipment for the architectural, engineering, and construction industries closes the gap between design (that is, by definition, preconceived), real-time adaptation, and open-ended transformation. It represents a convergence of multiple developments in environmental sensors, robotic systems, digital fabrication, simulation, software development, and even building codes and legislation.[2] The landscape engineering and construction industry is in the early stages of using autonomous earth-moving equipment, bringing digital fabrication to the scale of the landscape. As a construction method that operates explicitly with procedures over time, it holds the potential for working with the ever-changing and uncertain environments in which landscape architecture operates. Utilizing a real-time feedback mechanism between found material and designed performance, such equipment can autonomously direct and maintain the course of dynamic processes in the landscape. Autonomous earth-moving equipment will transform the way we design and build large-scale landscapes.

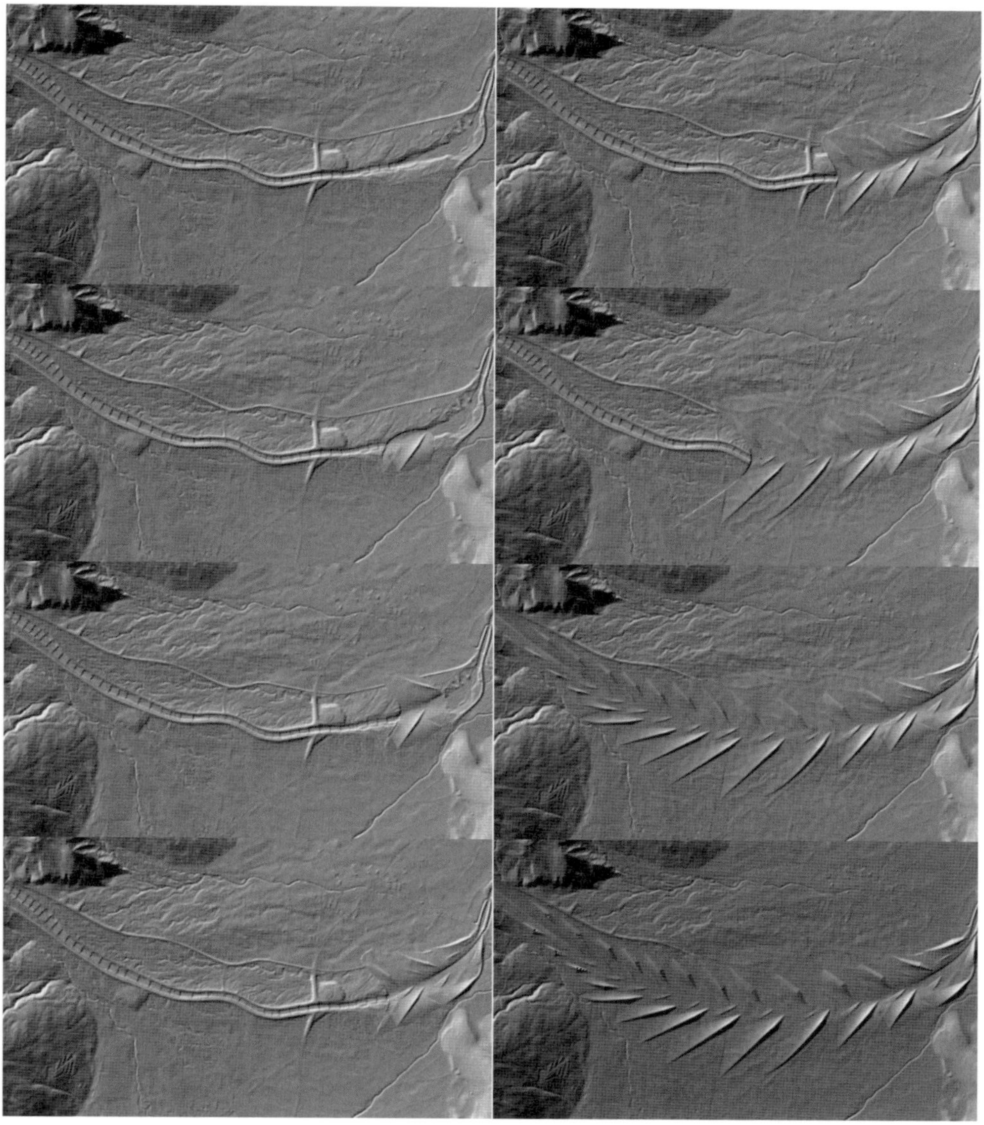

T 0.0 T 1
T 0.1 T 5
T 0.2 T 10
T 0.5 T 20

Digital model of a construction sequence at intervals over 20 years. During this period, check dams are dismantled or eroded away and subsequently reconstructed into large earthworks designed to attenuate debris flows of up to 200,000 cubic meters per event. Seasonal debris flows are projected to deposit 50,000 cubic meters of material annually. Consequently, the timing of construction phases directly corresponds to the volumes of sediment accumulating on-site over the years and is subject to change.

Drone view of the robotic excavator HEAP (Hydraulic Excavator for an Autonomous Purpose), a customized Menzi Muck M545 12-ton walking excavator developed by the Robotic Systems Lab, ETH Zurich.

In landscape architecture, terrain and its structure are key to organizing space, functioning as a load-bearing material for civilization. The recent increase in natural hazards, such as rising sea levels, landslides, floods, and drought points to the delicate balance between our settlements and our environment. Responding to these challenges is becoming more urgent because of escalating climate variability and related uncertainties. In the ever-increasing superimposition of natural and urban systems with declining resources and increasing demand for space, a structural and circular approach to construction becomes necessary.

This chapter promotes the real-time integration of information, design, and fabrication to enable an adaptive and sustainable landscape transformation. This integration starts with the information phase, captured using surveying instruments capable of relaying various sensory data of the physical world (geometric, climatic, and tactile, among others). The design phase analyzes this data and creates a purposeful and conscious response to a spatial and material reality encoded in a new composition. Finally, with the advent of robotic construction equipment, the fabrication phase transforms the found materiality into a new structure, a new terrain. This integration can be described as a robotic system that combines information, design, and fabrication using sensors, actuators, and human interfaces to produce change by interacting with its environment. This *in situ* method promotes sustainable and site-specific landscape design and construction.[3] In addition, autonomous construction equipment can be used to create complex and intricate designs that would otherwise not be possible with traditional methods. It allows us to capture and respond to relations between form and processes in the landscape, underscoring how spatial proximities in surface structures influence ecological performance and the movement of people and animals. The use of locally resourced materials can transform the ground into topographic structures that are more resilient to natural disasters, such as floods and debris flows, as well as help create formations and material ecologies of any kind. By embracing technological advancements and understanding them as interconnected with humans, animals, and plants alike, these complex modern systems might become fundamental to a sustainable organization of our environment.[4]

Instead of the traditional linear phasing of a landscape architectural project (from survey to design to construction to maintenance), the process described below collapses these phases into single moments in time that repeat indefinitely. This recursive and ongoing process poses challenges to the design discipline itself. It would be advantageous to make many design decisions at the time of construction, giving agency to the found materiality of a site and letting it guide its potential formal outcome. This process might be well supported by in-time simulation of the projected change. With the temporal nature of the landscape in mind, design becomes a time-critical operation. Instead of preconceiving a form, one must design the processes by which that form will be created. The type and sequence of these processes then determine their duration. Some might take milliseconds, some hundreds of years. To consider a truly site-specific and adaptive construction method, the following paragraphs outline an initial approach to time-sensitive landscape design in operation. The examples below show practical applications in field tests and illustrations that chart design decisions over various magnitudes of time.[5] Ultimately, the aim is to establish a dynamic construction approach that aligns with an inherently dynamic environmental condition.

Milliseconds–Seconds

The robotic feedback mechanism relies on various onboard sensors to operate in changing environments. These sensors enable a robotic excavator to know its position in space relative to the existing and designed topography. Sensors include GNSS for accurate position data, lidar for the terrain, and various inertial measurement units (IMUs) and joint sensors for continuous position data of the excavator's chassis, arm, and bucket. Together, they inform the state estimation of the machine at a rate of 100 Hz, operated on the computer's memory for speed. The motion planning of the excavator, whether it needs to traverse terrain or perform a digging or dumping cycle, is controlled by an algorithm that calculates the difference between the existing and desired state. From here, actuators spring into motion to physically alter the landscape. When encountering unstable terrain or muddy conditions that cause its wheels to slide, the Hydraulic Excavator for an Autonomous Purpose (HEAP) immediately recognizes the state change and adjusts its control.[6] When digging in loose and sandy soil, the motion cycle can automatically perform a deep and steep digging motion, filling the bucket. However, on hard ground full of rocks, the force-feedback on the shovel initiates a different motion path, one that is more like scraping over the ground, adapting to changing ground conditions. This near-real-time adaption to terrain enables traversing and manipulation in uncertain environments and changing site conditions.[7] The direct relation between sensing, environment, and manipulation forms the basis for all *in situ* formation

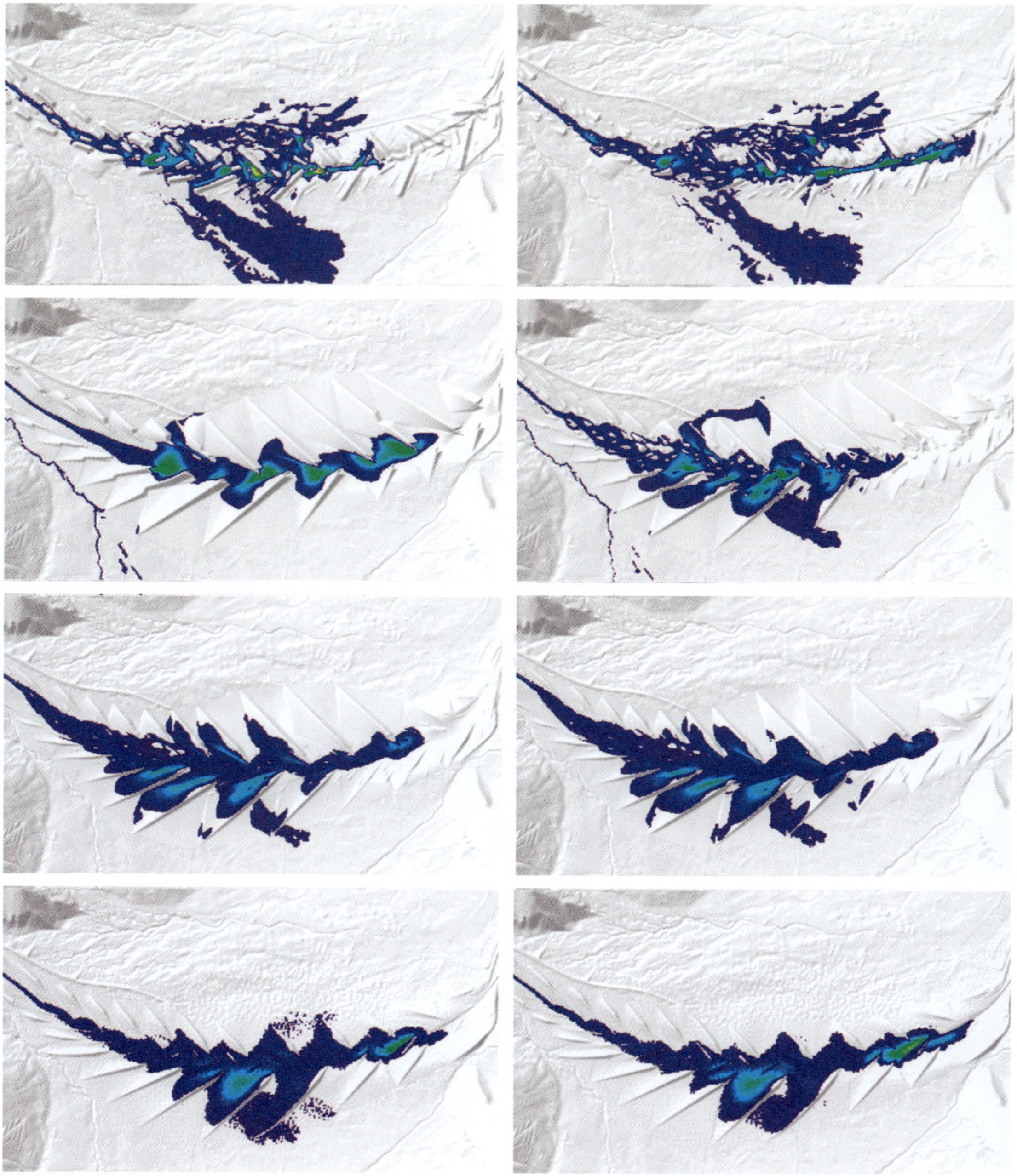

Muddy and debris-laden flow simulations throughout the design process highlight a possible scenario after 20 years. The topographic design is continuously adapted using iterative simulations to create a valid landscape structure capable of performing on structural, ecological, cultural, and aesthetic levels. Inputs include volume, flow depth, bed erosion, deposition, speed, and duration.

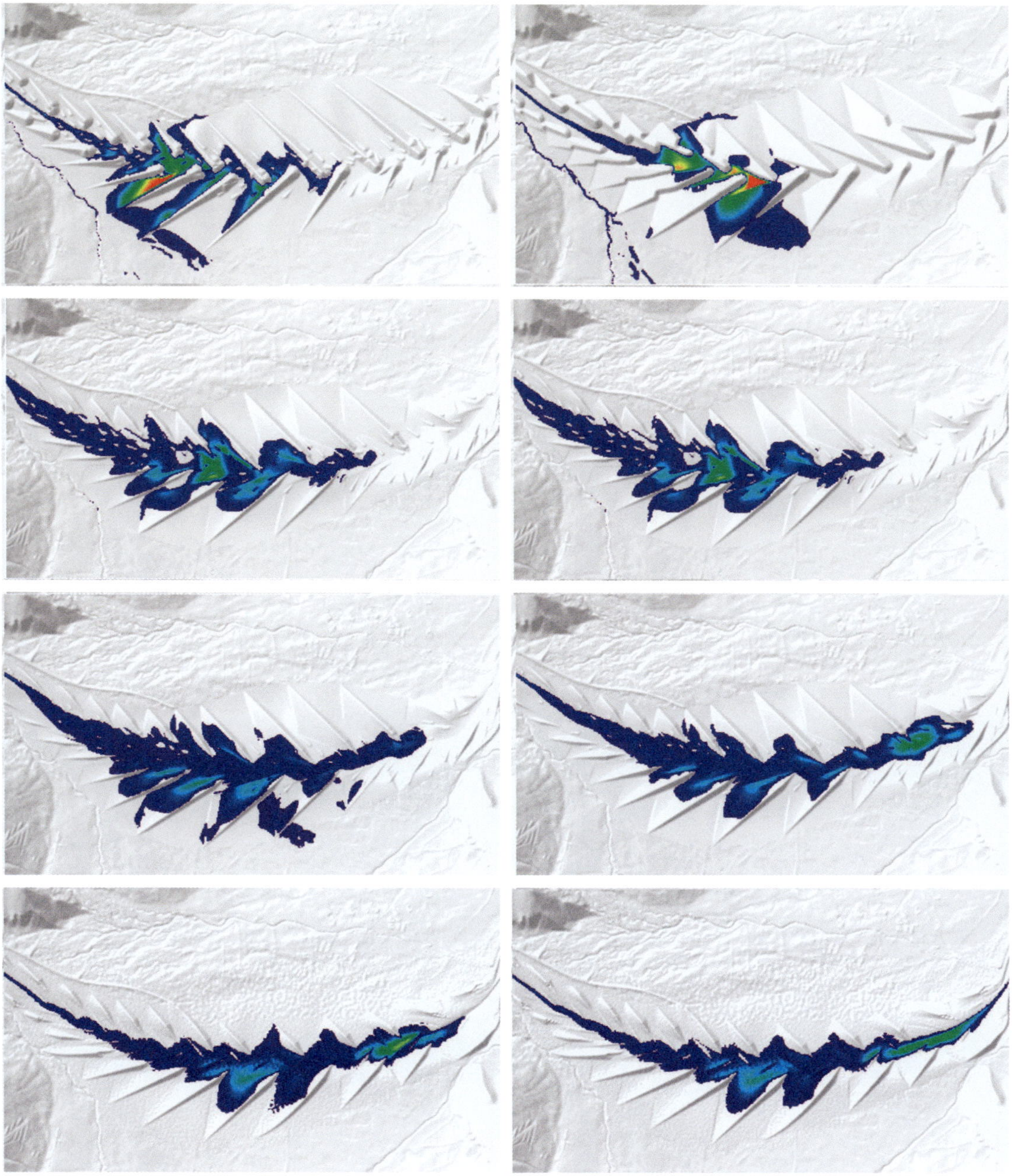

of local soil with heavy robotic equipment. A reflexive approach to grading translates well to the manipulation of granular materials in landscape structures, as their variability changes widely over a site and with time.

Relaying information on volume balance, slope angles, and the excavated terrain's general shape is critical for dynamic adaptation. Instead of removing and applying external fill, transforming local materials yields many benefits, from minimizing material handling and transport, to supporting existing processes and ecologies, to strengthening existing spatial identities and experiences. Technically, this can be accomplished using the open-source robotic framework, Robot Operating System (ROS).[8] Every few seconds, an analysis is made to follow the volume balance of the design, along with an analysis of the overall geometry and chemical makeup. It enables different responses to various changing conditions one might find when digging in the ground. For example, when encountering clay, a stiff and sticky fine-grained substance, one can achieve steeper slope angles with more erosion resistance.[9] On the other side of the soil texture triangle, one may encounter sand. This granular substance has a much lower stable slope angle and tends to erode easily, even by wind.[10] In the example of the Robotic Embankment Prototype, the goal was to achieve a new structure using digging and dumping cycles in local soil with a neutral soil balance.[11] However, up-front determination of the swell factor of soils is very difficult to estimate.[12] Roughly two-thirds into the construction of the prototype, a change was triggered. The desired geometry of the embankment was adjusted to incorporate a new swell factor and crown lowering while maintaining the south-facing slope angle and swale. In this manner, the form can be completed while maintaining a neutral soil balance and functioning structure.

Minutes-Hours

We are transitioning to processes that are less time-sensitive to human supervision and monitoring of the autonomous material handling playing out in the field. As robots gain capabilities in sensing and actuation, implications of the robot's role in collaborative tasks, autonomy, and decision-making in shared environments become pertinent, as well as strategies for safe interaction with humans and animals during task execution.[13] Together, human–robot collaboration (HRC) should realize robustness and intelligence in unstructured environments. To achieve this, various information is relayed to the operator for visual feedback and interactive guidance. There are many reasons for this; however, when we focus on design decisions that need to be made within the production cycle itself, we can think about the incorporation of larger boulders that are found during the excavation process or the identification of substantial design changes that need to be incorporated later. With the appropriate interface, the design model can be adjusted to accommodate these encounters.

The described shared workspace of a robot and a human supervisor will involve HRC through digital twins, where the interaction model may ask for human input to complete the specific task at hand.[14] In this way, the autonomous fabrication process, skilled workers, and designers work together to create an adaptive structure combining machine power, human experience, and creativity. The combination of human expertise and skillfulness with the accuracy and power of hydraulic machines is promising to enhance the efficiency, adaptability, and resilience of autonomous fabrication processes in the landscape.[15]

From a technical perspective, machines require hourly care for oil changes, charging, and other operations crucial to their sustained functionality. This aligns with procedures of operations management, aiming to maximize cycle production and efficiency. Safety and environmental concerns also start to play a role, with a focus on harmonizing robotic operations with other activities on site. Apart from these functional activities that take place within hourly timeframes, examples of the Robotic Landscapes Research Studios might help to communicate this new reality of autonomous construction and maintenance. Tasked with the construction of a dynamic topography aimed at flood prevention and capable of handling significant sedimentation, a fleet of robotic excavators maintained a balanced material flow crucial to tending to the natural processes on site. In this example, maintenance was required to establish an equilibrium in a river system so as not to rely on large-scale concrete infrastructures. Similar to maintaining and operating robot equipment, ecological restoration practices like soil remediation, revegetation, and habitat creation require critical time management.

Integrating robots into the landscape will undoubtedly be received with distrust initially because of limited technical understanding, algorithm bias, work displacement, and cultural beliefs. However, the opposite can also be true. The closure of the largest active storm surge barrier operates explicitly without human intervention in case of a flood to reduce the risk of human error and reliability in extreme events. Of course, this new relationship among nature, humans, and machines will be particularly apparent at community scales and have spatial implications because dynamic landscapes require more space than hard infrastructure like a concrete-lined channel. While we have become accustomed to behaving safely within risk-prone environments, it may be clear that our interaction with robotic excavators cannot rely on past experience. Encounters between humans and construction robots will certainly have to be governed.

Days–Weeks

As we scale up in time, we also scale up in space. While the excavation and deposition cycles have reached maturity, an unexplored research area lies in investigating the redistribution of locally sourced granular materials at the scale of the site. Large-scale material flows within national borders have been effectively implemented, yet direct and local, project-based resource management is in its early stages. There is a risk that standard solutions will proliferate over site-specific responses, ecological diversity, and the cultural identity of a place. Creating adaptive design strategies within the execution phase of a project is often viewed as risky, given standard certification norms and licensing. However, it is precisely where I foresee the most substantial impact on circular construction with a large potential to develop emergent site-specific topographies. The circular application of as-found materials will also minimize loading/unloading steps and transportation. Instead of designing the material characteristics of the infrastructure (for example, dikes or river and coastal-protection structures), it would encourage designing the geometry of such infrastructures to the found materials on site. This creates genuinely

0–1 m
1–2 m
2–3 m
3–5 m
5–15 m
15–20 m
20–30 m
30–40 m
40–50 m

4D speculation of vegetation canopy and extent as it recovers from disturbance events from year 0 (t=0) to year 20 (t=20). Disturbing soil horizons will benefit nutrient cycling, soil aeration, seed germination, and stimulate microbial activity. The proposed construction method initiates these natural successional processes that lead to a more resilient and diverse ecosystem in the long term.

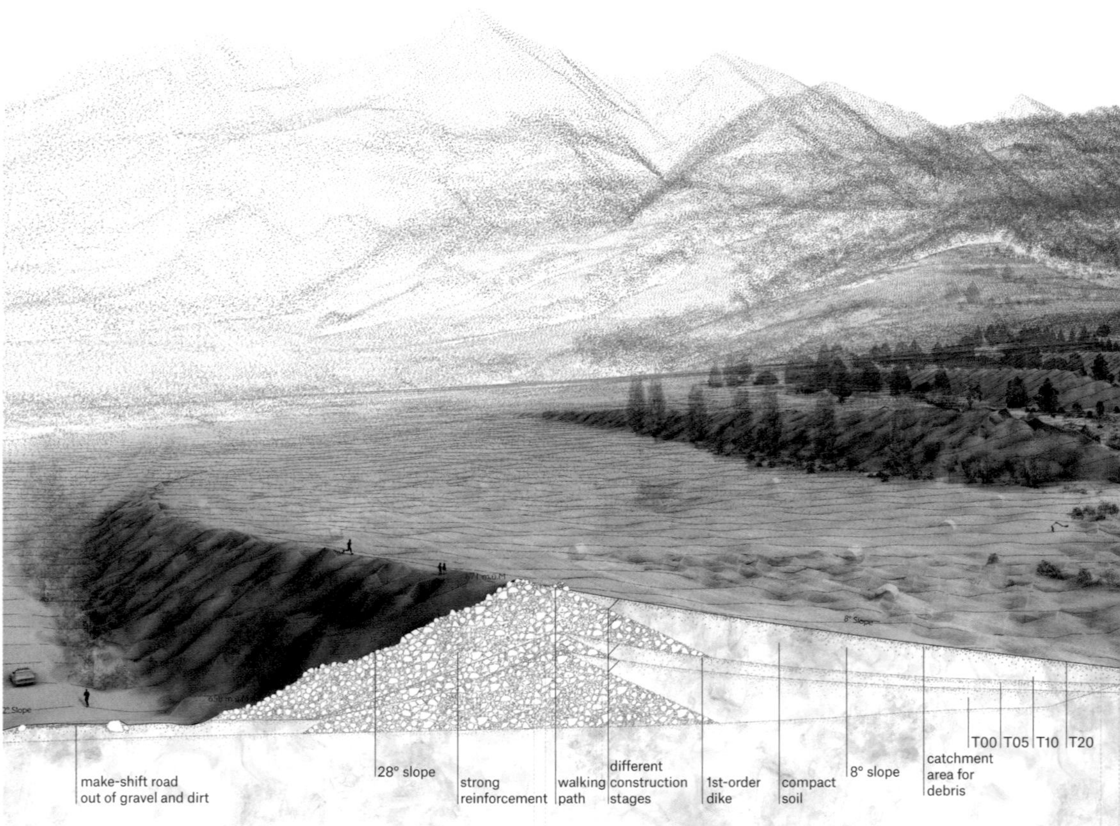

Drawing depicting how a riverbed prone to flooding and debris flows in spring and early summer can be maintained over time.

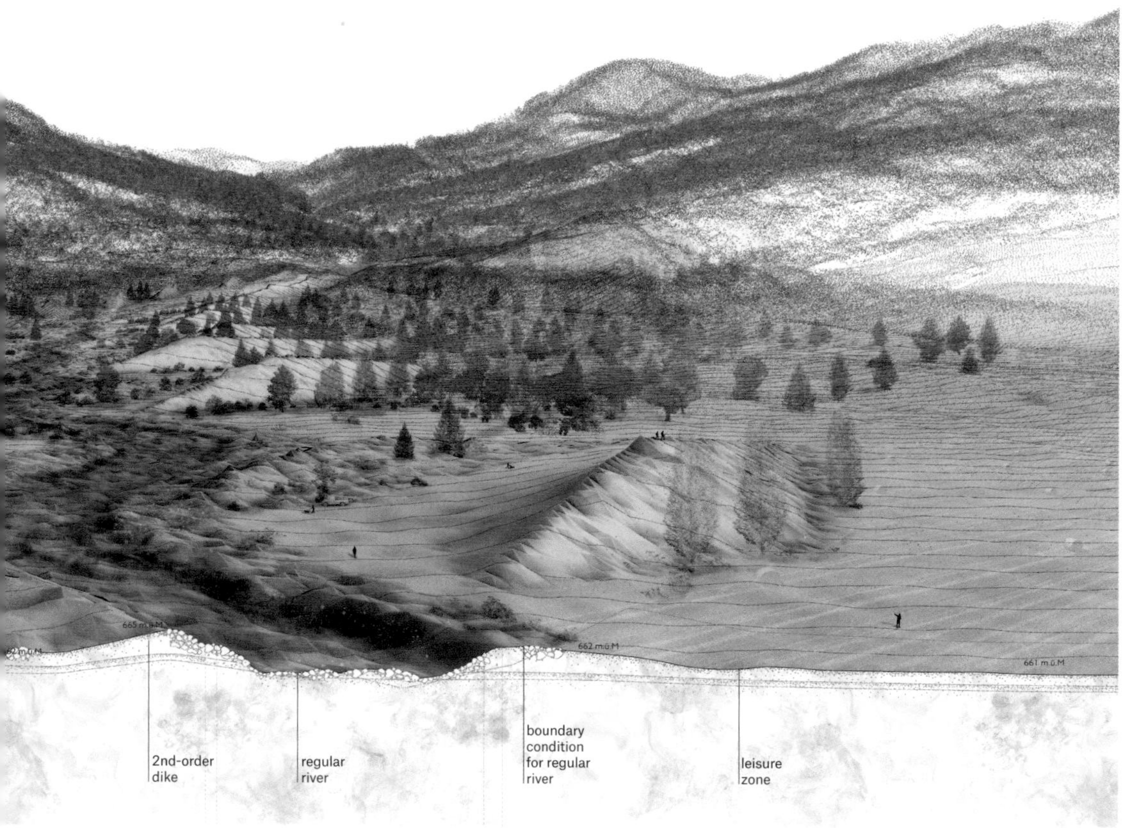
2nd-order
dike
regular
river
boundary
condition
for regular
river
leisure
zone

site-specific topologies embedded into the local material ecology and enables a truly local and circular material flow with minimal material downgrading.[16] During the excavation cycles, material types can be deducted using reinforcement learning techniques, then selected, and finally directed toward a suitable application within the project.[17]

As the first larger structures start to emerge from the earth-moving cycles in the span of weeks, design adaptations can still be implemented in the model through concurrent engineering of the desired outcome. This was the case in the construction of the Circularity Park, where the design and construction ran simultaneously, instead of consecutively. To achieve this, the desired terrain model was a piece of code that formed a topological network of points and paths. While this topological network itself was scaleless, parameters could change width, height, slope, and curvature to give the model a three-dimensional shape. As all of this was done in code, the design no longer consisted of drawings or geometric models but was an evolving codebase made of classes, functions, and variables.[18] As expected, the autonomous excavator HEAP followed suit and dynamically adapted its procedures to include changes in the landscape.

Months–Years

Timescales of the physical production process and natural processes, such as erosion and revegetation, start to make a real impact on the site. The first indications of soil stability and sedimentation emerge, along with new habitats for plants and animals on the newly shaped terrain. Particularly apparent are seasonal influences, not only for the operation windows determined by cold weather or significant stormwater events, but also for the first functional indications of newly established terrain structure. Seasonal erosion patterns can bring large volumes of sand, cobbles, and boulders from upstream onto the site because of the costs associated with maintaining concrete check dams and channels or an unstable upper reach. For example, one of the Robotic Landscape Design Research Studios investigated a site on a debris cone with a riverbed lined with check dams and a channel. Removing these static structures would wash over 5,000 cubic meters of material per check dam downstream. The change in riverbed slope would also increase erosion, and an unstable upper reach would contribute an estimated annual sedimentation of approximately 50,000 cubic meters per year, with a maximum event reaching 200,000 cubic meters. The construction must start from a new topographic situation with extra material to distribute over the site. This material can be sorted by size and placed onto new structures to grow in proportion and strength to accommodate next year's events when the seasonal cycle begins again. Other timely processes involve upscaling fine sediments through ripening processes into clay or minimizing the negative effects of construction disturbances to support maturing soil profiles and biodiversity. These highly local site-time approaches leverage existing performances and ecologies as well as the cultural and aesthetic context of landscape design, aiming to integrate processes, materials, and formal considerations with respect to the identity of the site. As such, they align both to quality in function, environment, and aesthetics, as well as address challenges from ongoing climatic shifts.

Over years, design becomes a project of never-ending maintenance. While landscape architects are accustomed to designing and then producing a finished state of nature, the reality is that we can only propose a change in the direction of a continuous succession taking place in the environment. Just like robotic procedures, landscapes are made of and in time. While we generally know when things were made (for example, when a project was finished or a hazard event happened), it is quite challenging to grasp how long it took for a material ecology to establish a recognizable form.[19] The process described thus far is not about setting the duration of a transformation, but about an open interaction between the existing landscape and a desired goal, and allowing the design processes to unfold over time. Allowing natural and robotic processes to play out slowly over time may also benefit social processes. In large-scale engineering works, often the challenge lies in governance and environmental management, not in technological achievements per se. While tasks like stakeholder management, compliance with regulations, and engaging in a participatory process with the local community often require a significant amount of time, the gradual transformation of dynamic maintenance may provide the necessary conditions for these processes to unfold. This implies that these processes can occur simultaneously or concurrently, potentially speeding up overall progress, despite their individual time-intensive nature.

Proposing to transform existing static systems like channeled rivers or coastal defense structures into open and dynamic landscapes while allowing this transformation to take place over many years is challenging. As such, it is not vital to focus on the outcome but on the initiation of a process of local material movements. The new system's performance can be encoded in a dynamic landscape topology capable of adapting to change over time while functioning at every stage of construction. Instead of creating a single visionary image, it is more about a continuous triangulation between the landscape architect, the robot, and the cultural landscape.[20]

Decades

Engineers are used to operating in timescales of decades. The lifespan of large-scale infrastructures is usually set between 50 and 100 years. Take the example of risk prediction of extreme weather events. Statistical modeling, empirical analysis, or data-driven approaches have been overtaken by actual hazard events over the last years. While recurrent neural networks show promising results in making these predictions more reliable, 10 years from now, it may be clear that we will have access to new paradigms because of evolving scientific insights.[21] With the recent rapid developments resulting from climate change, we cannot predict the environmental future beyond very short timeframes and probable return periods of extreme events. The key point here is that attempting to predict changes over longer timeframes is not necessary or even desirable. I am advocating letting site-time dimensions of such infrastructures compress down to the millimeter and millisecond or expand over thousands of kilometers and into centuries. Let each design determine a temporality, a sequence of events, a process. Equipped with sensors, digging tools, and a landscape topology stored in memory, the robotic feedback loop enables the act of design to happen, not only on the drawing board, but also in the field.

A Novel Approach

Throughout history, working with terrain has always been fundamental to supporting civilization. The recent increase in extreme natural events resulting from rapid climate change calls for an increased focus on the structural organization of our settlements relative to our environment. At the extremes, we find a total retreat to safe ground or attempts at total control. Although the second option has been tried and tested over the second half of the 20th century, it has left us in an increasingly precarious situation, causing destruction without the capacity for self-regeneration. Modifying dynamic landscapes poses the problem of the impossibility of foreseeing their future evolution, as computation and simulation can only reflect a small subset of outcomes involved in nature's dynamics. Through dynamic construction processes, a continuous adaptation of the terrain becomes possible. As such, the formation of terrain by natural and mechanical forces can evolve over ever-changing site conditions, capable of adapting to future needs.

This shift toward performance and material ecology over a formal approach in landscape architecture contributes to and is accelerated by the development of sensory instruments and robotic manipulation. A new landscape design and construction process can be established through the combination of real-time environmental data, topological design, and autonomous actuation. Here, the focus for design lies not foremost on composition or experiences but rather is occupied with experimentation, the flows and transformation of materials, and the processes of making. This approach integrates the physical specificity of a site into a timely design and fabrication process. Here, the original form of a terrain acts as an initial catalyst and ordering principle to evolve into different dimensions over site and time. While continuous evolution of a site can enhance its resilience, we can also create conditions for a new, extraordinary experience to emerge. It is essential to situate ourselves within the entropic processes of the landscape by actively working with them to adapt to inevitable change. As landscape architecture has always been at the forefront of site-time investigations, now is the moment for real-world experimentation in the field. Existing methods fail to address the conditions within which we work. I am confident that a time-critical design approach will unlock previously unthinkable design possibilities in shaping 21st-century landscapes.

Notes

1. Lidar is an acronym for Light Detection and Ranging, a remote sensing technology that uses laser light to measure distances and generate three-dimensional elevation data or point clouds of the Earth's surface. It consists of a laser sensor mounted on either an aircraft or a terrestrial platform and is combined with a GNSS receiver and an IMU for accurate position data.
2. Lauren Vasey & Achim Menges, "Potentials of Cyber-physical Systems in Architecture and Construction," in Anil Sawhney, Michael Riley & Javier Irizarry (eds), *Construction 4.0: An Innovation Platform for the Built Environment* (Routledge, 2020), 90–112.
3. Ryan Luke Johns, et al., "A Framework for Robotic Excavation and Dry Stone Construction Using On-Site Materials," *Science Robotics* 8, no. 84 (November 22, 2023).
4. Bruno Latour, "Love Your Monsters," *Breakthrough Journal* 2 (2011): 19–26.
5. This chapter draws from experiments of the Robotic Landscapes research project encompassing various experimental and design research investigations, such as the Robotic Embankment Prototype, the Robotic Landscape Research Studio, and the Circularity Park. Part of the research has been published in Ilmar Hurkxkens, Fujan Fahmi & Ammar Mirjan (eds), *Robotic Landscapes—Designing the Unfinished* (Park Books, 2021) based on research conducted

between 2017 and 2022 at ETH Zurich. See also Ilmar Hurkxkens, et al., "Robotic Landscapes: Designing Formation Processes for Large Scale Autonomous Earth Moving," in Christoph Gengnagel, et al. (eds), *Impact: Design with All Senses* (Springer International Publishing, 2019), 69–81.

6. HEAP, the Hydraulic Excavator for an Autonomous Purpose, used in the Robotic Embankment Prototype and the Circularity Park, is a customized Menzi Muck M545 developed for autonomous use cases as well as advanced teleoperation. Dominic Jud, et al., "Autonomous Free-Form Trenching Using a Walking Excavator," *IEEE Robotics and Automation Letters* 4, no. 4 (October 2019): 3,208–15.
7. Near-real-time refers to a minimal delay in the processing and delivery of information and is short enough to be practical for a robotic system to interact effectively with its environment and carry out tasks, typically between 1 and 100 milliseconds.
8. ROS - Robotic Operating System, https: //www.ros.org/ (accessed on January 12, 2024).
9. Occupational Safety and Health Administration, *OSHA Technical Manual Section V: Chapter 2–Excavations: Hazard Recognition in Trenching and Shoring*, https://www.osha.gov/dts/osta/otm/otm_v/otm_v_2.html (accessed 07/16/2019).
10. For instance, clay has a maximum slope angle of 53 degrees, while sand has a maximum of 33 degrees.
11. Dominic Jud, et al., "Robotic Embankment: Free-form Autonomous Formation in Terrain with HEAP," *Construction Robotics* 5 (June 23, 2021).
12. The swell factor denotes the volume expansion of soil following excavation or disturbance, attributed to aeration and loosening; it is the ratio between the volume of excavated material and the volume of the material in its initial, undisturbed condition.
13. Sami Haddadin, et al., "Towards the Robotic Co-Worker," in Cédric Pradalier, Roland Siegwart & Gerhard Hirzinger (eds), *Robotics Research vol. 70* (Springer Tracts in Advanced Robotics, 2011), 261–82, https://doi.org/10.1007/978-3-642-19457-3_16.
14. A digital twin is a virtual representation of a physical object or system, created from the design model and using data from sensors and actuators. It allows for real-time monitoring, analysis, and optimization of robotic procedures, enabling informed decision-making and predictive maintenance.
15. Daniela Mitterberger, "Augmented Human and Extended Machine: Adaptive Digital Fabrication and Human-machine Collaboration for Architecture" (PhD thesis, ETH Zurich, 2023).
16. Lauren Vasey, et al., "Circular Robotic Construction," in Catherine De Wolf, Sultan Çetin & Nancy M. P. Bocken (eds), *A Circular Built Environment in the Digital Age* (Springer International Publishing, 2024), 151–70.
17. Pascal Egli, et al., "Soil-Adaptive Excavation Using Reinforcement Learning," *IEEE Robotics and Automation Letters* 7 no. 4 (October 2022): 9,778–85.
18. In the computer programming language Python, variables are used to store data, functions perform specific tasks or operations, and classes provide a way to structure code. See Ilmar Hurkxkens & Mathias Bernhard, "Computational Terrain Modeling with Distance Functions for Large Scale Landscape Design," *Journal of Digital Landscape Architecture* 4 (2019): 222–30, https://doi.org/10.14627/537663024.
19. Timothy Morton, *All Art is Ecological* (Penguin Books, 2021), 104.
20. Christophe Girot & Ilmar Hurkxkens, "The storm, the Architect, and the Robot: Landscape Maintenance in the Age of Robotic Intelligence," in Hurkxkens, Fahmi & Mirjan (eds), *Robotic Landscapes—Designing the Unfinished.*
21. Jonathan M. Frame, et al., "Deep Learning Rainfall–Runoff Predictions of Extreme Events," *Hydrology and Earth System Sciences* 26, no. 13 (July 5, 2022): 3,377–92.

Regenerative Techno-Ecosystems in Urban Landscapes

Christopher Streb and David Blersch

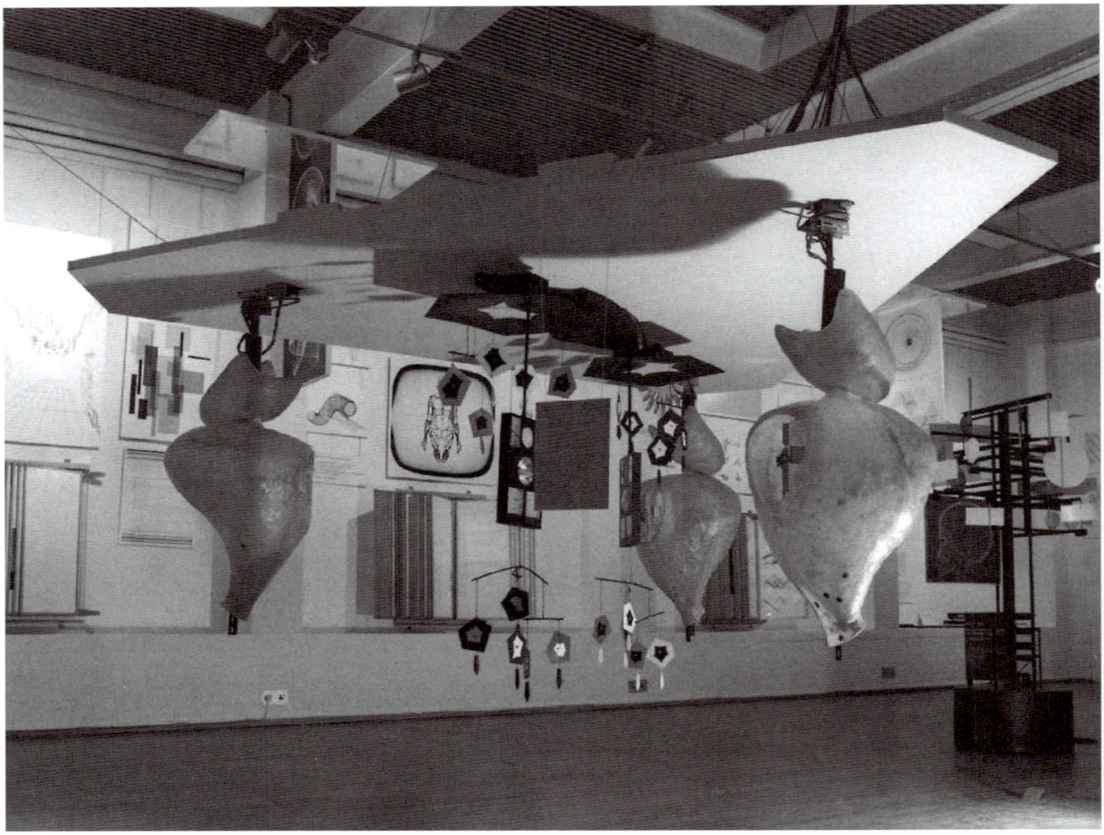

Gordon Pask, *Colloquy of Mobiles*, Cybernetic Serendipity Exhibit, ICA London, 1968. Pask's groundbreaking installation was an early demonstration of the feedback loops in cybernetic principles.

The Earth has experienced five previous mass extinction events over its four-billion-year history. Following each of these events, biodiversity gradually rebounded, with new species and communities creating a new dynamic equilibrium lasting for tens of thousands to millions of years. The unraveling of natural system stability induced by human activity appears to be causing a sixth such event; a dubious distinction given that this is the first mass extinction to be caused by a species.[1] Assuming that past is prelude, biodiversity will recover in time, requiring decades to centuries. Information and technology have given humanity the power to destabilize the biosphere; however, the question remains as to whether the species that destabilized the entire biosphere can garner its technology to support the recovery of the ecosystems that sustain us.

This chapter focuses on forms of digital media that facilitate the translation of environmental information into methods for monitoring, managing, and sustaining landscapes. Human bias may consider information the domain of civilization—books, music, art, film, etc.—however, information in nature catalyzes critical feedback loops that enable communities of species and ecosystems to self-organize and self-regulate. Nevertheless, the rapid growth and expansion of human activity—resource extraction, land conversion, habitat fragmentation, waste disposal, and the liberation of fossil carbon sources into the atmosphere—has triggered feedback loops at multiple scales, impacting the climate, forcing species extinctions, and degrading the ecosystems that support a diversity of life.

Scientists have projected dire outcomes associated with the climate crisis, including more frequent flooding, wildfires, extreme heat, declining freshwater reserves, coastal erosion, and sea level rise. Outcomes that were projected well into the future are already occurring, sooner than expected, only highlighting our tenuous predicament. Rather than consign us to the trajectory of ecological collapse, biodiversity loss, and decline of civilization, the following project examples explore how the application of information and technology may be used to document, analyze, support, and stabilize ecosystems, perhaps incorporating technology as part of nature itself.

Feedback Loops and Information in Ecosystems

Information existed well before the evolutionary arrival of *Homo sapiens*; living systems have always been shaped by information and communication. Honeybees scouting for pollen return to their hives and conduct a waggle dance to direct other worker bees to the source

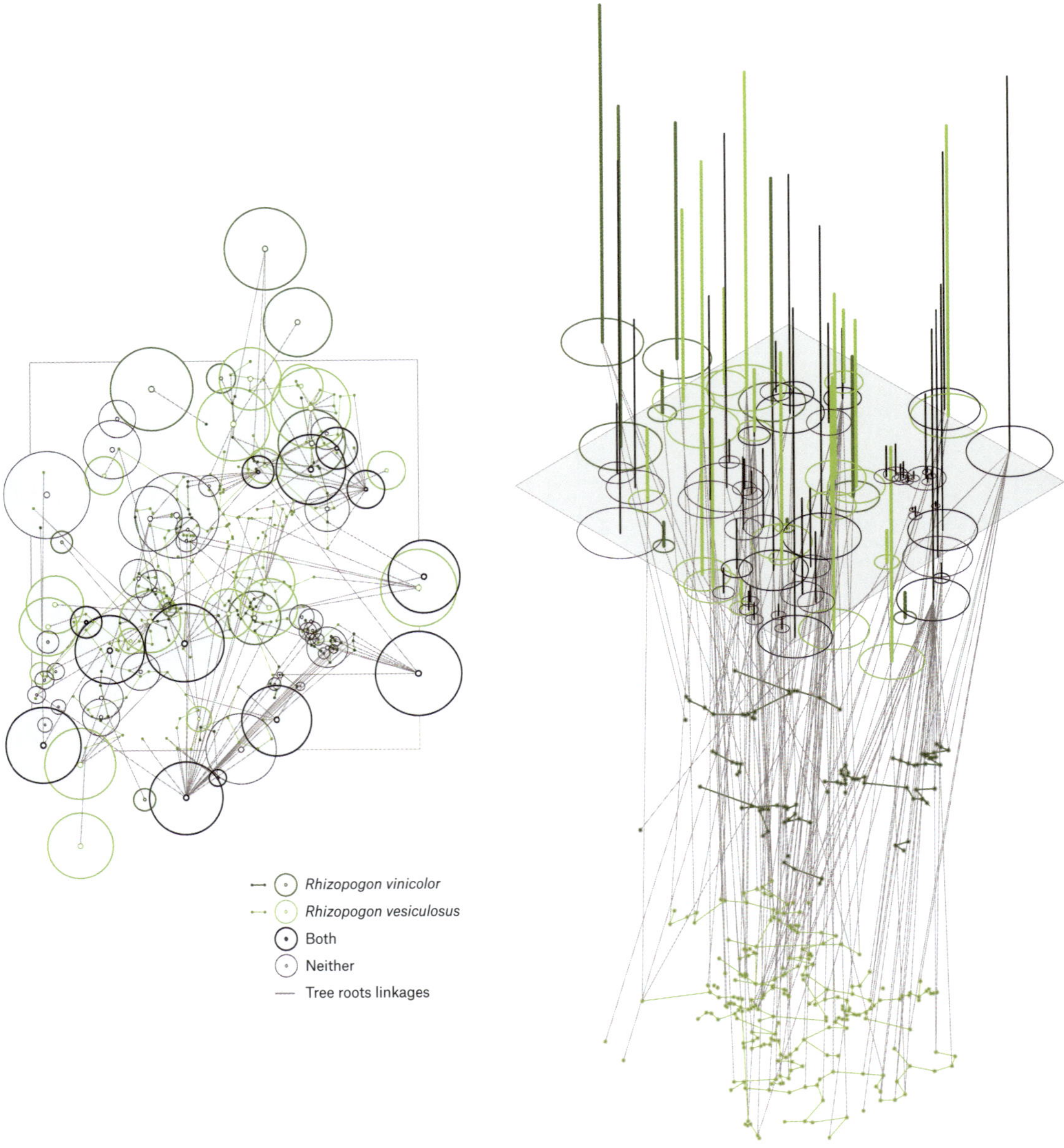

The plan (left) and exploded axonometric depict underground mycorrhizal networks among tree species. These networks are increasingly recognized as mediators of tree survival, growth, and competition. Of 401 *Rhizopogon* ectomycorrhiza samples (small light and dark green dots), 338 were linked to two or more trees within a 30 x 30 m plot of 67 Douglas fir trees. The light and dark green lines represent different individual fungal genotype samples (*Rhizopogon vesiculosus* and *Rhizopogon vinicolor*) and related tree connections above ground.

of pollen. Flowering plants attract bees to their flowers through aromatics and color, so the bees will produce fertilized seed and reproduce. These instructions, in the flower and in the bees, are all packed into their genomes.

Ecosystems are collections of species and communities interacting with a locale's geology, topography, orientation, and climate. A key attribute of ecosystems is reinforcing feedback loops. Feedback loops in a system are defined as any flow from a system's output that informs, affects, and regulates its input, amplifying or reinforcing changes within a system and leading to either a self-reinforcing loop of growth or a decline.[2] These feedback mechanisms play a crucial role in shaping the dynamics and stability of ecosystems. A vivid example of this dynamic involves plant and animal feedback. "Masting" refers to the phenomenon in which certain tree species, including oak trees, exhibit synchronized and intermittent patterns of seed production. In other words, masting is the episodic and highly variable production of large seed crops by a population of trees, followed by periods of low seed production. This pattern occurs at irregular intervals, often spanning several years. Oak trees, for example, will have several years of low seed production, and all at once, across species, the trees will produce a bumper crop of acorns. Producing a large mast of acorns satiates the consumers, like squirrels, and with such ample food, allows excess acorns to be forgotten and germinate into saplings. Bumper crop years also lead to more offspring for the consumers. But with fewer acorns the following fall, the population of consumers must decline in reaction to the scarce food supply. This feedback illustrates how the abundance and distribution of seed consumers impact the regeneration and population dynamics of the tree species involved, and how tree masting can influence the population of seed consumers.

Although scientists understand the why of this strategy in trees, the how of trees (across species) knowing when to mast is not clearly understood. Theories include ideal nutrient resource availability and weather conditions, triggering a mast year. But might other information be at play? Suzanne Simard, a forest ecologist, proposed the "tree communication hypothesis," which suggests that trees in a forest communicate with each other through a vast underground network of mycorrhizal fungi. This network, described as the "wood wide web," allows trees to exchange information, such as chemical signals and nutrients. According to Simard, trees can form symbiotic relationships with mycorrhizal fungi that attach to their roots. These fungi act as conduits for the exchange of water, carbon, and other nutrients among trees. Simard found that older, more established "mother trees" can transfer resources to younger, neighboring trees, particularly during times of stress or when one tree is in need.[3]

This communication system is thought to facilitate mutual support and cooperation among trees within a forest. For example, if a tree is under attack by pests or facing environmental stress, nearby trees can receive chemical signals through the mycorrhizal network, enabling them to activate defense mechanisms or allocate resources more efficiently. Although we are only beginning to study communication among trees, the evidence suggests that information exchanges occur throughout nature to regulate resource allocation.

Information exchanges among individuals, species, and communities in ecosystems indicate that living systems are maintained by causal feedback loops, an attribute that helps to steady and regulate the system from changing environmental conditions and episodic disturbances so that a dynamic stability of its structure is sustained over time. Although ecosystems often demonstrate incredible resiliency to change, there are limits, and with enough stress, either acute or chronic, stabilizing causal feedback loops may break down, while destabilizing feedback loops emerge. Such instances can push an ecosystem into an alternate, nonoptimal state. Such breakdowns in ecosystem function and structure are readily observable where anthropogenic disturbances are most intense: in and around cities.

Cybernetics and Ecosystems in Cities

In urban ecosystems, where natural feedback and controls have been severed and system stability is either dependent on or influenced by human activity, deploying sensors, computers, and mechanical systems is emerging as a potential strategy to monitor and regulate resources delivered to the landscape during periods of climate-induced stress, such as drought, flooding, and extreme heat. In essence, the deployment of technology in urban landscapes may serve as an ecological prosthetic, mimicking biological feedback mechanisms, like the wood wide web, that are difficult to jumpstart in a created environment. Landscape architects Bradley Cantrell and Justine Holzman recognized this potential for landscapes augmented with computers and hypothesized that new "natures" may spawn by coupling machines and biology.[4] Though lurid and futuristic, this notion of landscapes—part biology and part machine—as cybernetic ecosystems is not new. In fact, the theory of ecosystems being cybernetic (without technological assistance) has been researched since the 1950s. The history of cybernetic concepts and ecological processes explains much about the potential for conceptualizing the combination of technological and ecological systems.

Cybernetics is a field of study focused on causal feedback systems across a wide spectrum of disciplines, including ecosystem science. Cybernetic systems require information, communication, and mechanisms for control. The concepts of cybernetics were formally developed by Norbert Wiener in the mid-20th century as a system of analysis of feedback in emerging control systems for technological machinery.[5]

Early electronic sensors, controls, and communications, interfaced with the physical entities of the world, led to the formal development of control systems theory as a computational approach for accounting for the regulating effect of feedback dynamical systems and their components. Control systems engineering has since become an integral part of systems design throughout the technological world. Biologists and ecologists at the time recognized the role of feedback in biological systems as well. Observed phenomena such as autonomous neurological control systems of individual organisms, or the materials loops in growing communities in environmental and ecological systems, suggested the influence of feedback concepts in supporting and maintaining biological systems. The role of feedback in biosystems can be seen as providing control for trajectories of organization—growth and maturation of an individual organism, say, or successional patterns in structure and function of an ecosystem—that prompted investigations into the cybernetic aspects of natural systems.

Indeed, in the near past, there has been periodic academic questioning and research addressing the cybernetic nature of ecosystems. The primary question, "Are ecosystems cybernetic?" was first asked in the 1950s and remains to be answered fully.[6] Counterarguments in later decades focus on the loose coupling between organization and information in ecological systems, which negates the cybernetic interpretation.[7] Recent speculations rely on cybernetic interpretations to unify human agency with ecosystem organization.[8] As such inquiry advances, the cybernetic interpretation remains a fundamental direction of inquiry and understanding through modeling the organizational patterns of ecosystems. Coterminous with the technological developments in cybernetic systems and the later extension to biological systems, ecosystem theory was being formalized through earlier efforts at reconciling concepts of general systems theory, itself based in the thermodynamics of prior decades, with observations from natural philosophers of the same era. The work of Alfred J. Lotka in the early 20th century expressed the constraints of thermodynamics on the organization of ecological systems, determining limits based upon energetic principles from the fundamental laws of thermodynamics.[9]

The work of E. P. Odum through the mid-century formalized these into coherent ecological theory, with observations on systems-level organization and expressed characteristics from ecological science, laying the foundations for systems ecology that incorporated an understanding of linkages between internal components and external environmental forcing on ecological organization.[10] H. T. Odum formalized the analytical approaches even further through the development of energy circuit diagramming to represent energetic and material transfers within dynamical ecological systems, incorporating thermodynamic laws and constraints into a rational approach for representing and analyzing connections and components within complex organizing systems.[11] Importantly, by accounting for all real transactions in a system through energetic transformation, H. T. Odum extended his conceptualization of complex organizing biological systems beyond natural ecosystems to include human-dominated or human-built systems as part of the overall self-organizing system of the planetary biosphere.[12] From here, it was one more conceptual step in recognizing the information-processing power and characteristics of human systems, having the effect of accelerating information exchange and material process manipulation on real systems, human and natural ecological alike, which culminated in the definition and conceptualization by H. T. Odum of the *techno-ecosystem,* the combined ecological and technological components of the natural and human subsystems that organize together in directions novel to the biosphere, although not necessarily in new processes or ways.[13]

The concept of the techno-ecosystem formalizes the feedback linkages between what we might call natural and synthetic components of the complex organizing biosphere on the planet. The question remains as to whether the techno-ecosystem concept is functionally real at the global scale, and what the implications for long-term techno-ecosystem organization might be. Experimentation to demonstrate techno-ecosystem self-organizational behavior has been accomplished at only limited scales in the laboratory, using technological feedback systems to attain goal setpoints on ecological microcosms.[14] In these experiments, ecological components organized rapidly to take advantage of newly available information pathways

The raised deck of the EcoCommons (Georgia Institute of Technology) provides space for outdoor classes and information about, and access to, the water and air quality monitoring within the stormwater catchment feature.

supplied by technological components in ways that maximized energy availability to the whole system. Signatures of self-organization to the new energetic reality were observed at the component level, where one species or taxon outcompeted others and thus dominated the community, and, at the systems level, where measures of ecosystem-level metabolism, such as primary productivity and respiration and their relative ratio, were seen to shift in response to the novel feedback pathways. These results give an indication of what is expected of natural systems in the biosphere, but they lack any indication of scalability to larger systems.

Indeed, in response to the altered landscapes of human systems, feedback processes that favor certain species over others are present–for example, *Phragmites* giant reed being more competitive and dominant in hydrologically disturbed areas proximate to human infrastructure. These might be thought of as a first-level passive response feedback, generally describing a one-way response of biological components to a change in environment resulting from human activity. The second-level active feedback response is rarer, where active sensor networks monitoring the condition of a biological system afford control over one or more energetic inputs to the system, and the ecological system thus organizes favoring components that respond positively to the input energies made available by the feedback network itself. These systems presumably require input of a setpoint or range of favorable conditions to target and, thus, are inherently teleological and goal-seeking, necessitated by the choice of monitoring and parameter setpoints determined by the human designers of the system. Systems beyond this are not known to exist but are functionally possible, such as those with tight feedback loops between ecological and technological components that include rapidly responsive sensor networks and materials systems response. An example of this might be where the survival or operation of technological components are directly dependent upon a favored state of an ecological component—for example, sensors that draw power from maintenance of an oxidation potential in stratified wet sediments. However, these patterns might be observable only at the largest, global scale, where a significant part of the human enterprise is dependent upon the ecosystem services provided by regional- or global-scale ecological phenomena.

Therein we recognize the role of feedback control in human–natural systems organization across all scales. Implementation of feedback control scenarios at the local scale, say, the instrumentation of a wetland system for control of water levels, can be seen to have near-immediate effects on the state of the wetland, and presumably affect the performance of the system through changes in the ecological functions of the system itself. Positive or negative feedback to the human component is partially buffered by choice and valuation systems, and by extant access to other systems and components of the larger human economic system that can provide alternate energy and material sources. Scaling up considerations to the planetary biosphere, there is no denying the emergence of a technological overlay to the extant ecosystems themselves, and data collection at the planetary scale through remote sensing affords full-system knowledge upon which control actions can be taken (although often these are short-circuited by inefficiencies and misinformation in economic and political systems). The emerging global techno-ecosystem must be recognized as being cybernetic, with countless novel feedback pathways emerging as technology advances, and as inherently teleological and by nature bent toward optimization of the human condition.

Emerging Techno-Ecosystems

With the expansion of urbanization and its associated infrastructure throughout the world, fragmentation of natural ecosystems has greatly increased, making these systems more vulnerable to ever-increasing climatic extremes (heat, precipitation, floods, fires, wind) and biotic stressors. Prior to land use transformation, many of these ecosystems contributed to the provision of clean fresh water, flood attenuation, temperature regulation, and pollination, and they supported biodiversity. Stressed ecosystems have been observed to reach thresholds, where reinforcing feedback processes accelerate a breakdown in the processes and structure of the overall system, accelerating further decline. If ecosystems that were once able to self-organize, respond to change, and provide ecosystem services are too impaired to recover, technology is now available to function as a prosthesis to replace those processes.

Environmental monitoring using microsensors is becoming increasingly prevalent and normalized. These sensors can tell us the temperature, the humidity, the pollen count, the presence of a person at our door, or show us if a groundhog is eating vegetables from the garden. Even more intimate than monitoring our homes and gardens, people are wearing sensors to track their heart rates, steps, calories burned, sleep patterns, and movements across the landscape. The thirst to digitize the world by adding more sensors, along with the ability to store the data they generate on huge data farms, is seemingly unquenchable. The rationale for collecting so much data may be due in part to an over-exuberance for technology, a "because we can" mentality, without a specific purpose. But it is also true that the growing network of sensors, along with cloud computing and controls, the so-called Internet of Things (IoT), is yielding important information that can be used not only to monitor conditions, but also to provide feedback that helps us to optimize performance and attain desired outcomes, including ecological functions and ecosystem services.

Using sensors to monitor specific environmental parameters has been a tool in ecology for decades and has provided important insights about ecosystem processes. As the technology has advanced over the past few decades, the cost of sensors has dropped an order of magnitude; data can be transmitted wirelessly and stored in the cloud. The technology is now accessible for homeowners to set up their own weather stations, check in on their gardens from their phones, and control inputs, such as irrigation. This represents an adoption of a simple techno-ecosystem by individuals to gather information and control responses. Large-scale farms deploy more sophisticated versions of a techno-ecosystem, incorporating remote data collection to identify where fertilization is needed most to optimize a crop's yield, representing a further decoupling of the agricultural system from natural inputs. By extension, it is no longer unimaginable to create landscapes that are given agency to regulate their inputs to optimize performance, whether it be carbon sequestration, flood control, or support for biodiversity.

What seems clear is that the field of ecology is no longer a field of study that only observes, theorizes, analyzes, and reports on species and natural systems that are in decline. It must also offer evidence that tells us whether conservation, restoration, and adaptive management practices are helping to steer us back on track to regenerating our living planet. The emergence of environmental sensors, cloud computing, and controls represents a frontier in applied ecology whereby techno-ecosystems are capable of optimizing the throughput of energy and matter to maximize the yield of ecosystem services. In some instances, giving ecosystems additional information and agency to control their throughputs can help to protect them from increasingly frequent extreme events associated with climate change and large-scale landscape disturbances. In cities, the greatest beneficiaries of high-functioning, resilient landscapes are the members of the apex species in that landscape: human beings.

A project by Biohabitats, where one of us is employed, serves as an example. The firm was retained by the Waterfront Partnership of Baltimore to address landscape and water quality challenges as part of the Healthy Harbor Initiative. The goal of Healthy Harbor was to make the Inner Harbor swimmable and fishable (a goal that after 13 years has very nearly been realized). At the receiving point of the Jones Falls River watershed, every opportunity to implement interventions was explored to improve water quality and to provide habitat and refugia to prevent fish kills, while increasing public awareness of these issues. One idea involved reclaiming and transforming the derelict Chase Pier into a "wet wharf," a waterfront feature that would simultaneously serve as cultural artifact, habitat, water filter, and sentinel to engage the public in enjoying the harbor and learning about its health. In addition to building a constructed tidal marsh on the top of the pier deck, the proposal included a series of waterfalls cascading around the perimeter of the pier to combat the harbor's low dissolved oxygen, called "dead zones," which can lead to fish kills. Given the episodic nature of low dissolved oxygen events, the waterfalls were designed to activate only when sensors detected perilously low oxygen levels. In this manner, the waterfalls assumed the role of a visual indicator for poor water quality while simultaneously providing a refuge, or "life zone," for aquatic organisms during these life-threatening occurrences. To manage public expectations in the event the waterfalls were not active, options to activate the wet wharf, either by a smartphone app or by stationary bikes along the promenade, were considered. This idea enabled a kind of engagement, making the techno-ecosystem an entity and partner. The neighboring Mr. Trash Wheel—a solar-powered, semi-autonomous machine with googly eyes that removes floatable debris from the harbor and trash talks—has become so popular that it generates its own revenue through branding and social media.

The Chase Pier project was never built, but the IoT is automating management for enhanced ecosystem services in an urban environment at the Georgia Institute of Technology campus in Atlanta. Georgia Tech wants to reduce the annual volume of stormwater runoff from the campus by 50%, and it looked to the EcoCommons, a performance landscape and living laboratory, to help. The seven-acre site, designed by a team that included Biohabitats and landscape architecture firm Nelson Byrd Woltz, receives stormwater runoff from two small, urbanized catchment basins, and is intended to serve as a sponge and evapotranspiration machine for the drainage area above it. As a result, irrigation is provided throughout the site by using rainfall and condensate harvested from buildings in large underground cisterns. Soil moisture sensors installed throughout the landscape keep continuous tabs on the availability of water for plants. If soil moisture drops too low, harvested rain will be called to irrigate. As the plants mature into a Piedmont forest, increasing volumes of water will be evapotranspired into the atmosphere, helping to cool the site and temper the urban heat island. Finally, as the roots grow deeper and the soils become more porous, it is hypothesized that infiltration will improve with time. The landscape is also being used as a classroom and as an experiment. When compared to a traditional campus quad of mown grass, rather than emit greenhouse gases, require fertilization, pollute stormwater, and provide little habitat, this techno-ecosystem successional Piedmont forest has the potential to regenerate ecosystem services, while producing few environmental impacts at no additional maintenance cost. It was constructed in 2020, and the information collected with sensor technology is influencing landscape management and appears to be yielding benefits: a return of wildlife, a cooler microclimate, and a place for the campus body to learn or rest.

Aerial view of a 930 m2 floating wetland in Baltimore's Inner Harbor. An advanced hydraulic system helps replicate the function of shallow water flow, which plays a crucial role in water oxygenation and marsh grass aeration.

Cybernetic Techno-Ecosystems of the Future

Natural areas and open spaces within urban landscapes provide vital links for recreation, respite, and habitats for city dwellers, including people, plants, and wildlife. The emergence of environmental sensors, cloud computing, and controls represents a frontier in landscape design: the consideration and design of techno-ecosystems, capable of optimizing the throughput of energy and matter to maximize the yield of ecosystems services. Giving ecosystems additional information and automatic agency to control their throughputs is likely to become increasingly important to protect the systems from increasingly frequent extreme events associated with climate change or human activity.

Although ecosystems exhibit cybernetic properties, such as self-organization and self-adjustment in response to changes through species interactions, information can be limited to localized abiotic and biotic sources. The ability of species to adapt and survive has evolved over time within a narrower range of climatic patterns. Moreover, ecosystems are not teleological, do not set goals, and have limited agency to anticipate and protect themselves from changes in the patterns to which the community has evolved. The availability of vast geospatial datasets, combined with localized environmental sensors, allows for the design of landscapes that can anticipate and prepare for climate extremes without direct human management. Moreover, with additional information and agency, cybernetic ecosystems may be capable of maximizing the delivery of critical ecosystem services through reinforcing feedback loops that develop resilient community structure. As technology and human development advance and techno-ecosystem feedback pathways harden into requisite mutualized co-dependency, we might expect transitions to new states and perspectives on ecosystems themselves.

What might the future state of emerging near-global techno-ecosystems look like? The fusing of technology as ecological components is imminent, with a blurring of boundaries as technology becomes part of nature. True techno-ecosystems may not emerge until sensors and information processing are so common they seem invisible. This suggests a system state in which sensor production and maintenance are integral to the energetic feedback of the ecosystem itself, or are persistent over the long term, akin to geologic substrates with some awareness of their surroundings, so that they remain effective within the ecosystem over relevant time scales. Can techno-ecosystems be designed as such? Or can we expect to see them emerge as part of human–ecological integration expected over time? Information processing is likely to be global and ubiquitous soon, as cloud storage and communications (Wi-Fi, cellular, satellite, merging to form universal information fidelity or "in-fi") reach pan-global capabilities. With universal data generation, storage, processing, and computation, is it possible for all states of ecosystems to be known and acted upon? What then of the system's organization, and in what directions for future states?

Here is where teleology returns for consideration of the potential for future techno-ecosystem design. While not inherently goal seeking, ecosystems can be recognized to have preferred states that convey healthy function and relate to services provided. Human mentation provides valuation to the emerging techno-ecosystems and can map onto goal seeking by way of design. For the purposes of long-term sustainability in the global system, thus defining and necessitating sustainability at regional and local scales, emerging technology should be focused on regenerative processes in ecosystems rather than the extractive processes adopted since the Industrial Revolution. Identifying and recognizing prioritized ecosystem function, designing and implementing sensor perception that interfaces at strategic parameters of measure, and designing control actions that are robust, resilient, and scaled for the condition are key to shepherding the emerging techno-ecosystems to those that are mutually provisioning for natural and human needs. Valuation development into goal-seeking trajectories can likely be imprinted into emerging artificial general intelligence (AGI), thereby turning over management questions from human activity to our *in silico* proxies. Given the scaling potential for data access and processing of these near-future AGI managers, the potential exists for techno-ecosystem development that is managed beyond our capacity to understand the details. We had better get the questions around valuation and goal-seeking right from the beginning, to forestall or prevent the unintended consequences of automation beyond our control. Should we now think to define the new Three Laws of Techno-Ecologics, applicable to scales far beyond what Isaac Asimov could at the time imagine?[15] The rapid merging of technology and ecology appears unstoppable, but the opportunities for their sustainable symbiotic co-dependence provide a trajectory for the design of a future sustainable world that is supportive and affirming of the human–natural state that is necessary for our long-term survival.

Notes

1. Kundaranahalli R. Shivanna, "The Sixth Mass Extinction Crisis and its Impact on Biodiversity and Human Welfare," *Resonance* 25, no. 1 (2020): 93–109.
2. Barry Richmond, *An Introduction to Systems Thinking: STELLA Software* (ISEE Systems, 2013), https://iseesystems.com/resources/articles/download/intro-systems-thinking-chapt-1.pdf.
3. Suzanne Simard, *Finding the Mother Tree: Discovering the Wisdom of the Forest* (Knopf Doubleday Publishing Group, 2021).
4. Bradley Cantrell & Justin Holzman, *Responsive Landscapes: Strategies for Responsive Technologies in Landscape Architecture* (Routledge, 2016).
5. Norbert Wiener, "Cybernetics," *Bulletin of the American Academy of Arts and Sciences* 3, no. 7 (1950): 2–4.
6. Bernard C. Patten, "An Introduction to the Cybernetics of the Ecosystem: The Trophic-Dynamic Aspect," *Ecology* 40, no. 2 (1959): 221–31.
7. J. Engelberg & L. L. Boyarsky, "The Noncybernetic Nature of Ecosystems," *The American Naturalist* 114, no. 3 (1979): 317–24.
8. Søren Nors Nielsen, "Second Order Cybernetics and Semiotics in Ecological Systems—Where Complexity Really Begins," *Ecological Modelling* 319 (2016): 119–29.
9. Alfred J. Lotka, "Contribution to the Energetics of Evolution," *Proceedings of the National Academy of Sciences of the USA* 8 (1922): 147–51.
10. Eugene P. Odum, "The Strategy of Ecosystem Development: An Understanding of Ecological Succession Provides a Basis for Resolving Man's Conflict with Nature," *Science* 164, no. 3877 (1969): 262–70.
11. Howard T. Odum, *Environment, Power and Society* (John Wiley & Sons, 1971).
12. Howard T. Odum, "Self-Organization, Transformity, and Information," *Science* 242, no. 4882 (1988): 1,132–39.
13. Howard T. Odum, *Ecological and General Systems: An Introduction to Systems Ecology* (University Press of Colorado, 1994).
14. John E. Petersen, "Adding Artificial Feedback to a Simple Aquatic Ecosystem: The Cybernetic Nature of Ecosystems Revisited," *Oikos* 94, no. 3 (2001): 533–47.
15. Isaac Asimov, "Runaround [1942]," in *I, Robot* (Doubleday, 1950), 40.

Forests as Environmental Media: Vegetalizing a Smart Forests Atlas

Jennifer Gabrys

A screenshot of the Smart Forests Atlas homepage shows the tag network structure and clustering of related tags. Clicking a tag opens a side panel, which displays contributions related to it.

Environmental digital technologies are now planetary in scope, monitoring oceans and farms, cities and atmospheres. Remote sensing satellites and *in-situ* sensors, lidar, and environmental robots are deployed to monitor, manage, and transform environments. In this context, forests have also become increasingly digitalized. Digitally monitored forests connect to expanded networks for documenting and managing a changing planet.[1] Whether to prevent deforestation or enhance carbon storage, smart forest technologies are often programmed to optimize or augment forest services for addressing the climate crisis.

While digital media are transforming forests, forests are themselves a kind of environmental media. Environmental events course through them as they record long durations of environmental change and sense seasonal variations in ways that offer a different form of analog computation. Forests are environmental processors, sensing and responding to their milieus to provide expanded models for how computation occurs or could be conceptualized.

As I have previously written, forests are not just media but also operate as computers of sorts.[2] Analog and biological computing are processes that encompass more than the input/output model of computing. More than merely sending signals, forests are entities that analyze and shape their milieus. They perceive and take decisions based on their surroundings. They communicate operational states, respond to environmental events, and transform their milieus. These modes of computation involve intervention and transformation over extensive stretches of space-time. Here is a mode of computation that transcends the descriptive and managerial aspects of digital computing to signal toward other registers of computational media within and as ecosystems. While forests are increasingly monitored by "smart" technologies, they are also (computational) media that remake designations of what counts as computation. I refer to this as "vegetalizing" digital technologies, where the mediality of forests can serve as a provocation to rethink the diagram of digital technologies – including their operations, materiality, and power structures.

In response to this collection's objective to investigate the "dual meaning" of environmental media in landscape architecture, this chapter explores how forests operate as environmental and planetary media while also investigating the extent to which digital technologies tune in to the mediatic operations of forests. Drawing on research from the Smart Forests research project, this discussion extends work that investigates how environmental digital technologies constitute different social-technical worlds. From the way that machine vision parses camera trap data to the processing of acoustic sensor data, different forest processes are made sense-able and actionable through digital technologies. At the same time, the processing that forests undertake can serve as a kind of dataset for training digital technologies to detect, analyze, and manage distinct ecological events and relations.

The chapter first provides an overview of the Smart Forests Atlas, our research project infrastructure and digital media experiment that uses "digital gardening" methods and four wayfinding devices to map, narrate, log, and connect digital forest knowledges and practices.[3] Through this exploration, the chapter considers three instances from the Smart Forests Atlas where forests circulate within and as environmental media across digital and vegetal operations. Drawing on these examples, it proposes how forests could vegetalize digital technologies to monitor environments and work with and through more expanded environmental operations. How do smart forests, as a concatenation of digital technologies, align with forest processes and intelligences? How do forest media exceed or redirect practices and understandings of computation toward more vegetal and pluralistic practices? The digitalization of environments is never a singular, one-way project. This chapter looks at the milieus and worlds that smart forest projects would build and the vegetal processes that challenge prevailing digital logics.

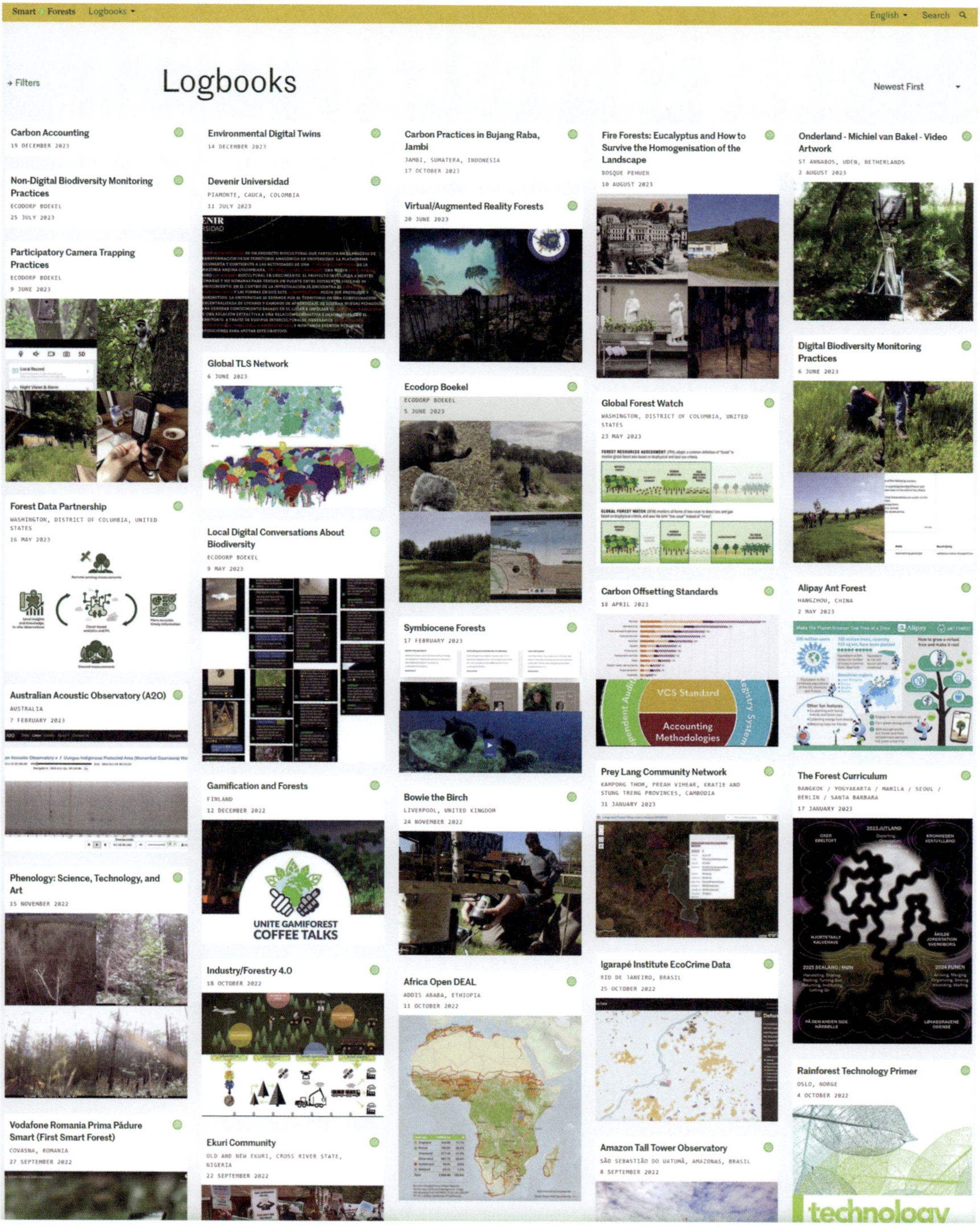

A screenshot of the Logbook overview page. Logbooks are an open format where contributors can add data, fieldwork findings, thoughts, and questions.

Pluralizing Environmental Media with a Smart Forests Atlas

The Atlas is a pervasive genre within spatial and environmental projects. It is a form of environmental media that precedes and exists alongside contemporary geospatial technologies. Indeed, this text could analyze the Atlas as a medial project that is a distinct environmental medium. However, the Smart Forests project has already been written about at length with regard to this topic, and this collection includes meditations on environmental atlases to which readers can also refer.[4] Instead, this analysis first provides a sketch of the Smart Forests Atlas practice-based research infrastructure as it has been developed in its first two years, as it continues to take shape, as it is activated in this chapter, and as it might continue to materialize through ongoing contributions and interventions.

The Smart Forests research group has developed the Atlas with the support of a London-based digital tools cooperative, Common Knowledge. Initiated in March 2021 and launched in the summer of 2022, the Atlas is a research repository, environmental network, and participatory infrastructure for sharing, exploring, and cross-referencing materials about the rise of smart forest projects. The Atlas is less a static archive than a changeable array of materials and participants engaged with forest technology topics. External researchers, practitioners, NGOs, governmental institutions, and more-than-human entities connect with the platform both to document projects and to activate collaborations.

Organized through four "wayfinding devices," including logbooks, a radio, stories, and a map, the Atlas allows participants to navigate the site through different points of entry and across different associated topics in the form of changing tag clouds. This structure presents a pluralistic, cross-fertilizing approach to site content and forest technologies, which unsettles the usual ways of understanding digital technology through big-tech company projects operating through processes of more singular environmental monitoring and management. What filters through this more lateral and associative structure is a dynamic set of environment-technology projects and practices, some of which raise questions about centralized or distant and colonial power structures, some of which demonstrate how different eco-social collectives can remake technical practices and technicity.

Sequential sections of Scotch pine from the coast of Norway (left, center) and southern England (right). Among other things, growth rings indicate fluctuations in precipitation levels over time.

If you search, filter, and follow the tags "environmental media," "sensing," "alerts," and "carbon" on the Smart Forests Atlas, you will find a collection of entries aligned with and developed for this chapter. These tags signal environmental media's dual and pluralistic meanings by working through three instances of sensing, alerting, and carbonizing forests through and as multiple computational media. This collection of materials, discussed below, further reflects the design principles of the Atlas, which span the construction of a relational commons, epistemic justice and data plurality, participation and more-than-human data, digital infrastructures and sustainable computation, wayfinding within the unexpected, and moving to praxis through open data.[5] The next section develops three instances of environmental media that explore how to pluralize and vegetalize forest technologies and data.

Forest Media: Sensing, Alerting, Carbonizing

Sensing

This overview of the Smart Forests Atlas shows how different forest media constitute and transform forest worlds. We can consider how sensing technologies constitute forests by zooming in and out, from sensors to satellites. Sensing is one of the most prominent operations within forests as environmental media. From satellites to the Internet of Things (IoT) networks, camera traps, motion sensors, soil sensors, smoke sensors, and more: digital infrastructures are observing, constituting, managing, and transforming forest worlds through how they "tune in" to them.[6] Not just individual variables and organisms but also broader events, such as deforestation, drought, wildfires, and dieback, are sensed through sensors and datasets gathered across space and time.

Yet who or what is sensing forest worlds? The development and uses of digital technology tend to be concentrated within spaces of corporate technology and expert science, often far from the lived environments of forests.[7] However, communities living within forests are often best placed to sense these environments and to understand how forests are already sensing environmental change. Moreover, different sensing *demos* might materialize at this juncture through different configurations of sensing and praxis.[8]

The Atlas includes multiple examples of sensing as it unfolds across entities and devices. One such in-depth discussion, documented in a Smart Forests Radio episode, includes work by the Technology for Wildlife Foundation in Goa, India. In this conversation with Shashank Srinivasan, director of the Foundation, sensing emerges as a topic of discussion since the group frequently uses drones to monitor forest environments. The topic of conversation involves more than how drones allow the foundation to document encroachments due to development or road construction. It also includes the different sensory configurations that materialize when conservation researchers deploy drones to study landscapes. Responding to the question of whether drones have changed his sensory practices, Srinivasan says:

> That's a very interesting question because, again, it's something I'm conscious of. So, I go to a forest quite often; that's one thing that I like being based where I'm currently based. I go to Mollem at least like once or twice a month. And there's other forests... I know what they all look like from space... depending the scene, I look at a Google Map of it on my phone,

> right, so I have a sense of what it looks like. Again, I can use the Google Earth Pro timeline as well to go back in time, forward in time and see what the forests look like.[9]

As Srinivasan further describes, different aerial views travel with him in his fieldwork, but so, too, do different grounded observations, engagements with local forest dwellers, and understandings of forest change. These are not binary approaches to forest worlds. Instead, they assemble into a more pluralistic and multi-perspectival set of engagements with and understandings of forest worlds. Rather than an all-seeing aerial view of forests, here sensing happens in numerous registers, across multiple participants and entities, including forest organisms. While remote sensing technologies might, at first, seem to overdetermine forest engagements, here forest events and relations are continually co-calibrating with digital analysis through multiple, situated, and distributed forest perspectives. Environmental media proliferate, rather than consolidate, into technologies and technical practices, lived forest worlds and sensed conditions, and forest entities and processes across space-time.

2000–2021
Driest since 1520

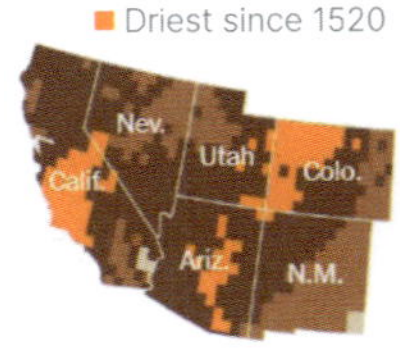

Alerting

One of the most common ways that sensor technologies, from satellites to IoT, are put to work in forest landscapes is as an alerting system. Deforestation, wildfire, and wildlife alerts can signal different forest events and assemble forest actors and actions in response. As the Smart Forests Atlas documents through numerous logbook entries, there are monitoring tools for Indigenous communities in the Amazon to respond to deforestation events.[10] These events can be documented through remote sensing or through acoustic sensors that signal when events correspond to chainsaws or heavy equipment. Working together with Rainforest Connection, Vodafone has claimed to have developed one of the "first" smart forests with its technology in Romania, which detects the sound of logging in the Carpathian Mountains. Acoustic sensors send alerts to apps used by foresters and rangers, who can locate the site of potential illegal activity through location sensors.[11]

Global Forest Watch is one project that has worked extensively to join up remote sensing datasets with near real-time alerts, communicating across geospatial platforms and apps to send warnings to forest dwellers about forest encroachments.[12] Once alerts are received, rangers and defenders can visit sites to document illegal deforestation and increase patrols in these areas. Often, the alerts are too late to stop deforestation while in action, but this could also avoid live conflicts with the agents of deforestation. The near real-time quality of alerts can activate further monitoring of specific forest areas within large reserves or expanses. Yet it also orients forest dwellers to a position of monitoring and defense, which requires resources, people, time, and often extensive travel to document ongoing forest loss.

Such real-time immediacy of alert and response contrasts with how forests, as environmental media, might sense alerts within and through ecosystems.[13] Whether signaling ongoing drought, the encroachments of pests, wildfire conditions, or carbon storage, forests are, in numerous ways, indicating and alerting to environmental change. As environmental media, forests register different space-time measures of environmental change while indicating transformations in ecological relations. Many forest dwellers tune in to these different modes of alerting that forests activate to understand more extensive

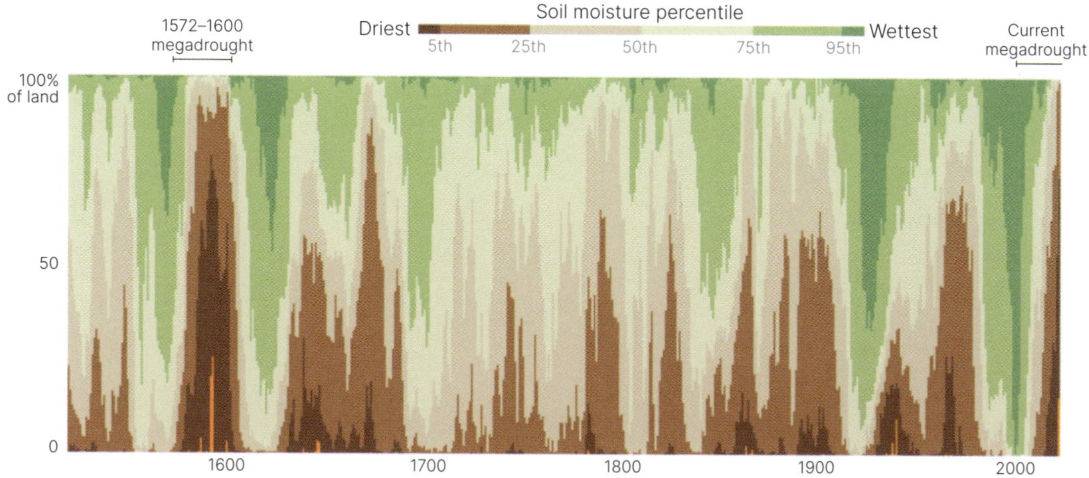

Chart showing the cumulative effects of rain and drought in the Southwest over the past five centuries. Decade-long measurements help climatologists recognize megadroughts. Image by A. Park William, Benjamin I. Cook, and Jason E. Smerdon, courtesy of the *New York Times*. © (December 5, 2022) The New York Times Company. All rights reserved, used under license.

environmental changes taking place over time, across ecological relations, and within organismal processes. Deforestation alerts attempt to stop the loss of forests due to one type of encroachment, but climate change is contributing to the loss of forests through increased heat, aridity, and disease, which can affect forests even as they are preserved in place.

Tuning in to forests as environmental media—and as computers—is a way of vegetalizing a forest alerting system, documenting significant forest events beyond the immediate and machine-readable, accounting for changes over time, and registering eco-social transformations. Yet this perspective also requires rethinking what a computer is or could be. As the Devenir Universidad project and platform developed by Ursula Biemann with Inga Indigenous communities demonstrates, a forest can be a "living cognitive territory" that requires ongoing learning, exchanging, cultivating, and transforming across human and more-than-human inhabitants. This continual calibration toward reciprocity and mutual flourishing is, in many ways, a more robust model for what an environmental computer is or could be.[14]

Carbonizing

One of the most pervasive modes of forest sensing, monitoring, and observation is less about a type of technology or media and more about the object being studied, primarily in the form of carbon. Forests storing carbon are monitored and documented by satellites and sensors, lidar and terrestrial laser scanning (TLS), drones and GIS, maps and transects. Forest carbon is monitored and modeled, and data on carbon levels are combined with other datasets to document possible ecological impacts on carbon levels. The goal of these projects is to identify and maximize carbon storage, often for the purposes of selling carbon offsets or profiting from carbon credits. Forests, in this sense, come into view primarily through a singular element. Practices of monitoring, management, preservation, and expansion guide forests toward carbon stores as their primary contribution.

The monitoring, measuring, and communicating of carbon in forests can be a key aspect of how forest ecology research unfolds or how forest restoration and tree planting operations take place. As the Smart Forests Atlas demonstrates through logbooks, stories, radio episodes, and mapped locations, carbon can become a primary target and objective: sensors measure carbon stocks, technologies automate and optimize tree planting for carbon storage, and carbon offsets work to value forests based on their potential to mitigate carbon-emitting activities elsewhere.[15]

The Carbon Tree is a project and website that monitors and documents the carbon flow of a Scotch pine at the Hyytiälä Forest Field Station in Finland. By monitoring the real-time flow of carbon dioxide while allowing for the modification of environmental conditions to observe changes in carbon flow, the project seeks to increase public awareness about the dynamics of carbon exchange.[16] Environmental science projects worldwide are now monitoring and documenting carbon flux with the use of remote sensing, *in-situ* sensors, and laser scans. The storage of carbon becomes a primary rationale for preserving and expanding forest environments.

Forests are, however, more than carbon.[17] At the same time, ecological relations can influence carbon levels over time and in relation to specific events. Invasive vegetation can create conditions that are conducive to wildfires, even as this vegetation might store carbon over time. Yet this same carbon can be released as emissions during a fire event. One indicator, such as carbon, cannot easily be isolated as a single metric of forest health. Carbon benefits might be differently realized—and vegetalized—if understood as part of the more extensive flourishing of forests across multiple space-time registers. Carbon can activate different approaches to valuing forests, as the Yurok Tribe's carbon offset project suggests, where the longer durations of forest inheritance and memory guide and transform eco-social relations and practices.[18] Yet carbon offsets have also become the target of considerable scrutiny for the climate fictions that they potentially produce.[19]

Conclusion: Vegetalizing a Smart Forests Atlas

Forests are becoming "smart" environments, joined up by digital networks. However, the environmental media that assemble here are not straightforward artifacts or operations. This chapter considers the multiple forms of environmental media that materialize through the digitalization of forest environments. By walking through examples of smart forest technologies in the Smart Forests Atlas site, this chapter suggests it is possible to vegetalize technology when engaging with the dual or multiple meanings of environmental media in landscape architecture and aligned fields. Technologies are co-constituted together with their environments. They do not merely act on environments but, rather, take shape through mutual influence. A practice of vegetalizing technology foregrounds how forests as media—and as computers—can remake (computational) technologies beyond the managerial and optimized.

Technologies compute forests. But forests also compute. Forests detect and process environmental inputs, generate outputs, and provide indicators of environmental change. Forests also transform and remix multiple ecological relations, influencing environments and the organisms within them. They rework understandings of intelligence, cognition, exchange, reciprocity, relation, and space-time inheritances. As both computing entities and environment shapers, forests offer new possibilities for environmental media. By drawing attention to the actions, relationships, and mutual adaptations within their ecologies, forests offer an array of vegetal qualities that are suggestive of alternative designations and practices of environmental media.

Acknowledgment
This project has received funding from the European Research Council (ERC) under the European Union's Horizon 2020 research and innovation program (grant agreement No. 866006).

Notes

1. Jennifer Gabrys, *Program Earth: Environmental Sensing Technology and the Making of a Computational Planet* (University of Minnesota Press, 2016).
2. Jennifer Gabrys, "Forests that Compute," in Jane Prophet & Helen V. Pritchard (eds), *Plants by Numbers: Art, Computation, and Queer Feminist Technoscience* (Bloomsbury Press, 2023).
3. Michelle Westerlaken, Jennifer Gabrys & Danilo Urzedo, "Digital Gardening with a Forest Atlas: Designing a Pluralistic and Participatory Open-Data Platform," *PDC '22: Proceedings of the 17th Participatory Design Conference 2022 – Embracing Cosmologies: Expanding Worlds of Participatory Design* 2 (August 2022): 25–32.
4. Westerlaken, et al., "Digital Gardening." See also: Heather Houser, this collection. See also: Anna L. Tsing, et al. (eds), *Feral Atlas: The More-Than-Human Anthropocene* (Stanford University Press, 2020); Laura Kurgan, *Close Up at a Distance: Mapping, Technology, and Politics* (Zone Books, 2013); Anuradha Mathur & Dilip da Cunha, *Mississippi Floods: Designing a Shifting Landscape* (Yale University Press, 2001).
5. Westerlaken, et al., "Digital Gardening."
6. Gabrys, *Program Earth*.
7. Jennifer Gabrys, et al., "Reworking the Political in Digital Forests: The Cosmopolitics of Socio-technical Worlds," *Progress in Environmental Geography* 1, no. 1–4 (2022): 58–83.
8. Jennifer Gabrys, *Citizens of Worlds: Open-Air Toolkits for Environmental Struggle* (University of Minnesota Press, 2022).
9. Shashank Srinivasan & Trishant Simlai, "Shashank Srinivasan: Conservation Technologies in India," https://atlas.smartforests.net/en/radio/shashank-srinivasan (accessed November 18, 2023). Note all other references to the Smart Forests Atlas were referenced on this date.
10. Jennifer Gabrys, Kate Lewis Hood & Danilo Urzedo, "Monitoring Tools for Indigenous Territories in the Amazon," https://atlas.smartforests.net/en/logbooks/monitoring-tools-for-indigenous-territory-in-the-amazon/#rainforest-alert.
11. Kate Lewis Hood, "Vodafone Romania Prima Pădure Smart (First Smart Forest)," https://atlas.smartforests.net/en/logbooks/vodafone-romania-prima-padure-smart/#prima-padure-smart-technology.
12. Mikaela Weisse & Amy Pickens, "GLAD Deforestation Alerts, Explained," Global Forest Watch (September 2, 2020), https://www.globalforestwatch.org/blog/data-and-research/glad-deforestation-alerts (accessed November 18, 2023); Yuti Ariani Fatimah, "Global Forest Watch," https://atlas.smartforests.net/en/logbooks/global-forest-watch/#global-forest-watch-datasets.
13. For an extended discussion of temporality in smart forests, see Kate Lewis Hood & Jennifer Gabrys, "Keeping Time with Digital Technologies: From Real-Time Environments to Forest Futurisms," *Environment and Planning D: Society and Space* 42, no. 2 (2024): 254–74.
14. See Devenir Universidad, https://deveniruniversidad.org (accessed November 18, 2023); and Kate Lewis Hood, "Devenir Universidad," https://atlas.smartforests.net/en/logbooks/devenir-universidad.
15. See, for instance, Jennifer Gabrys, Kate Lewis Hood & Danilo Urzedo, "Digital Tree-Planting Operations," https://atlas.smartforests.net/en/logbooks/digital-tree-planting-operations/#precision-forest-restoration-pfr; Kate Lewis Hood, "Industry/Forestry 4.0," https://atlas.smartforests.net/en/logbooks/fpinnovations-forestry-40/#smartforest; and Ed Cooper, Jennifer Gabrys & Danilo Urzedo, "Ed Cooper: Nature-Based Solutions in West Berkshire, UK," https://atlas.smartforests.net/en/radio/ed-cooper.
16. Michelle Westerlaken, "Hyytiälä Forestry Field Station," https://atlas.smartforests.net/en/logbooks/hyytiala-forestry-field-station/#carbon-tree; Carbon Tree, https://www.hiilipuu.fi/index.php/en/home/.
17. For an overview of carbonizing forests, see Esther Turnhout, "The Forest Multiple: Esther Turnhout," https://atlas.smartforests.net/en/radio/the-forest-multiple-esther-turnhout.
18. Jennifer Gabrys & Kate Lewis Hood, "Indigenous Forest Technologies, Digital Practices, and Data Sovereignty," https://atlas.smartforests.net/en/stories/indigenous-forest-technologies.
19. Yuti Ariani Fatimah, "Carbon Offsetting Standards," https://atlas.smartforests.net/en/logbooks/carbon-offsetting-standards/#verra.

Model Ecologies—On Disassembling and Reassembling Landscapes

Paolo Patelli and Jussi Parikka

Climate variability and change, habitat fragmentation, overexploitation, and pollution pose a threat to both human society and natural ecosystems.[1] The urgent need to understand the impact of increasingly relevant anthropogenic factors on the biological world has, therefore, intensified a quest for predictions.[2] The ability to forecast how ecosystems, components of ecosystems, and the so-called "services" we derive from them will respond to such changes entails understanding how complex systems will adapt locally to large-scale environmental changes.

Landscapes, already fundamentally multiscalar, are at the hinge of such mutations as sites for observation and manipulation. In this context, a landscape is not just a physical expanse of land, but also a complex mosaic of interacting ecosystems, communities, and landforms. Different "patches" and elements are connected through the movement of matter, organisms, gene flow, energy, and information.[3] The spatial arrangement and composition of these elements influence ecological processes; therefore, the focus of multidisciplinary teams working in landscape ecology is understanding the patterns, processes, and dynamics of such spatial arrangements and their ecological implications.

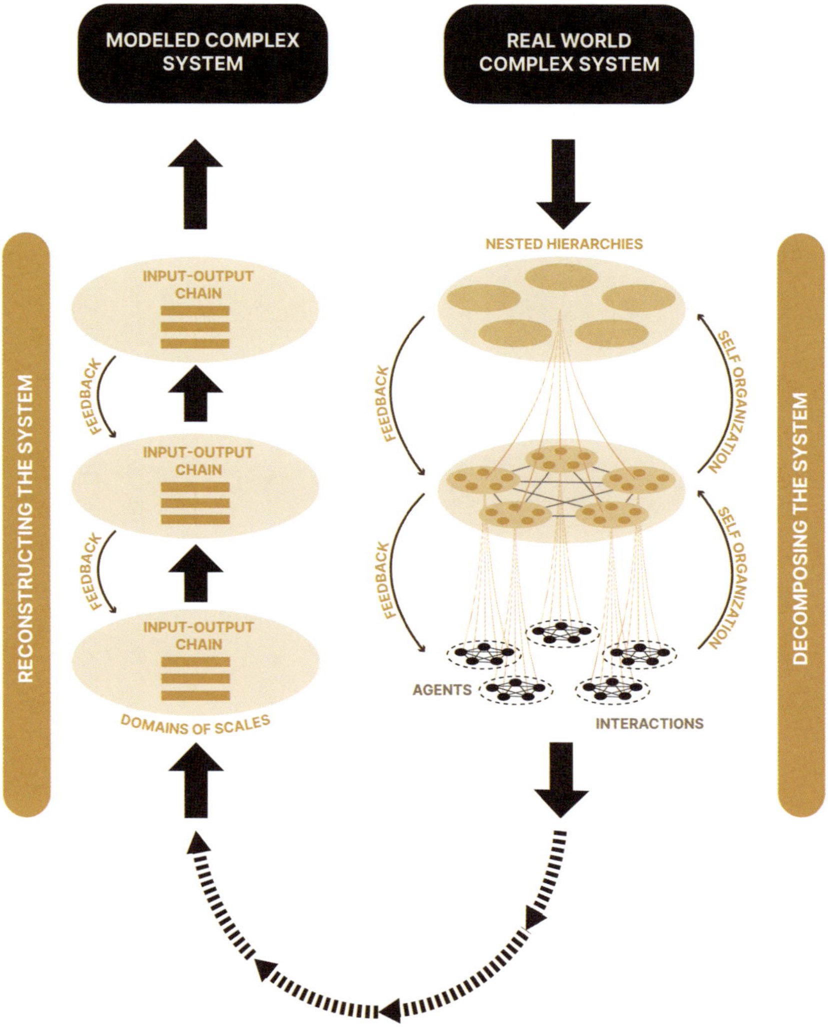

The nested hierarchical network structures of complex adaptive systems arise from the bottom-up self-organization of many interacting agents.

Models of such landscapes are widely used as they provide a powerful toolset to study complex interactions and dynamics. Models are more than just representations of knowledge about the world; they serve as epistemic tools for comprehending and interpreting the world. In landscape modeling, computational tools and mathematical representations are used to simulate and analyze the spatial and temporal dynamics of landscapes, but they also function as media for generating ideas, as reflexive human constructions about both the world we live in and the structure of our knowledge about it. These models are designed to understand and predict ecological processes, patterns, and the impacts of environmental changes across heterogeneous landscapes. In scientific practice, however, models only partially map onto the world, and different models do so in different ways.[4] The landscape appears as a unified object of knowledge only through the patchy grafting of code around a simulation core within a model system. Yet, as scientific agents must be included in the picture, such objects only ever represent the agent's intention to represent a part of the world, for some purpose.[5]

The operative modeling of a landscape, in relation to spatial planning, policymaking, or other forms of instrumentalization, often differs from scientific aims and methods, though the operational and the scientific conjoin in many aspects. Among the shared characteristics is a reliance on a set of data and parameters that are inherently dynamic at vastly different spatial and temporal scales, from geological structures to water patterns or weather recurrences. Computational landscape models are spatially explicit, as they incorporate spatial information considering, for example, the arrangement and distribution of different land cover types, habitats, or ecosystems within a given area. This spatial explicitness allows researchers to study—and practitioners to grasp—how spatial patterns influence ecological processes over time.

Many different computational methods have been deployed since the second half of the last century, each with their mediating function of how to represent and thus understand the world. Cellular automata models, for example, represent landscapes as a grid of cells, with each cell transitioning between different states based on predefined rules. These models are useful for studying dynamic processes, such as land cover change over time. Agent-based models instead simulate the behavior and interactions of individual entities or "agents," such as plants, animals, or even humans, within a landscape. These models are valuable for understanding emergent properties and complex dynamics that arise from individual-level interactions.

Animal and plant populations are thus also an essential part of a landscape as they become models within a model when the twofold movement of first analyzing and then synthesizing a landscape is attempted. Physical, chemical, and biological behaviors are interconnected across scales, from individuals to populations, species, communities, ecosystems, and the biosphere, with fluctuations at various scales interacting with one another.

Jane Hutton's pithy line that "landscapes are models *in situ*" is a rewarding way to appreciate the complexity of multiscalar events that constitute any landscape as mediation.[6] Anthropogenic landscapes can be interpreted in themselves as models of human–nature relations, physical and virtual spaces supporting forms of life, and "models of being with, working with, and interacting with all that is more-than-human."[7] Landscapes are also always experimental testing grounds: they are models of human relationships while also materially embodying their conditions of existence. The agencies of both systems have ambiguous effects, a peculiar instance of middle voice; shaping and being shaped by the material and human influences in the system.

We are, however, interested in the paradoxical yet continuous work of picking landscapes and their constitutive populations apart in order to put them back together. Computation plays a key role in the process of recomposing a view of the landscape. Faster computers now serve as catalysts for innovations in understanding ecological and climatic phenomena.[8] Hybrid models integrate multiple methods to capture the complexity of ecological systems by combining spatially explicit models with management models and dynamic population models to provide insights into how ecosystems respond to anthropogenic disturbance - be it land use changes or local climate change. We are interested in models as the central hinge through which ecological specification takes place, with a special eye on questions of scale within computational and software-based models.

Different models produce and contain different epistemologies; each carries forward different assumptions as to what a landscape *is*. We narrate this through selected episodes from the history of calculation and modeling where some of the landscapes and ecologies are mobilized through software and programs, some as mathematical patterns. Landscapes become coded content. To showcase some of the complexity of these intricate practices, we end the chapter with current scientific work using the example of the Animal, Landscape and Man Simulation System (ALMaSS), developed at Aarhus University. ALMaSS provides a multitude of interacting agents built in C++ code for the purpose of "investigating the effect of changes in landscape structure and management on the population size and distribution of animals," themselves individually reproduced as encoded protocols, models of programmed affordance.[9] Here, code-based entities such as classes and objects, with their methods and variables, feature as their natural counterparts, such as rabbits, mice, birds, and spiders. Among the 19 modeled species currently available for ALMaSS, we focus on the field vole (*Microtus agrestis*), a relative latecomer in the articulated history of animals and computing, but one with its own history as a laboratory and research animal.

Counting Rabbit Ears

In *Liber Abaci*, published in 1202, Leonardo Fibonacci devised a formula to calculate how many pairs of rabbits would be born from a single pair, knowing that each month from one pair, another pair is born and that each pair starts breeding in the second month of life. The solution was simple: in a given month, the number of pairs was the sum of the pairs in the previous two months. In the Fibonacci sequence, each number is the sum of the two preceding numbers. Given the initial conditions—the existence of a pair of rabbits in the first month—an algorithm can automatically compute the system's state at any moment in time, as it is only dependent on previous

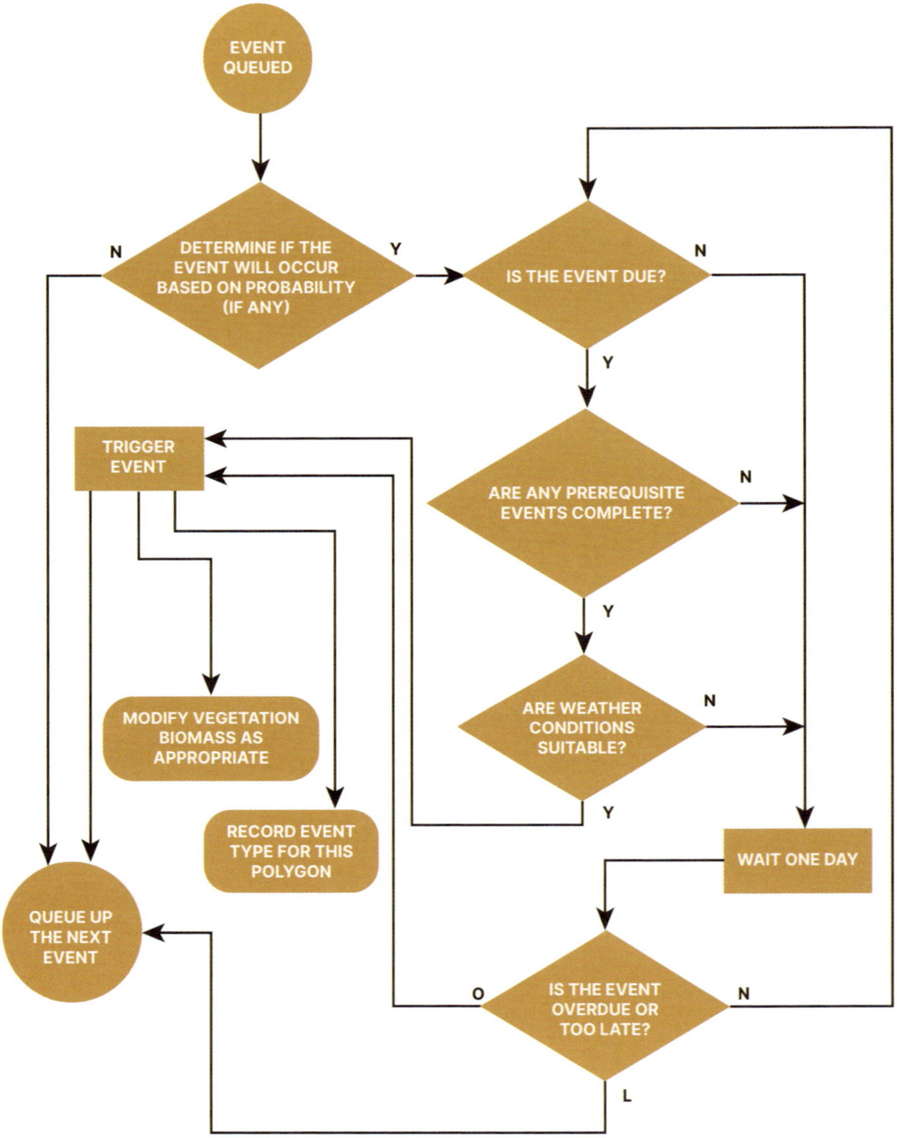

An example of a decision tree structure showing the sequence of events on a hypothetical farm.

states. The execution of the procedure is aimed at an effective result in a finite number of steps, but in the time and space of a computer's memory, where an infinite number of steps is perfectly plausible, the population will also tend to infinity, as it will always increase, unbounded, constantly following the golden ratio.

The recursive sequence is possibly the most aesthetically effective series of numbers ever imagined—as an approximation of the golden ratio, it can be found in works by Leonardo da Vinci or Hokusai. As a population model, though, Fibonacci's formula is biologically unrealistic, and intentionally so. Most obviously, in his model, the rabbits never die and, equally importantly, they do not relate to their surroundings. As a description of the relationship between two variables, it exemplifies how a scientific problem can be resolved, with interrelations providing the basis for prediction and control. Taking the sequence as a model, a world analogous to the one we know emerges, populated by idealized forms and processes.

While it is known that the Fibonacci numbers have inspired a number of efforts in more or less esoteric fields—from tarot interpretation to gematria—the knowledge of such algorithms and their limitations will ultimately lead us away from the superstitious elevation of a model to an oracle. As already noted by Norbert Wiener (1945), the computer does not really allow us to rest while it does the job; rather, it forces us to face the innumerable problems it constantly poses.[10] Automating ecological processes requires the control and evaluation of the accuracy of the analog processes, also in relation to their referents. This point can be linked to the broader study of artificial life—of statistical and computational models that meaningfully approximate basic life processes—abstracting, with just the needed accuracy, both space and bodies.

During the second half of the 20th century, the significant progress made by biology in descriptive research led to further developments in quantitative research with the ultimate goal of predicting organic responses to specific conditions. In this context, the methods developed by ecologists intersect with those from computer science. Empirical observations may guide the production of models, but models may also become realities in their own right, which need to be constantly examined, reflected upon, and managed. In this manner, the question of models was already early on—in computational discourses of scientific modeling—seen as "aesthetic." As John von Neumann, one of the founding fathers of artificial life, wrote:

> It is a relatively good approximation to truth—which is much too complicated to allow anything but approximations—that mathematical ideas originate in empirics, although the genealogy is sometimes long and obscure. ...But, once they are so conceived, the subject begins to live a peculiar life of its own and is better compared to a creative one, governed by almost entirely aesthetical motivations. ...As a mathematical discipline travels far from its empirical source,...it becomes more and more purely aestheticizing, more and more purely *l'art pour l'art*. This need not be bad...if the discipline is under the influence of men with an exceptionally well-developed taste.[11]

In short, models might be premised on empirical observations, but they also become second-order representations to be evaluated as art and media. As Marshall McLuhan noted in 1967, the computer is admirably suited to the artistic programming of an environment, of which the planet has become the content. The task of programming the environment is itself a work of art, something between imagination and representation.[12] Following McLuhan, if ecology is a background condition, ecological models produce "anti-environments" as different modes of perception, revealing the invisible nature of the environment we live in—or rather, the different ideas we have of it.

As environmental media, such models and software take up the interesting connection between knowing and seeing, of epistemic and aesthetic effects of scientific and operational models. Following Sebastian Vehlken's take on models as media, models are not just representations of theory or empirical material; their value is in the aesthetic surplus for epistemic ventures or, in Vehlken's words, "models make representations conceivable that would not be conceivable within existing theories."[13] Hence, the medium of ecological modeling does not simply make ecology visible; rather, it invents worlds that become sufficiently interesting surplus to what we already know. This surplus starts to produce, interestingly, new views of the original source, the target system.

All Models are ~~Wrong~~ Pragmatic

Let us use the above heading as a starting point and complexify from there: models are idealized structures that we use to represent the world via resemblance between systems.[14] They are meant to give a simplified insight into a "target system" by an analog system that is easier to understand or analyze. Models are thus handles that allow a particular grasp; as such, they already imply the work of not just representation, but also intervention. Analog systems share dynamic properties with target systems, but analogs may differ from their real-world counterparts in terms of substance or structure. In principle, anything can be a model of something when useful relationships with a different type of system can be established – be they mathematical, physical, biological, computational, or other.[15]

The importance and potential of such relationships became clear to George E. P. Box when, as a chemistry student, he joined the British Army Engineers during World War II. He was assigned to conduct biochemical experiments on the effects of poisonous gases on small rodents – animal models of humans.[16] Because the results of his experiments were too variable, he realized that the fundamental expertise needed to analyze them was not that of a chemist but a statistician. As a consequence of that realization, he changed the course of his career and, in a 1976 paper, he wrote what became a familiar trope, initially referring only to statistical models but sometimes applied to scientific models in general: "All models are wrong, but some are useful."[17] Box's aphorism recognizes that models always fall short of the complexity of reality but can still be usable – or that they are usable exactly because of their operative capacity to simplify. At the same time, models are only useful if they provide additional information beyond what is already known. Quantification focuses on trying to discern the effects of parameters of interest within noisy, real-world systems. Models cannot be true; all models are wrong,

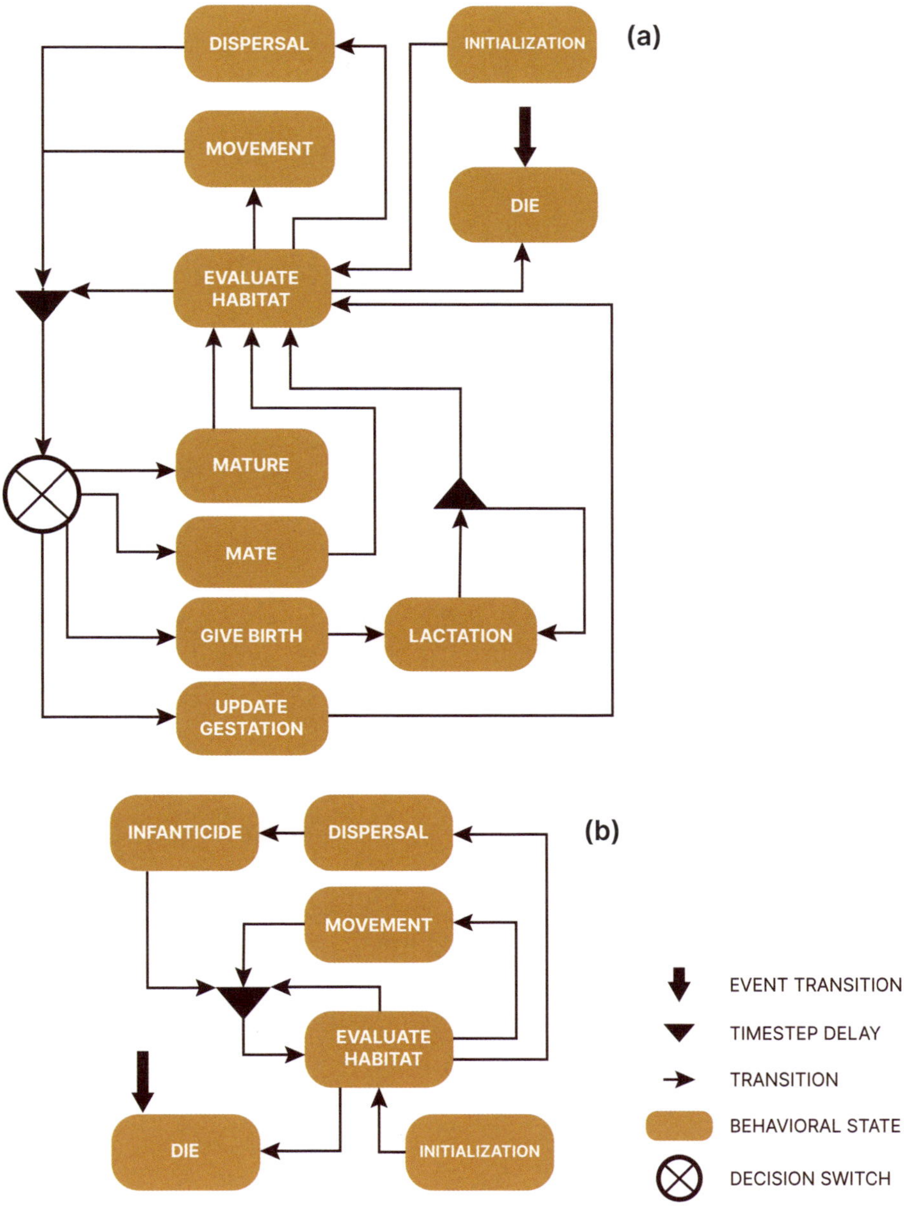

Agent-based simulation of behaviors for female (a) and male voles (b).

but what matters is that scientists be alert to what exactly is wrong, evaluating according to scientific "taste." Models allow researchers to manipulate environmental factors carefully to understand how they contribute to their development, behavior, and health. While there can never be an exact linear relationship between any model and any aspect of reality, "cunningly chosen parsimonious models often do provide remarkably useful approximations."[18] At the end of the day, models are pragmatic, even cunning, defined by what they can do and show.

Landscape Disassembly

In the field of simulation models, when scientists and engineers began exploring mechanical devices in the 1870s and electronic analog computers in the 1930s, they embodied mathematical, physical, and geometrical relations analogous to those of their target phenomena. Like maps, these models embodied a logic of navigation, though their medium was voltage. Mechanics and circuitry anticipated our current day's computation, defining the foundational metaphor of the "system" - a composition of elements interconnected through relationships. Such diagrammatic reasoning influenced the constitution of ecology as a discipline. Historically, the models that should make up a landscape's ecology have fallen into separate classes: for example, those that model surface dynamics (geomorphological models); the cycling of carbon, water, and nutrients (biogeochemical models); or population ecology (competition and population models). To assume a system is also to project and fabricate the component as an analytical, epistemic unit. Once a landscape is disassembled as a series of models, hundreds of components and many more feedback loops—not to mention different approaches and beliefs—make it difficult to put the system back together.

A fundamental divergence of approach lies in the consideration of the role of the environment in the ecology of animal and plant populations, which showed its philosophical significance and even captured the public imagination when the world's first televised scientific debate took place in 1954 on one of Australia's most popular television programs. In this case, history was made in the field of ecological population modeling, as the audience members were glued to their television sets, taking sides between two opposing schools of thought, one led by Herbert Andrewartha and Charles Birch, and the other led by Alexander John Nicholson. The prevailing view at the time was that populations—no matter where they were—were self-regulating based on competition for limited resources; that, as argued by Nicholson, populations were controlling themselves through density-dependent internal relations. Birch and Andrewartha posed a radical challenge to that interpretation. They argued that populations were controlled by their environment and that external processes (density-independent forces), driven by weather and other types of disturbance, were exceedingly important in controlling the numbers and distribution of animals.

The long, bitter battle effectively split the field of ecology. In the end, the Nicholson school won with a mathematical solution that could show that its theories worked in the form of differential Lotka-Volterra equations that had a long history in economic theory. Using this mathematical formula, it was able to show that its hypothesis was like physics, an observational science. It could do experiments in Petri dishes and in small cages. The other school could not produce anything that resonated with the science at the time; it did not have models with such powers of demonstration. The consequences of this duel were far-reaching: for many years, ecology remained focused on the idea that one can represent populations with very simple equations and with density dependence as an inherent property.[19] In some ways, many generations after Fibonacci's first pair of rabbits, Nicholson's creatures still resembled those that were "put in a place surrounded on all sides by a wall," to use Fibonacci's words, free of external conditions, devoid of context: a controlled laboratory-type setting instead of an open field. In contrast, the worlds generated by models based on Andrewartha's and Birch's theories help to explain the numbers in any population as a result of five components: the weather, resources, members of the same species, members of other species, and hazards. Recent agent-based models, including ALMaSS, which we discuss later, have emerged from this debate. They show that, just as Birch and Andrewartha did not have the models and level of mathematical sophistication as Nicholson's, to some extent, we still do not have this capability. It is complicated to describe how populations are constrained by their environment because this happens in many ways, and many models that translate these interactions use different mechanisms and codes. By contrast, Nicholson's world was encapsulated in a relatively simple equation, with density linked to the rates of reproduction and mortality.

Scales of Change

In the late 1970s, a series of models was developed to compute and simulate landscape evolution. A mesh of grid cells was used to represent a landscape and channel network. These models simulated landscape evolution by routing water across this mesh and changing the grid cell elevations to represent fluvial and slope erosion. Later, more enhanced models revealed how a larger set of interactions among, for example, hydrology, fluvial erosion, slope processes, tectonic uplift, climate, and lithology influence the drainage network and catchment form. These models introduced a holistic view, in which hydrology can determine geomorphology and geomorphology can alter the hydrology. Today, hydrological models remain technically and computationally challenging because they do not consist solely of surfaces; they continue underground, where water moves across and between layers, and they extend into the atmosphere. They are also economically challenging, requiring enormous resources and access to some of the most powerful computers.

Modeling landscape evolution is difficult due to the large number of processes operating over a wide range of spatial and temporal scales. Fundamentally, the challenge is how to address scales of change. For example, soil creep, the slow mass-wasting process of soil on a slope under the influence of gravity, may be inconsequential during a single season, but it can cause massive changes over thousands of years. Conversely, the exact location of a braided river section may prove irrelevant when considering thousands of years of valley aggradation, but very important when considering shorter timescales, such as where to build a bridge.

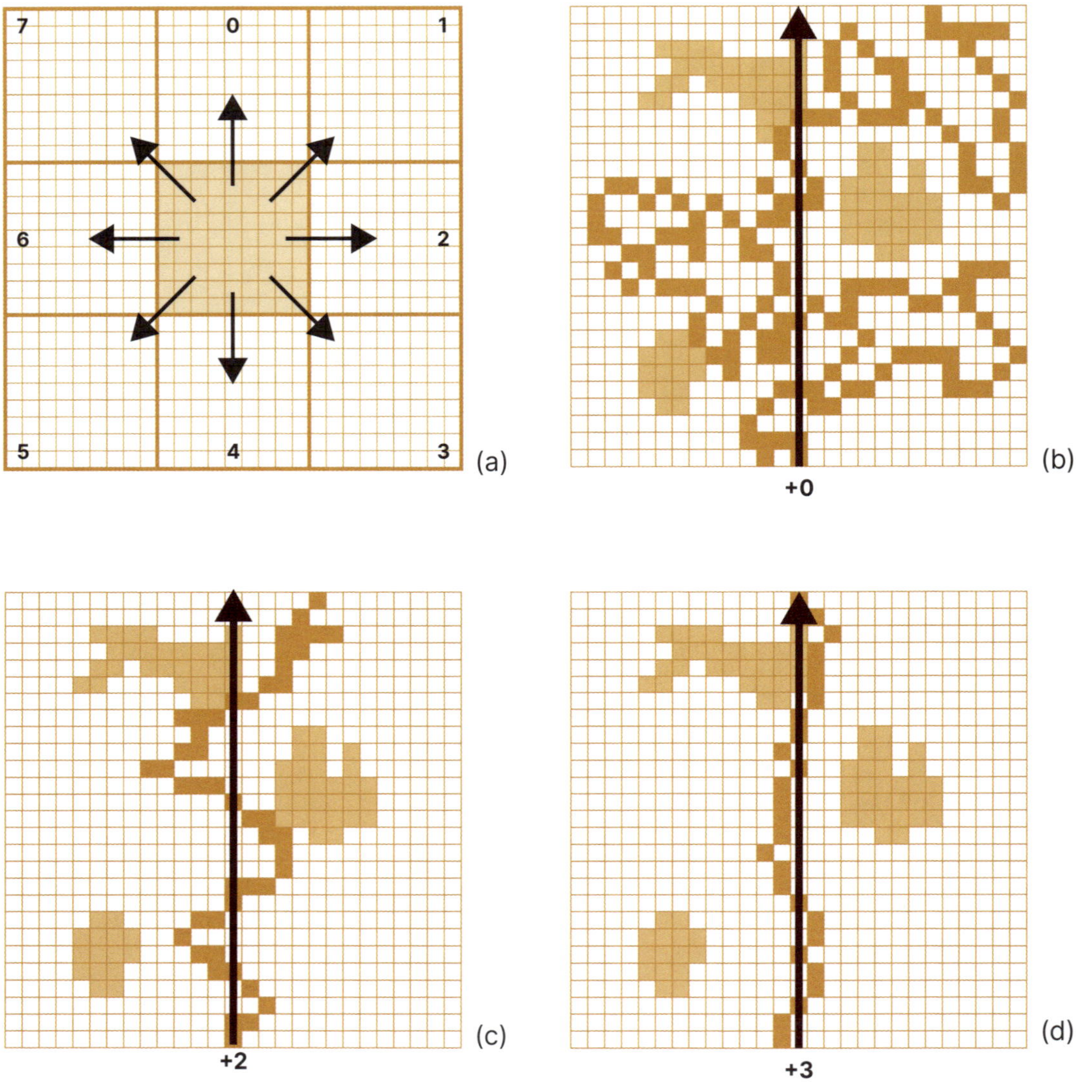

Agent-based simulation of potential animal movements across a landscape. Directional choice vectors for movement (a) and potential movements (b–d, dark ochre) based on weighing how close the movement adheres to the preferred direction (black arrow). Light ochre cells are considered unsuitable habitats.

To overcome the difficulties with changing spatial scales, models incorporate different techniques.[20] Some, like GOLEM, use a sub-grid cell representation, while others use irregular meshes. Areas with frequent change have more nodes, and thus more detail, than areas affected by slower processes. Other models, like CAESAR, distribute time, rather than space, differentially using a large mesh where most of the model's time is concentrated on active cells, while the relatively more stable ones are checked only periodically. In SIBERIA, when in any cell a threshold determined by the resistance of the slope material is exceeded by the discharge volume, material moves from one cell to another along the steepest line of descent, giving shape to the evolution of the landform.

Several of these landscape analysis programs can be obtained by following instructions on their respective websites. They usually provide an executable file, examples, and a manual showing how the physical structures of the landscape are broken down into operational units, interrelated variables, and flowcharts that highlight how such components are operable and possibly integrable. Still, these types of models do not include considerations of living forms that also recursively modify the environment and engineer their own niches.

A world that regulates itself through interactions between living organisms and their inorganic environment must account for variables in both the organisms and their environment. To map continuities across the biogeochemical strata, across life and non-life, complex loops, conditions, and causalities must be modeled, theorized, and, sometimes, just assumed. The first in-depth account of a living ecosystem described graphically as a model, which used the symbolism and aesthetics of electric circuit diagrams, was produced in the 1960s by Howard Odum. Systems Ecology had begun to develop since the 1953 publication of Eugene and Howard Odum's *Fundamentals of Ecology*, which was firmly committed to bringing both natural and human ecosystems into accord with the laws of ecoenergetics (the flow of energy through a system).[21] The central role of energy in all life processes brought thermodynamics closer to ecological processes, the tenet here being: "all equations equal zero." Solar radiation is captured through photosynthesis; chemical energy is ingested, assimilated, transformed, released through decomposition, stored in sediments, and exchanged as radiation and heat, as changes in states of matter and pressure, which is to say: weather. Ecologists and planners alike started to visualize the complex loops of energy, matter, and information flowing through natural, human, and technological systems using computer engineers' icons and circuit diagrams. Howard Odum even developed an analog of Ohm's Law, which was intended to be a representation of energy flows, except that instead of voltage, he pictured an "ecoforce."[22] This representation was designed to create a coupled system between organisms and their environment. While it proved influential as an energy-centered ecological theory, for example, in the later development of Gaia Theory and Earth System Science, it faced a fundamental problem in trying to describe ecosystems within a framework that only had one-dimensional currency at its core.[23] Within these limits, the Odumian paradigm could not produce a method that fully respects the complexity of the objects studied.

The Vole Protocol

Making predictions about how noisy ecological systems will respond to noisy large-scale environmental changes is extremely difficult, but it is precisely such promise to predict the future—or rather, plausible versions of it—that constitutes the surplus of computational models. Through careful patchwork and codework, they become interesting as a form of knowledge work that cultivates a taste for second-order realities. Such models allow different kinds of disciplinary knowledge to be grafted together through code and incorporated into a synthetic view of ecological patterns, where analytical knowledge is assembled into synthetic forms. Synthesis is enabled by turning knowledge into software, as simulations in a cybernetic flow of information in development.

ALMaSS, an agent-based model for animals in temperate European landscapes designed in the 1990s at Aarhus University and continuously developed on an ongoing basis by a wide network of researchers, is a predictive tool for answering policy questions regarding the effect of changing landscape structure or management on key species in the Danish landscape.[24] It integrates a landscape model with a farm management model, designed to service agent-based animal models with all the data they require about their surroundings, including events triggered by humans. According to Professor Christopher Topping, ALMaSS is not a model, but a model system: there are many models, and they can have very different purposes. The models all run through the same landscape simulation, a central core that is trying to replicate the reality "out there" as closely as possible. In an agent-based model system like ALMaSS, all the models are mechanistic: higher-level organizational patterns appear from the mechanisms introduced at lower levels or at a smaller scale. The model introduces a certain amount of food to simulate the evolution of a certain population. The individuals who are in the right place at the right time will be able to obtain the food, while once the food is depleted, other individuals will not be able to access it. This may result in a penalty for an individual, such as a reduced ability to reproduce or even starvation and death. Information from different disciplines can be integrated through these mechanisms: biological knowledge about how a species grows, ecological knowledge about how it chooses its habitats, physical-chemical relationships about how aspects of the environment change, and how pollutants or pesticides decay or travel in the environment. The world of ALMaSS is modular: it has been designed with a strong object-oriented paradigm to allow for the incremental addition of new features to the existing 100,000 lines of code without causing disruptions.

As the main code developer and scientist involved in ALMaSS, Topping explains how the system emerged in the late 1990s amid the proliferation of agent-based modeling. He likens the work of the system to an operative prototyping of sorts, where specific instances of modeling are "like cardboard boxes [that] are discarded or recycled after use."[25] While emphasizing such a pragmatics of modeling, ALMaSS is claimed to differ from usual ecological modeling in that it "involves including all real behaviour and mechanisms that are needed to describe the system to be modelled, such that we aim for a realistic systems representation."[26] This is quite different from the usual maxim used in ecological modeling, i.e., an application of

Ockham's razor, which focuses on simplicity as a value in itself.[27] ALMaSS is closer to an engineering approach in which a simulation is built to a specification. The very nature of the model, in fact, derives from its purpose: if a general modeling approach aims toward basic understanding, applied use demands a detailed simulation. ALMaSS simulations are, therefore, primarily aimed at supporting real-world decision-making and policy rather than general concepts. However, the models can also contribute to the underlying theoretical science, particularly where the key role of context in ecological system responses is concerned.[28]

The vole, already an "artifice" as a laboratory and research animal in its own environment, is one of 19 species modeled within ALMaSS. As a paradigmatic object in a simulated landscape, its synthetic form is defined by an ecological protocol of possible events and reactions within the fabric of its environment. Analyzing its behavior within the medium of the model might resemble a form of myomancy, the old practice of reading omens from the behavior of rats or mice, a "theriomantic" method of divination.[29] It might also remind us of rodent-related cautionary tales for children, populated by abstract objects as fictional characters; yet a model cannot warn against something that might happen; it only says that something will happen with a certain probability.

In ALMaSS, all initial parameters have been set when a vole has been weaned and enters the simulation as a new vole object: its life can be paraphrased from the project documentation. The model vole becomes a second-order object of ethology: it will evaluate its territory for habitat quality; if it is the breeding season, males will use the number of females present as a measure of quality. As a number of space steps are allowed for each time step with a given directional vector, the vole will also explore neighboring habitats and assess the quality of the territory there, using evaluation criteria that vary depending on the age, sex of the vole, and season. Once it has established a territory, the mature vole is capable of breeding. The female will mate with the nearest mature male whose territory overlaps her own. When young are produced, they enter initiation. The female will remain in the nest and feed her young, but dispersing males may attempt to kill unrelated young in their territory. When it dies, the vole is removed from the simulation.[30]

The vole—along with others such as the brown hare, the gray partridge, and the linyphiid spider—is an element of programmed landscapes that attempt to draw in the multitude of analytical bits of landscape information to create what was lost in the process: a living, dynamic system of interactions among different scales of agents and their material conditions.[31] Voles, moreover, are an excellent indicator of ecosystem health already in their organic—as opposed to synthetic—selves and, as such, models *in situ* of their environment: field monitoring of these species is already in place, providing valuable indications for ecosystem management.

The multiplication of landscapes through models and model systems does not in any way replace what Hutton signaled as the fundamental multiscalar richness of a landscape's original material dynamics. Instead, surplus software and code-based landscapes feature in a chain of comparative possibilities where making sense of disassembly and reassembly are inherent processes of knowledge and design.

The art and media of evaluating such computational epistemologies, even aesthetics in von Neumann's parlance, becomes a matter of trained taste, a particular sensibility of reading not only landscapes, but also the modeling media of such landscapes. The art of composing is thus crucial as components and systems do not pre-exist in this process.[32] Emphasizing the operational uses of models does not imply that coded environments are flattened onto the same ontological level as material landscapes; however, these models do track the interlinking chain of determinations. This also implies a fundamentally nonrepresentational mode of understanding ecology as always being a model about some order. When the model becomes the medium, its most fascinating aspects are not found in the results but in the process of practical examination, representation, and enactment of the complex interrelationships among its various components. This highlights how both human and nonhuman formations might come into existence through mutual dependence; an ever-changing and ever-evolving system of interactions and adaptations across diverse spatial and temporal scales.

Acknowledgment
The research and writing for this chapter was supported by the Aarhus University Research Foundation (AUFF) grant, Design and Aesthetics for Environmental Data (2022–2024).

Notes

1. Intergovernmental Panel on Climate Change (IPCC), *Climate Change 2022–Impacts, Adaptation and Vulnerability: Working Group II Contribution to the Sixth Assessment Report of the Intergovernmental Panel on Climate Change* (Cambridge University Press, 2023), https://doi.org/10.1017/9781009325844.
2. James S. Clark, et al., "Ecological Forecasts: An Emerging Imperative," *Science* 293 (2001): 657–60.
3. Joseph Engelberg & Louis L. Boyarsky, "The Noncybernetic Nature of Ecosystems," *American Naturalist* 114, no. 3 (1979): 317–24; Bernard C. Patten & Eugene P. Odum, "The Cybernetic Nature of Ecosystems," *American Naturalist* 118, no. 6 (1981): 886–95.
4. Julia Gouvea & Cynthia Passmore, "'Models of' Versus 'Models for.' Toward an Agent-Based Conception of Modeling in the Science Classroom," *Science & Education* 26, no. 1-2 (2017): 52.
5. Ronald N. Giere, "An Agent-Based Conception of Models and Scientific Representation," *Synthese* 172, no. 2 (2010): 269–81.
6. Jane Hutton, *Reciprocal Landscapes: Stories of Material Movements* (Routledge, 2020), 11.
7. Ibid.
8. Howard Veregin, "Computer Innovation and Adoption in Geography," in J. Pickles (ed.), *Ground Truth: The Social Implications of Geographic Information Systems* (Guilford Press, 1994), 93.
9. ALMaSS, "Short Introduction to ALMaSS," https://projects.au.dk/almass/ (accessed February 22, 2024). See also Farzin Lotfi-Jam. "Scales of Realtime," presented at the Transmediale, Berlin, 2022, https://2023.transmediale.de/en/event/scales-of-realtime; Jussi Parikka, *Insect Media: An Archaeology of Animals and Technology* (University of Minnesota Press, 2010).
10. Norbert Wiener, *The Human Use of Human Beings: Cybernetics and Society* (Houghton Mifflin, 1950).
11. John von Neumann, "The Mathematician," in Robert B. Heywood (ed.), *Works of the Mind* (University of Chicago Press, 1947), 180–96.
12. Marshall McLuhan, "The Invisible Environment: The Future of an Erosion," *Perspecta* 11 (1967): 161–67; Roman Frigg & James Nguyen, "The Fiction View of Models Reloaded," *Monist* 99, no. 3 (2016): 225–42.
13. Sebastian Vehlken, *Zootechnologies. A Media History of Swarm Research* (Amsterdam University Press, 2019), 185.
14. Ronald N. Giere, "Using Models to Represent Reality," in Lorenzo Magnani, Nancy J. Nersessian & Paul Thagard P (eds), *Model-Based Reasoning in Scientific Discovery* (Kluwer/Plenum, 1999), 41–57.
15. Derek Robinson, "Analog," in Matthew Fuller (ed.), *Software Studies* (MIT Press, 2008), 21–28.
16. George E. P. Box, *An Accidental Statistician: The Life and Memories of George E. P. Box* (Wiley, 2013). The British were anticipating possible chemical attacks in a similar manner to those that had been widely mobilized in WWI.
17. George E. P. Box, "Science and Statistics," *Journal of the American Statistical Association* 71, no. 356 (1976): 791–99.
18. George E. P. Box, "Robustness in the Strategy of Scientific Model Building," in Robert L. Launer & Graham N. Wilkinson (eds), *Robustness in Statistics* (Academic Press, 1979), 201–36.
19. Interview with Christopher Topping, conducted by the authors on December 13, 2023.
20. T. J. Coulthard, "Landscape Evolution Models: A Software Review," *Hydrological Process* 15 (2001): 165–73.

21. Eugene P. Odum, *Fundamentals of Ecology*, 2nd ed. (W. B. Saunders, 1959); Mark G. Madison, "'Potatoes Made of Oil': Eugene and Howard Odum and the Origins and Limits of American Agroecology," *Environment and History* 3, no. 2 (1997): 209–38.
22. Howard T. Odum, "Ecological Potential and Analogue Circuits for the Ecosystem," *American Scientist* 48 (1960): 1–8.
23. B. Å. Månsson & J. M. McGlade, "Ecology, Thermodynamics and H. T. Odum's Conjectures," *Oecologia* 93, no. 4 (1993): 582–96.
24. Chris J. Topping, et al., "ALMaSS, an Agent-Based Model for Animals in Temperate European Landscapes," *Ecological Modelling* 167, no. 1 (September 1, 2003): 65–82.
25. Chris J. Topping, "The Animal Landscape and Man Simulation System (ALMaSS): A History, Design, and Philosophy," *Research Ideas and Outcomes* 8 (2022): 6.
26. Ibid., 4.
27. Chris J. Topping, et al., "Per Aspera ad Astra: Through Complex Population Modeling to Predictive Theory," *American Naturalist* 186, no. 5 (November 2015): 669–74.
28. Chris J. Topping, "The Animal Landscape and Man Simulation System (ALMaSS)."
29. Ze Hong & Joseph Henrich, "The Cultural Evolution of Epistemic Practices: The Case of Divination," *Human Nature* 32 (2021): 622–51, https://doi.org/10.1007/s12110-021-09408-6.
30. Topping, et al., "ALMaSS, an Agent-Based Model," 65-82.
31. Chris J. Topping, "The Animal Landscape and Man Simulation System (ALMaSS)"; Ross E. Adams, "Landscapes of Post-History," in Ed Wall & Tim Waterman (eds), *Landscape and Agency: Critical Essays* (Routledge, 2018), 7–17.
32. Celia Lury, *Problem Spaces: How and Why Methodology Matters* (Polity Press, 2021).

More Than Just a Tool: Remote Sensing Potential for Transforming Landscape Research and Practice

Iryna Dronova

Progress in remote sensing and Earth observation technology over the past four decades has reshaped our ability to read, interpret, and create landscape information. Developed primarily for military and weather-related surveillance historically, remote sensing has evolved into a rich plethora of applications that have significantly improved the scientific understanding and monitoring of our environment.[1] Advancements in spaceborne satellite instrumentation have revolutionized how we analyze change via repeated imaging over vast regions, a task that is unfeasible using field surveys.[2] In turn, airborne instruments, including piloted aircraft and unoccupied aerial vehicles (UAVs), increasingly offer a bird's-eye perspective with unprecedented spatial detail.[3] At the same time, spatial data-processing tools have become more diverse and accessible, enhancing the efficiency of both research and communication.

Contrast in spatial detail between remote sensing images from an unoccupied aerial vehicle at 0.1 m spatial resolution (left) and Landsat-8 satellite at 30 m spatial resolution (right), displayed as true color spectral band composites. The area shown represents the western edge of a restored wetland site on Twitchell Island, Sacramento–San Joaquin Delta, California, in late June 2019.

Landscape researchers and professionals have welcomed the resulting shift from spatial data scarcity to an almost overabundance, creating new capacity for problem solving and knowledge discovery. This shift signifies a major breakthrough in the tradeoff between "reach and richness" of spatial knowledge.[4] Historically, high costs of data generation, storage, and communication made it extremely difficult to deliver rich information to large numbers of users. In contrast, modern data infrastructures, along with progress in remote sensing technology and products have facilitated the delivery of timely information via the internet and digital and print media to unprecedented audiences.[5] Open-access imagery has enabled novel capacities outside government—such as the commercial sector, NGOs, and the public—empowering socio-environmental activism and decision support in environmental disaster and hazard monitoring.[6] The abundance and versatility of remotely sensed information have strengthened landscape mapping, monitoring, and modeling and enabled collaborative, cross-disciplinary integration of landscape science into management, policy, and planning.[7]

These opportunities are raising important questions about how advances in remote sensing are strengthening landscape research, practice, and multi-stakeholder collaborations on wicked challenges entrenched in spatial decision-making. Are we taking full advantage of this potential? How is this progress changing our relationship with our environment and our ability to interpret and influence landscape states and their dynamics? What does this new capacity mean for our disciplinary relationships at a time when cross-field collaboration is crucial to prepare us for the environmental and social challenges of the 21st century? This chapter discusses these questions through the lens of a researcher-centric perspective by reviewing major advances, persisting caveats, and emerging strategies.

The New Landscape "Truth"

A recent state-of-the-art airborne remote sensing observatory equipped with imaging spectroscopy with light detection and ranging (lidar) has yielded a massive amount of new data across the Amazon tropical forest region, offering an unprecedented outlook on its ecosystems, biodiversity, and ecological threats.[8] Some have referred to the superpowers of such cutting-edge technology as "the new truth": high spatial detail accurately represents fine and complex landscape entities, complementary optical and lidar signals reveal the structure and vigor of vegetation, and broad observation footprints holistically capture entire regions.[9] Such capacities are becoming available to more and more users, and the opportunities for their customization are growing.[10]

Enhanced landscape recognition has been a critical breakthrough in both human and computer vision, enabling new mapping ontologies that downscale thematically coarse "cover types" to more nuanced landscape "objects" and "realistic" ecological networks.[11] This helps to overcome the nefarious challenge of distinguishing land use from land cover by highlighting fine-grained anthropogenic features, infrastructures, and natural and human-created vegetation alignments, thus enriching the knowledge base of environmental planning and design. It also provides critical new perspectives on understudied "mesoscales" at which traditional field surveys become prohibitively laborious, yet research goals require spatially explicit and comprehensive assessments. Such phenomena may include urban heat hazards mediated by the whole fabric of warmer and cooler landscape features and their mutual configuration, plant invasions where every new patch can contribute to further spread, and many more.[12]

"New truth" also means new "truthing," i.e., opportunities to verify spatial information and representations created by various analyses of imagery. Historically often called "ground-truthing," such validation relies on statistical comparisons of maps, image analyses, or predictive spatial models with the data collected *in situ* from discrete landscape samples—survey stops, plots, transects, or their combinations.[13] Comprehensive coverage and visual readability of new image products amplify the traditional truthing capacity in two significant ways: first, by augmenting field sampling with additional examples selected from the imagery, and second, by enabling alternative truthing strategies comparing not only identities, but also shapes, extents, and boundaries of mapping targets, thus widening the portfolio of truthing metrics for greater robustness.[14]

However, the benefits of new spatial richness come with an ordeal of excessive spectral noise, as small pixels convey variability in colors, illumination, surface roughness, and entities unrelated to observation

A high-spatial-resolution aerial photo of an oak woodland site in California, US (left), is classified using pixel-based mapping (middle) versus object-based mapping (right).

goals. A human brain may use such details as visual interpretation cues or ignore them. For instance, when observing sun glares and shadows, we can cognitively associate them with landscape objects and surfaces. However, computer-based mapping algorithms may struggle with excessive detail since traditional pixel-based mapping approaches have little information to work with besides pixel spectral values or "color." Accordingly, maps from high-resolution imagery can exhibit notorious artifacts showing fuzzy boundaries, irrelevant detail, or "salt-and-pepper speckle" noise due to the mislabeling of multiple classes in a single landscape element.[15]

An example of urban vegetation detection from high-spatial-resolution imagery illustrates that a pixel-based map contains some artifacts of spectral noise and does not account for spatial context in pixel assignment to classes. For instance, some landscape elements, such as lawns, have inclusions labeled by the map as "non-vegetated" due to the presence of dry grass or temporary objects (e.g., picnic blankets). In turn, some tree crowns that contain deep shadows are incorrectly labeled as non-vegetated surfaces. These issues are substantially improved by using an alternative technique, known as object-based image analysis, in which image pixels are grouped into small regions (objects) prior to being assigned a class label by the analysis algorithm. This strategy reduces spectral noise by averaging pixel properties at the object level and increases the alignment between mapped and real-world features by operating on local spatial neighborhoods rather than isolated pixels.

These issues echo the famous and timeless mapping challenge—balancing the conveyance of information with the necessary simplification of reality. As there can often be more than one way to achieve such balance, even high-accuracy mapping products may exhibit ontological vagueness or indeterminacy due to the inexactness

of map category definitions and imprecision of class boundaries relative to their respective real-world objects.[16] As remote-sensing-based maps and other products often aim to be multi-use, some degree of inexactness becomes inevitable across different possible applications. For example, "urban green space" maps are desired by diverse initiatives, including the assessments of biodiversity and ecological systems, models of urban microclimate and human thermal comfort, studies of public health and environmental justice, and many others.[17]

Notably, richer spatial and temporal information does not necessarily resolve spatial vagueness in relation to indeterminate or inexact object boundaries. In fact, abundant spatial detail in snapshot imagery is more likely to manifest fleeting moments in landscape states "truthfully" captured by the sensor, but not necessarily a lasting condition that may be sought by mapping. Shorelines with constantly moving waves are a great example of this challenge, forcing us to question how we define a water body and its edge and what spatial and temporal scales might best suit this definition. Similarly, some have questioned the terminology of urban "heat islands" (referring to warmer microclimates in cities compared to their surroundings) due to continuous changes in urban air temperatures on diurnal, seasonal, and long-term scales, making it difficult to establish a hard boundary.[18]

Not surprisingly, we often find that some degree of spatial and temporal aggregation is required to represent landscape conditions applicable to extended timeframes.[19] However, the resulting loss of information inevitably compromises visual recognition and communication. In contrast to quantitative analyses, where statistical methods can help to determine optimal spatial scales for image-based measurement and modeling, balancing relevant and irrelevant detail becomes an extremely complex task at the interface of data visualization and perception.[20] Novel geospatial analytical approaches and techniques show promise for developing such guidance; however, their advancement requires direct integration of multi-user perspectives and collaborative visualization.[21] Furthermore, to use the new remote sensing potential to understand landscapes more holistically, such developments need to be expanded from static maps and visualizations to analyses and representations of landscape change.

Understanding Landscape Change

The new information richness and data-handling powers of remote sensing technologies are fundamentally reshaping how we measure, monitor, and interpret landscape change, particularly with growing variety and access to repeated product time series. While repeated, statistically informed field data collection has long been a primary source of environmental "truth," the feasibility of such observations is necessarily constrained to specific, discrete "sites" and often only subsets of them. Simultaneous improvement in temporal frequency, spatial resolution, and, as with UAVs, customization of landscape sensing dissolves the tension between remotely sensed and ground "truths," making both critical facets of change assessment. Indeed, the superior capacity of remote-sensing-based analytical tools to address time has been highly praised by novel data integration platforms and other efforts to support landscape decision-making.[22]

Such possibilities are increasingly prominent in urban contexts where remote-sensing-based insights on landscape change can inform planning, design, and, ultimately, policies. For instance, mitigating globally exacerbating hazards of urban heat requires a firsthand understanding of landscape thermal performance and human exposure, where remote sensing technologies have been critical in three major ways. First, some instruments can directly sense landscape thermal properties such as surface temperature (now available as gridded products) and detect their responses to land use change and urban growth, including the evolution of the infamous city-level "heat islands." Second, remote sensing observations can detect some of the major sources of urban warming and cooling associated with the built environment, green and water spaces, and their spatial configuration and juxtaposition.[23] Finally, spatially comprehensive datasets can reveal inequities in human exposure to thermal hazards and in access to beneficial amenities such as vegetated parks, which can help to inform design and planning for environmental justice.[24]

Yet, important uncertainties remain with respect to the ontologies of change and how they respond to constraints in remote sensing capacity, particularly in geographic regions with sparse observations. For example, the high cost of frequent data collection or physical limitations of weather and cloud cover may lead to sparse inconsistent time series, where landscape differences between available dates may include both real and false appearances of "change" (e.g., phenological mismatches). Relatedly, a similar change process repeating across a landscape at different timeframes, such as vegetation stress, might look like many different types of change in a long image time series with a fixed start and end year.

Such issues can be somewhat alleviated by improving temporal frequencies of satellite observations and customized local airborne sensing, especially UAVs. At the same time, they call for novel "paradigms of change" capable of handling temporal noise and variable timeframes of similar phenomena. Such paradigms are rapidly evolving, expanding the scope of change analyses from classical map overlay approaches. For example, the idea of "dynamic cover types" treats landscapes as typologies of physically and ecologically plausible sequences of cover type transitions (rather than any possible cover type combinations).[25] Over multiple years, changes in mapped dynamic cover type zones could indicate shifts in landscape regimes shaped by ecological processes or human management. Other approaches allow the detection of similar types of changes occurring asynchronously over a landscape.[26] Such methods can isolate signals of transforming landscape events within longer time series, and they have started to inform the monitoring of complex urban land cover transitions.[27]

Frontiers of Landscape Research

New sensors and increasingly easier ways of data processing have started to reshape traditional research practices and the ways by which we investigate and communicate landscape information and academic and professional expert vision. A pertinent question arises about how these transformations change the frontier of landscape research and its relationships with disciplinary fields and

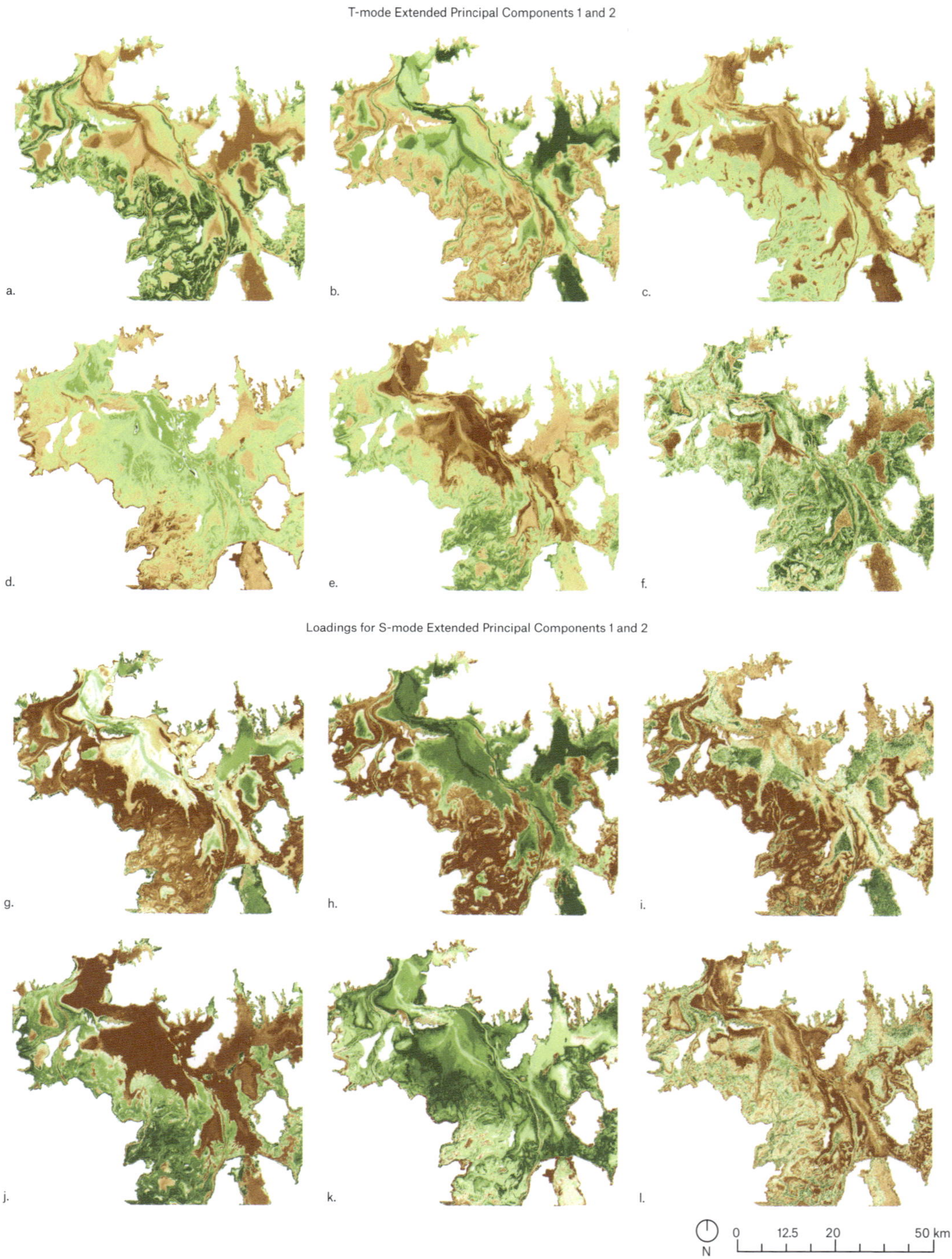

Visualizations of the spatiotemporal patterns highlighted through different machine-learning techniques (S-mode and T-Mode extended principal component analysis) to detect and classify changes in the Poyang Lake wetlands. Images a–f use T-mode and images g–l use S-mode.

nonacademic data users. In historically data-starved contexts, having some, albeit imperfect, landscape data has often been preferable to having none.[28] This constraint has forced both researchers and data users to seek compromises between their goals and the scopes of the available products. Empowered with new remote sensing technology, landscape researchers are now themselves becoming creators and stewards of spatial information, enabling other types of users to take advantage of its rich potential and to understand its constraints better. This has spotlighted the remote sensing potential to serve a wider range of societal needs and to improve quality of life including economy, governance, planning, and education. Indeed, remote sensing applications have propagated within traditional landscape disciplines as well as novel spheres that were not, historically, directly served by these technologies.[29] For instance, such applications have expanded in landscape architecture and planning from the use of raw imagery and lidar products for visualization to in-depth analyses of landscape character, aesthetic quality, and our perceptions of them.[30] This potential has also caught the interest of policy makers, as remote sensing has become a source of evidence on the impact of policies within various sectors, especially in regions with massive spatial data gaps. Comprehensive insights about environmental dynamics and human landscape activities across different scales have made remote sensing pivotal to the knowledge-building, problem-identification, and evaluation/monitoring phases of a policy cycle. This progress has brought hope that lessons learned through such evidence can be looped back into the cycle to strengthen new policies and inform landscape planning and action.[31]

Interestingly, however, the actual assimilation of remote sensing into real-world cycles of policy and decision-making has been lagging behind expectations. A review of remote sensing applications for urban planning, for instance, reported a still "limited integration between ecology, remote sensing, and urban planning," signaling that the full potential for this technology in guiding urban policies, planning, and public information has not been yet met.[32] Similarly, remote sensing contributions remain uncommon in policy formulation and application stages despite their prominence in the early phases of the cycle, with relatively little progress for over a decade.[33]

An immediate explanation for this discrepancy is that some of the most efficient and cutting-edge data-processing tools are still, perhaps, too recent to reach a diverse community of users. For example, navigating novel pools of abundant information and detailed imagery often requires "big data" capacities such as high-performance computing and spatial data infrastructures that are still evolving and not accessible among users equitably.[34] This barrier has been amplified by the lack of open science in terms of commercial data and software affordable to only a fraction of users. Fortunately, this situation is rapidly changing for greater transparency and data access both in the United States and worldwide as evidenced by public releases of global satellite-based products, e.g., by the American National Aeronautics and Space Administration (NASA) and the European Satellite Agency (ESA), alongside open-access geospatial tools including Python, R, QGIS, and web-based platforms such as Google Earth Engine and OpenStreetMap.[35] The proliferation of open-access tutorials and web-based materials is also helping to ease the learning curve for different users.

Yet another important barrier may lie in a still-significant demand for remote sensing expertise even for ready-to-use products. Robust applications in urban planning and natural resource management require an understanding of the physical characteristics of imagery (e.g., spatial and spectral resolutions), sensor and operation constraints (e.g., temporal frequency and sensitivity to clouds), and implications of error and uncertainty in maps or analyses in relation to user goals.[36] For example, using remote sensing to assess the heat-mitigating potential of green spaces must consider the seasonality of available imagery because vegetation-induced cooling depends on seasonally variable plant biomass and canopy structure. In some climates (e.g., Mediterranean), the hottest timeframes of the year coincide with the low-precipitation "dry" season when some common plant types may be senescent unless irrigated (e.g., annual grasses).[37] Using remote sensing data to detect the full extent of urban vegetation would therefore require imagery from cooler seasons to capture peak biomass and cover (e.g., spring to early summer in the Northern Hemisphere). However, such information may overestimate the cooling potential of non-irrigated green spaces for the hottest time of the year. In contrast, dry-season imagery would more realistically convey which vegetated areas remain green and participate in cooling but would be less useful for green-space mapping due to spectral confusion between dead vegetation and bare soil.

Product Creators and Product Users

The abovementioned challenges imply that to integrate seamlessly with landscape research and practice, applications of remote sensing must help to close the gaps in the flow of spatial information between data creators and users. Various stages of knowledge construction are critical to this purpose: converting the flux of raw data into usable information, optimizing the richness and reach of the deliverables, and comprehending error and uncertainty. The success, ultimately, depends on two key pillars of data quality: the accuracy of data generation, and the "fitness-for-use," or suitability for a given application.[38]

Accuracy embodies various well-studied dimensions of error and uncertainty (e.g., positional, thematic, electromagnetic) and defines the usability of mapping and change analysis products depending on the standards of a given application.[39] To this end, remote-sensing data vendors have substantially improved and streamlined the burden of data pre-processing including geometric, topographic, and sometimes atmospheric correction, at least for most popular satellite products. Data standards have been continuously evolving for spatial products in general. Finally, the rise of artificial intelligence (AI) and state-of-the-art machine-learning algorithms have also enhanced major data-creation workflows such as land cover recognition and mapping and integration of versatile remote sensing datasets into AI-based landscape analyses.

In turn, the "fitness-for-use" of spatial data critically depends on the ontological tradeoff between specificity and usability.[40] Advances in remote sensing have increased the demand and capacity for nuanced ontologies. For instance, urban green space monitoring may no longer be satisfied with generic cover types such as "developed, open space" in the US National Land Cover Dataset or global land cover products, targeting instead distinct entities such as parks, schoolyards, or greenways.[41] New high- and very-high-resolution imagery provides even finer-scale opportunities unfeasible for earlier studies. For instance, detecting and quantifying nuanced landscape elements within urban green spaces may help to explain differences in microclimate, social benefits, and ecological and health benefits even among nominally identical land uses such as "parks."[42] Yet, extremely specific definitions may limit the uses of a product, making it no longer "neutral across different data communities," unless a rigorous crosswalking takes place in parallel, which is a process for integrating disparate datasets.[43] The latter challenge may be addressed by using hierarchical ontologies capturing both coarser and nested finer levels of landscape and vegetation organization.

These issues underscore the critical importance of data representation, query, and visualization in fostering more effective researcher-user collaborations. Remote sensing data are now increasingly integrated into various forms of geo-visualization for both analytical and communication objectives. This heightens the risk of inappropriate or uninformed uses of visualization producing deceptive results. This can be illustrated, for example, by the effect of digital image stretching on the visualization of urban land surface temperature using a diverging color palette. Two depictions of the same dataset bound by identical minimum and maximum temperature values yield contrasting visual effects when using a similar maximum-minimum stretch rather than standard deviations, which results in greater dominance of a red color that may be intuitively perceived as hotter. Yet it is not easy to determine whether stretching distorts certain factual "truths" intended to be communicated by the map.

Related challenges arise when creative artistic approaches intended to enhance the perception of landscape information may inadvertently come up as data manipulation, distortion, or bias, smudging the divide between accuracy and cognitive effectiveness. Indeed, user misconceptions of geographic data as free of errors have often ascribed "undue credibility" to aesthetically attractive spatial products such as maps.[44] Incorporating some forms of "abstraction control" to vary the realism of spatial representations and creating "knowledge about scale" to support cognitive perception may help to mitigate these challenges and improve both fitness-for-use and guidance on spatial datasets.[45]

These issues are especially important given the growing plethora of data integration platforms in which remotely sensed information helps to communicate spatial information and connect researchers with other data users. Such platforms are a vivid testimony to technology's promises, ranging from sophisticated applied programming interfaces to innumerable web maps and tools for visual exploration and user-driven data extraction. There is a growing interest in facilitating collaborations and decision-making at different scales using new data-rich initiatives such as multidimensional data cubes, digital ecosystems, and digital twins of natural and anthropogenic environments.[46] Remote sensing is critical for these efforts by providing both data streams on landscape histories and state-of-the-art environmental indicators measured by sensors, such as vegetation health, air and water pollution, thermal hazards, and others.

Such data integration can support very specific landscape research and planning goals but also leave room for spontaneous collaborations, stakeholder engagement, data exchange and communication, and knowledge discovery and co-production.[47] Yet, echoing earlier discussed applications, these tools do not always take full advantage of the remote sensing advances, and the ones that do are not always equipped for multi-user support.[48] Indeed, most remote-sensing-centered tools require substantial technical expertise and thus may not adequately reach those in need, amplifying known inequities in access to geographic technology. One strategy to navigate this issue is supporting distributed local initiatives, where demand-oriented research brings together landscape scientists, municipalities, professionals, and other stakeholders.[49] Although such efforts critically depend on institutional means and incentives, they may generate lasting resources for training and knowledge dissemination tailored to decision support of their respective communities. They may also produce generalizable tools and blueprint models that can empower other initiatives and help to bridge broader gaps in expertise toward more seamless data integration and stakeholder collaboration.[50]

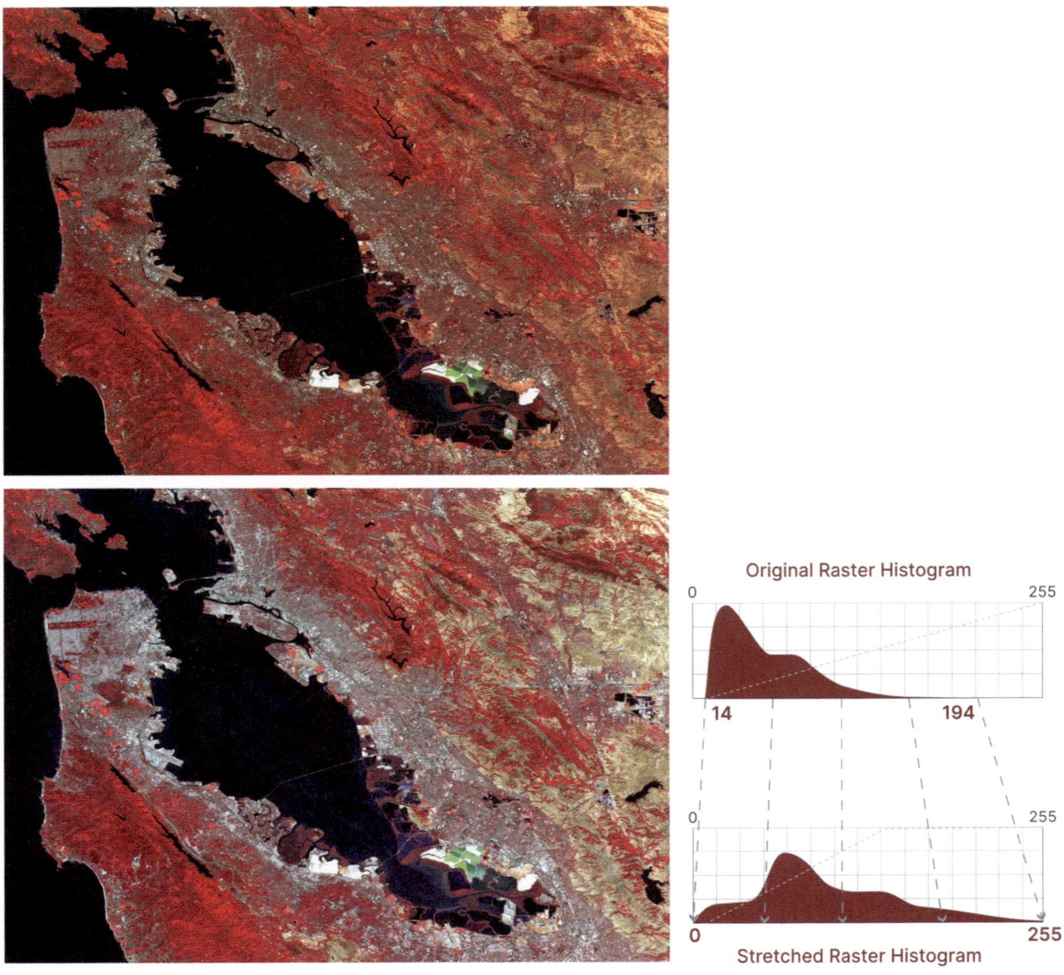

The effect of digital raster stretching (bottom) on a satellite-derived land surface temperature (LST) image (top) over a portion of Oakland, California, US. Raster stretching increases the difference among pixel color values to identify features more easily.

In summary, advances in and achievements of remote sensing technology hold a strong promise for supporting rich and multifaceted cross-disciplinary partnerships at a time when global landscapes are undergoing unprecedented change. Historically regarded as a special source of physical environmental data, remote sensing has clearly become "more than just a tool," enabling novel landscape questions and discoveries about novel types of change and interactions among their drivers. The reciprocity between remote sensing and field research becomes especially crucial in light of this progress, and proactive anticipation of the needs of research product users can help to identify such synergies and optimize their use more effectively.

This empowerment goes well beyond collective problem solving alone, creating new opportunities for activism, relationship building, and accountability between the public and governments. Yet, it is also clear that the full promise of rapidly advancing remote sensing technology has not been realized, in part due to barriers related to required expertise and the still-limited reach of truly accessible data, tools, and support. A critical priority for the scientific community and researchers working with remote sensing data directly is therefore to create more impactful and efficient data integration and sharing to help to navigate such barriers and to nurture stronger, productive, and seamless partnerships among researchers, professionals, policymakers, and publics.

Notes

1. Siamak Khorram, et al., *Principles of Applied Remote Sensing* (Springer, 2016), https://doi.org/10.1007/978-3-319-22560-9.
2. Susan L. Ustin & Elizabeth M. Middleton, "Current and Near-Term Advances in Earth Observation for Ecological Applications," *Ecological Processes* 10, no. 1 (January 4, 2021): 1, https://doi.org/10.1186/s13717-020-00255-4.
3. Karen Anderson & Kevin J. Gaston, "Lightweight Unmanned Aerial Vehicles Will Revolutionize Spatial Ecology," *Frontiers in Ecology and the Environment* 11, no. 3 (April 2013): 138–46, https://doi.org/10.1890/120150.
4. Khorram, et al., *Principles of Applied Remote Sensing*.
5. Vitor Gomes, Gilberto Queiroz & Karine Ferreira, "An Overview of Platforms for Big Earth Observation Data Management and Analysis," *Remote Sensing* 12, no. 8 (April 16, 2020): 1,253, https://doi.org/10.3390/rs12081253.
6. On activism, see John C. Baker & Ray A. Williamson, "Satellite Imagery Activism: Sharpening the Focus on Tropical Deforestation," *Singapore Journal of Tropical Geography* 27, no. 1 (March 2006): 4–14, https://doi.org/10.1111/j.1467-9493.2006.00236.x; on hazard monitoring, see Karen E. Joyce, et al., "A Review of the Status of Satellite Remote Sensing and Image Processing Techniques for Mapping Natural Hazards and Disasters," *Progress in Physical Geography: Earth and Environment* 33, no. 2 (April 2009): 183–207, https://doi.org/10.1177/0309133309339563.
7. On management see Robert E. Kennedy, et al., "Remote Sensing Change Detection Tools for Natural Resource Managers: Understanding Concepts and Tradeoffs in the Design of Landscape Monitoring Projects," *Remote Sensing of Environment* 113, no. 7 (July 2009): 1,382–96, https://doi.org/10.1016/j.rse.2008.07.018; on policy and planning, see Alexandra Bell, et al., "Scientific Evidence from Space—A Review of Spaceborne Remote Sensing Applications at the Science–Policy Interface," *Remote Sensing* 15, no. 4 (February 8, 2023): 940, https://doi.org/10.3390/rs15040940; Thilo Wellmann, et al., "Remote Sensing in Urban Planning: Contributions towards Ecologically Sound Policies?" *Landscape and Urban Planning* 204 (December 2020): 103921, https://doi.org/10.1016/j.landurbplan.2020.103921.
8. Gregory P. Asner, et al., "Quantifying Forest Canopy Traits: Imaging Spectroscopy Versus Field Survey," *Remote Sensing of Environment* 158 (March 1, 2015): 15–27, https://doi.org/10.1016/j.rse.2014.11.011.
9. Cameron Brinitzer & Etienne Benson, "Introduction: What Is a Field? Transformations in Fields, Fieldwork, and Field Sciences since the Mid-Twentieth Century," *Isis* 113, no. 1 (March 1, 2022): 108–13, https://doi.org/10.1086/718147.
10. Nicholas C. Coops, Tristan R. H. Goodbody & Lin Cao, "Four Steps to Extend Drone Use in Research," *Nature* 572, no. 7770 (August 22, 2019): 433–35, https://doi.org/10.1038/d41586-019-02474-y.
11. Elie Morin, et al., "The Promising Combination of a Remote Sensing Approach and Landscape Connectivity Modelling at a Fine Scale in Urban Planning," *Ecological Indicators* 139 (June 2022): 108930, https://doi.org/10.1016/j.ecolind.2022.108930.
12. See for example, Matthew

Maimaitiyiming, et al., "Effects of Green Space Spatial Pattern on Land Surface Temperature: Implications for Sustainable Urban Planning and Climate Change Adaptation," *ISPRS Journal of Photogrammetry and Remote Sensing* 89 (March 2014): 59–66, https://doi.org/10.1016/j.isprsjprs.2013.12.010; Iryna Dronova, Erica N. Spotswood & Katharine N. Suding, "Opportunities and Constraints in Characterizing Landscape Distribution of an Invasive Grass from Very High Resolution Multi-Spectral Imagery," *Frontiers in Plant Science* 8 (May 30, 2017), https://doi.org/10.3389/fpls.2017.00890.

13. Russell G. Congalton & Kass Green, *Assessing the Accuracy of Remotely Sensed Data: Principles and Practices*, 2nd ed. (RC/Taylor & Francis, 2009).
14. Nicholas Clinton, et al., "Accuracy Assessment Measures for Object-Based Image Segmentation Goodness," *Photogrammetric Engineering and Remote Sensing* 76, no. 3 (March 2010): 289–99.
15. Thomas Blaschke & Josef Strobl, "What's Wrong with Pixels? Some Recent Developments Interfacing Remote Sensing and GIS," *Geo-Informations-Systeme* 14, no. 6 (2001): 12–17.
16. Matti Eklund, "Deconstructing Ontological Vagueness," *Canadian Journal of Philosophy* 38, no. 1 (2008): 117–40; on indeterminacy, see John S. Pipkin, "Fuzzy Sets and Spatial Choice," *Annals of the Association of American Geographers* 68, no. 2 (June 1978): 196–204, https://doi.org/10.1111/j.1467-8306.1978.tb01190.x.
17. Wellmann, et al., "Remote Sensing in Urban Planning."
18. Eberhard Parlow, "Regarding Some Pitfalls in Urban Heat Island Studies Using Remote Sensing Technology," *Remote Sensing* 13, no. 18 (September 9, 2021): 3,598, https://doi.org/10.3390/rs13183598.
19. Iryna Dronova, et al., "A Review of Unoccupied Aerial Vehicle Use in Wetland Applications: Emerging Opportunities in Approach, Technology, and Data," *Drones* 5, no. 2 (June 2021): 45, https://doi.org/10.3390/drones5020045.
20. Alois Ferscha, "A Matter of Taste," in Bernt Schiele, et al. (eds), *Ambient Intelligence, Lecture Notes in Computer Science*, vol. 4794 (Springer, 2007), 287–304, https://doi.org/10.1007/978-3-540-76652-0_17.
21. Haoxuan Wang, et al., "Hierarchical Visualization of Geographical Areal Data with Spatial Attribute Association," *Visual Informatics* 5, no. 3 (September 2021): 82–91, https://doi.org/10.1016/j.visinf.2021.09.001.
22. Jenny Palomino, Oliver C. Muellerklein & Maggi Kelly, "A Review of the Emergent Ecosystem of Collaborative Geospatial Tools for Addressing Environmental Challenges," *Computers, Environment and Urban Systems* 65 (September 2017): 79–92, https://doi.org/10.1016/j.compenvurbsys.2017.05.003.
23. Alexander Buyantuyev & Jianguo Wu, "Urban Heat Islands and Landscape Heterogeneity: Linking Spatiotemporal Variations in Surface Temperatures to Land-Cover and Socioeconomic Patterns," *Landscape Ecology* 25, no. 1 (January 2010): 17–33, https://doi.org/10.1007/s10980-009-9402-4; Fanhua Kong, et al., "Effects of Spatial Pattern of Greenspace on Urban Cooling in a Large Metropolitan Area of Eastern China," *Landscape and Urban Planning* 128 (August 2014): 35–47, https://doi.org/10.1016/j.landurbplan.2014.04.018.
24. Bill M. Jesdale, Rachel Morello-Frosch & Lara Cushing, "The Racial/Ethnic Distribution of Heat Risk-Related Land Cover in Relation to Residential Segregation," *Environmental Health Perspectives* 121, no. 7 (July 2013): 811–17, https://doi.org/10.1289/ehp.1205919; Maimaitiyiming, et al., "Effects of Green Space Spatial Pattern on Land Surface Temperature."
25. Iryna Dronova, et al., "Mapping Dynamic Cover Types in a Large Seasonally Flooded Wetland Using Extended Principal Component Analysis and Object-Based Classification," *Remote Sensing of Environment* 158 (March 1, 2015): 193–206.
26. Robert E. Kennedy, Zhigiang Yang & Warren B. Cohen, "Detecting Trends in Forest Disturbance and Recovery Using Yearly Landsat Time Series: 1. LandTrendr—Temporal Segmentation Algorithms," *Remote Sensing of Environment* 114, no. 12 (December 15, 2010): 2,897–2,910, https://doi.org/10.1016/j.rse.2010.07.008.
27. Theodomir Mugiraneza, Andrea Nascetti & Yifang Ban, "Continuous Monitoring of Urban Land Cover Change Trajectories with Landsat Time Series and LandTrendr-Google Earth Engine Cloud Computing," *Remote Sensing* 12, no. 18 (September 5, 2020): 2,883, https://doi.org/10.3390/rs12182883.
28. A-Xing Zhu, "Research Issues on Uncertainty in Geographic Data and GIS-Based Analysis," in Robert B. McMaster & E. Lynn Usery (eds), *A Research Agenda for Geographic Information Science*, 1st ed. (CRC Press, 2004), 197–223, https://doi.org/10.1201/9781420038330-7.
29. Bell, et al., "Scientific Evidence from Space."
30. Aileen R. Buckley, Mark Gahegan & Keith Clarke, "Geographic Visualization," in Robert B. Mcmaster & E. Lynn Usery (eds), *A Research Agenda for Geographic Information Science*, 1st ed. (CRC Press, 2004), 313–33, https://doi. org/10.1201/9781420038330-11; Iryna Dronova, "Environmental Heterogeneity as a Bridge between Ecosystem Service and Visual Quality Objectives in Management, Planning and Design," *Landscape and Urban Planning* 163 (July 2017): 90–106, https://doi.org/10.1016/jlandurbplan.2017.03.005.
31. Bell, et al., "Scientific Evidence from Space."
32. Wellmann, et al., "Remote Sensing in Urban Planning."
33. Bell, et al., "Scientific Evidence from Space."
34. Palomino, Muellerklein & Kelly, "A Review of the Emergent Ecosystem of Collaborative Geospatial Tools for Addressing Environmental Challenges."
35. Ustin & Middleton, "Current and Near-Term Advances in Earth Observation for Ecological Applications"; Noel Gorelick, et al., "Google Earth Engine: Planetary-Scale Geospatial Analysis for Everyone," *Remote Sensing of Environment* 202

(December 2017): 18–27, https://doi.org/10.1016/j.rse.2017.06.031.
36. Kennedy, et al., "Remote Sensing Change Detection Tools for Natural Resource Managers."
37. Iryna Dronova, et al., "Spatio-Temporal Non-Uniformity of Urban Park Greenness and Thermal Characteristics in a Semi-Arid Region," *Urban Forestry & Urban Greening* 34 (August 2018): 44–54, https://doi.org/10.1016/j.ufug.2018.05.009.
38. Zhu, "Research Issues on Uncertainty in Geographic Data and GIS-Based Analysis."
39. Congalton & Green, *Assessing the Accuracy of Remotely Sensed Data: Principles and Practices*.
40. David M. Mark, et al., "Ontological Foundations for Geographic Information Science," in McMaster & Usery, *A Research Agenda for Geographic Information Science*, 335–50, https://doi.org/10.1201/9781420038330-12.
41. Owen Thian Seng Yeo, et al., "ABC of Green Infrastructure Analysis and Planning: The Basic Ideas and Methodological Guidance Based on Landscape Ecological Principle," *Urban Forestry & Urban Greening* 73 (July 2022): 127600, https://doi.org/10.1016/j.ufug.2022.127600.
42. Amir Reza Shahtahmassebi, et al., "Remote Sensing of Urban Green Spaces: A Review," *Urban Forestry & Urban Greening* 57 (January 2021): 126946, https://doi.org/10.1016/j.ufug.2020.126946.
43. Mark, et al., "Ontological Foundations for Geographic Information Science."
44. Zhu, "Research Issues on Uncertainty in Geographic Data and GIS-Based Analysis"; Ronald F. Abler, "The National Science Foundation National Center for Geographic Information and Analysis," *International Journal of Geographical Information Systems* 1, no. 4 (January 1987): 303–26, https://doi.org/10.1080/02693798708927819.
45. Nina Lam, et al., "Scale," in McMaster & Usery, *A Research Agenda for Geographic Information Science*, 93–128, https://doi.org/10.1201/9781420038330-4.
46. Gomes, Queiroz & Ferreira, "An Overview of Platforms for Big Earth Observation Data Management and Analysis"; Stefano Nativi, Paolo Mazzetti & Max Craglia, "Digital Ecosystems for Developing Digital Twins of the Earth: The Destination Earth Case," *Remote Sensing* 13, no. 11 (May 28, 2021): 2,119, https://doi.org/10.3390/rs13112119; Gordon S. Blair & Peter A. Henrys, "The Role of Data Science in Environmental Digital Twins: In Praise of the Arrows," *Environmetrics* 34, no. 2 (March 2023), https://doi.org/10.1002/env.2789.
47. Joanna Pluto-Kossakowska, et al., "Dashboard as a Platform for Community Engagement in a City Development—A Review of Techniques, Tools and Methods," *Sustainability* 14, no. 17 (August 30, 2022): 10,809, https://doi.org/10.3390/su141710809.
48. Palomino, Muellerklein & Kelly, "A Review of the Emergent Ecosystem of Collaborative Geospatial Tools for Addressing Environmental Challenges."
49. Harlan Onsrud, et al., "The Future of the Spatial Information Infrastructure," in McMaster & Usery, *A Research Agenda for Geographic Information Science*, 225–55, https://doi.org/10.1201/9781420038330-8.
50. Gomes, Queiroz & Ferreira, "An Overview of Platforms for Big Earth Observation Data Management and Analysis."

The Seeing Machine: Bending Drone Maps Down to Earth

Karl Kullmann

Plate from *Fabrica et usus instrumenti chorographici* (*The manufacture and use of chorographic equipment*) by Leonhard Zubler (c. 1607) demonstrating triangulation techniques in surveying. Zubler is credited with introducing the plane table, a foundational tool in modern land surveying.

I recall vividly the first time I saw a drone map. Early in the consumer drone revolution, I visited a Bay Area drone startup that had grown out of two hobbyists' garage experimentation with transplanting the inertial sensors from smartphones onto Meccano-like airframes. This innovation provided quadcopter formats with the airborne stability that was lacking in hobby radio-controlled helicopters and moved UAVs into the mainstream. In the pre-regulatory context of the time, the startup's engineers would routinely fly test missions from the fifth-floor rooftop, dispatching drones far and wide.

During my visit, a drone was deployed to test map the Albany Bulb, a decommissioned landfill of rubble, rebar, and self-seeded domestic garden plants that protrudes unnaturally into San Francisco Bay. With its erratic topography, entangled social trails, and recent history of clandestine inhabitation and artistic intervention, it is a place that had long fascinated me. It was also a site that steadfastly frustrated my efforts to survey or map it, with the Bulb's intricacies remaining concealed from satellite imagery, lidar models, and other readymade mapping media. With the assistance of my graduate students, we resorted to walking a series of transects and recording our three-dimensional traces with GPS in an (ultimately unsuccessful) mission to assemble an interlocking cardboard cutout skeleton of the Bulb's topography.

The drone's automated mapping route loosely mirrored our rudimentary transects, albeit from 120 m aloft, and using stereo optics in place of our handheld GPS to register the ups and downs of the Bulb's hummocky surface. Twenty minutes after dispatch, the drone reappeared on the rooftop with its digital payload of overlapping imagery, which was conveyed downstairs and crunched through a photogrammetric stitching process to create a high-fidelity aerial image and topographic mesh. I still recall my astonishment at seeing the high-definition orthophoto, which I likened to having my degenerative vision miraculously corrected – every leaf on every tree, every fist-sized chunk of rubble, contours that traced every nook and cranny, even picking up footprints in the sand. In that instant in my mind's eye, the deepest expression of the Bulb shifted from my explorative mental maps to the cartograph on the screen – that is, from the imagined to the medium.

In *The Vision Machine*, Paul Virilio examines how visual technologies such as cinema and photography shape how we see, and hence perceive—and ultimately imagine—the world.[1] Writing in the early 1990s, Virilio observed a new paradigm of "vision machines" "capable not only of recognizing the contours of shapes, but also of completely interpreting the visual field, of staging a complex environment close-up or at a distance."[2] Although Virilio was undoubtedly reacting to the then-military-only development of nap-of-the-earth avionics, his account also resonates with today's zeitgeist of autonomous navigation technologies. Prescient to our present-day reckoning with artificial intelligence, Virilio feared that vision machines would automate perception, creating a mechanized imaginary from which we are totally excluded. At the very least, these seeing machines would cleave a "splitting of viewpoint" whereby we ("the animate") share perception of the environment with the vision machine ("the inanimate").[3]

Vision machines that can recognize contours and interpret a visual field, close up and at a distance, that split the viewpoint between the viewer and the apparatus, similarly describe drones - also an artifact with military origins, albeit one that Virilio could never have foreseen. For now, drones augment rather than automate perception, although, as I experienced when first seeing the drone map of the Albany Bulb, drone imaging—like the vision machines that preceded it—is not an inert medium. Drone images are entwined with and, in some instances, usurp the stored images of our imaginations. Like the cinema and the camera, the drone shapes how we "see" the world and "foresee" our place in it.[4]

With a decade of hovering seeing machines to reflect on, there is now a substantial body of cross-disciplinary scholarship on the cultural impacts of the drone's weightless third-person bird's-eye viewpoint, which, in mimicking the gamer's perspective, blurs what distinctions remain between the virtual and the real (a distinction that preoccupied critical theory around the time of Virilio's *Vision Machine*). In this chapter, I focus on unpacking the consumer mapping aspect of drones, their agency, and their deficiencies as an environmental medium, specifically as it pertains to landscape architectural conceptual envisioning. Through my creative work, I advance an alternate mapping modality that blends the site-oriented scope of drones with the locality-oriented scope of chorography.[5]

Air-Truthing

The power of maps lies in their capacity to not only reflect and describe a territory but also shape it. If we comprehend the terrain as an encrypted dataset, maps both read the landscape and write it. Consider political lines drawn up from afar that, over time, calcify into the very real landscape. Or a planimetric map that omits topographic relief, clearing the way for landforms to be leveled to accommodate flatland-style development. For landscape architecture, the often-fraught relationship between territories and maps has an intermediary *plan* phase, the mandate of which is to bend maps to the designer's vision for the landscape. The landscape plan is a future-map, a measured guide for reimagining and remaking (a small piece of) the territory to a higher standard than if left up to the map's unfolding laissez-faire alternative. Like time-traveling map-whisperers, landscape architects portage seamlessly between maps and plans, leveraging the agency of the former through the instrumentality of the latter.

We can retrace this causal sequence back one phase to include the apparatuses that were used to create the maps in the first instance.

Without being deterministic, mapping instruments shape base maps, which in turn shape design outcomes. At one end of the technological spectrum, an on-site mud-map that is paced out and eyeballed is likely to produce an incremental assemblage of happenstance elements. At the other end, the surveyor's theodolite generates sparse geometric maps with pinpoint accuracy that clear the way for clean-slate designs. In both extremes, it is difficult to design for features that are omitted from the map or are recorded so abstractly that they remain formless. Somewhere in between, the *feature survey*—part theodolite, part fieldwork—served for most of the profession's modern history as the working standard for site base-mapping. Landscape architects were practiced at taking these skeletal surveys to the site to fill in the gaps, walking about holding pencils at arm's length: vertically to triangulate treetops and horizontally to deduce the lay of the land, emphasizing certain features and deemphasizing others.

Meanwhile, high overhead, incremental improvements in the coverage, fidelity, and accessibility of aerial and satellite imagery proved useful for cross-referencing the ground-truthing of incomplete basemaps. By the turn of the millennium, the saturation of online aerial and satellite imagery disseminated for the first time a coherent overview of landscape patterns, processes, interconnectedness, and materiality. A paradigm shift followed, whereby the use of satellite and aerial imagery to assist with the ground-truthing of site basemaps was supplanted by their use for *air-truthing* the wider landscape. This was transformative for the field, facilitating the interpretation of cities as organic systems and the wider landscape as a denatured machine. Characterizing urban processes in ecological, rather than built-formal, terms supported the emergence of the concept of landscape urbanism (or *satellite urbanism*) within the environmental design fields.[6] Beginning in the late 1990s through to the first decade of the 2000s, a cadre of creative cartography evolved around this burgeoning dataset and discourse, incorporating multimodal collages of satellite imagery, drafted linework, and other sampled images.

Notwithstanding these innovations, as a site mapping medium, aerial and satellite imagery is imperfect. The satellite's seductive gaze naturalizes the cultural landscape and smooths over differences. From the scenic overlook of low Earth orbit, the vacant lots of declining neighborhoods appear pastoral, and toxic plumes seem almost painterly. On this flattened-out canvas, the nuances and details that more closely approximate the three-dimensionality of grounded landscape experience remain concealed in the shadowed and interstitial spaces. A flat canvas enables plan-biased landscape design, which in turn perpetuates the recurrent critique of landscape architecture as a predominantly horizontal, two-dimensional discipline that eschews verticality.[7] Flatness is further magnified on the screen, where the easy convenience of online satellite imagery and mapping serves to insulate landscape architects from the discipline's traditions in on-site fieldwork.

In principle, drone imagery and mapping address some of the deficiencies of satellite mapping. The drone's capacity to hover and rapidly maneuver on all three axes enables exploration of the landscape as an unflattened, thickened, three-dimensional volumetric space.[8] As an environmental medium, the novel nearness of drone imagery reveals the landscape at a fidelity comparable to how we perceive it

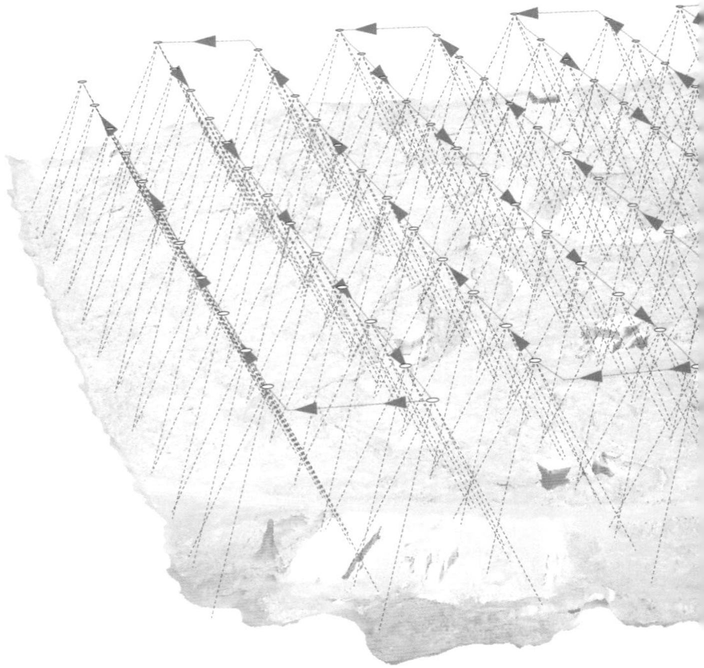

Diagram illustrating the drone pathing process for generating georeferenced images necessary for the stitching process in photogrammetry software.

from the ground. This familiar near-ground proximity ought to be less prone to the aestheticization and misinterpretation of the landscape that often plagues more distanced imagery.

As an instrument, the drone promises a digitally escorted return to the field that renews the discipline's foundational traditions of in-person, on-site fieldwork.[9] That landscape architects now have the capacity to travel back up the mapping chain to self-map a complex site in the moment in hyper-detail—untethered from the predetermined timeframes and parameters of satellite mapping data—should be groundbreaking. Just as ubiquitous satellite imagery sparked a reimagining of the upper limits of landscape architecture and urbanism's creative scales of operation, drone mapping potentially stretches those creative parameters downward, closer to the ground. This might manifest as more intricate and nuanced site-specific design that prioritizes amplifying existing site features and reinvigorating building craft. This focal shift is especially pertinent for design interventions on complex post-industrial wastelands and other similarly marginalized sites, such as the Albany Bulb.

In practice, the transformative promise of drone mapping is proving more complicated. Inconvenience is clearly a factor: drone site-mapping missions require far more effort and foresight than harvesting online satellite data (however inexact and outdated the latter may be). The tightening regulatory environment weighs on this convenience

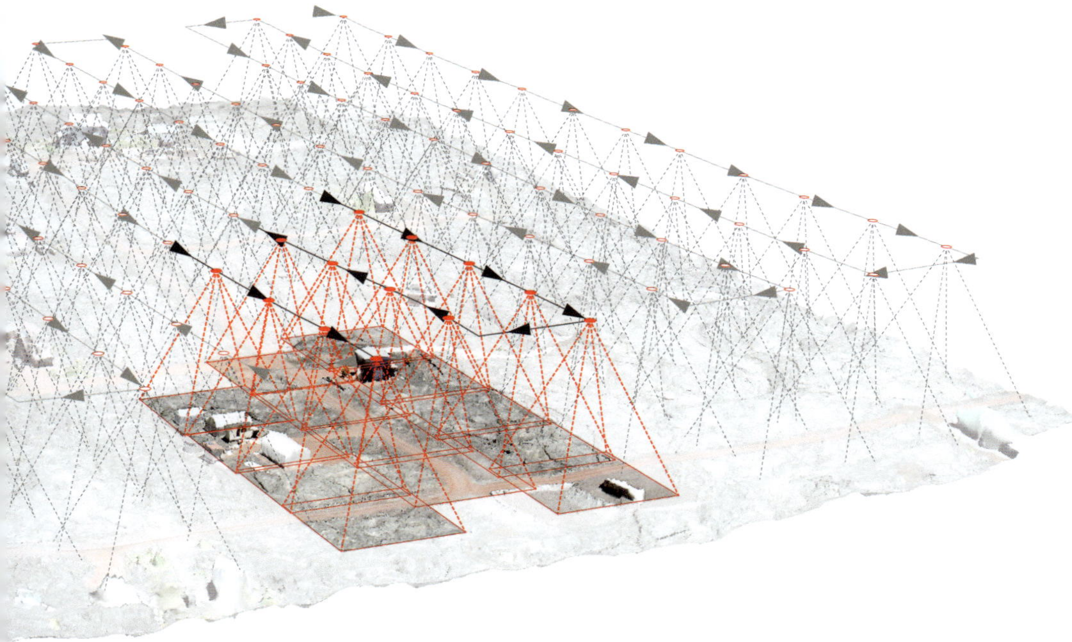

calculation, with aviation agencies and local ordinances now heavily restricting or, in many instances, prohibiting impromptu drone flight. This is with good reason, since drones not only *survey* but also *surveil*, fueling societal suspicion around a device that appears to cross the line in our social contracts, just as the Google Glass beta testers learned a decade ago in the streets and bars of San Francisco. Despite drones still being deployed sporadically, rather than systematically, it seems that we prefer our surveillers (which translates from the French as *overwatchers*) to remain up and out of sight, in orbit and in the cloud, where we can apply cognitive dissonance to the mass upload of personal data.[10]

Viewed from the other side of the UAV's disembodied eye, our unease at being drone-surveilled is reflected in the uncanniness of the drone survey itself. By this, I posit that site mapping traces the contours of the uncanny valley, a phenomenon first perceived in robotics and animation. As representations of familiar lifeforms become more lifelike, they become more engaging – but only until an abrupt inflection point, where they appear real yet not real and elicit a sense of unease. While the uncanny valley carries over directly to landscape design representation (to include, for example, perspective renders populated with 3D humanoids) with some adaptation, it also applies to landscape architectural mapping. Site mapping, including site models and imagery, becomes more conducive as it becomes more lifelike, which is to say higher fidelity. But only up to an inflection point, where, as it approaches J. L. Borges' fabled 1:1 map of the territory, it ceases to be conducive to design, becoming less an instrument of abstraction than a virtual world unto itself.[11]

In this scenario, the uncanniness of high-fidelity drone mapping and imaging materializes through beholding the familiar from an unfamiliar near altitude. This disembodied position differentiates the uncanniness of high-fidelity mapping from high-fidelity ground-based images, which explains why we have no issue consuming ultra-high-definition eye-level images. A base map that is almost real engenders *stickiness*: not in the sense of data refresh lag, but in terms of the map user being mesmerized by the minutiae to the point of inaction. Just as an abstract survey plan devoid of site specificity clears the way for a heavy-handed *tabula rasa* design, a hyper-real site model clutters the designer's mind's eye with particulars such that they tread on virtual eggshells, unable to intervene in the status quo. At worst, this variation of analysis paralysis encourages trivialization of the rich texture of a site into superficial pattern making.

The mapping medium abrades against the parameters of the craft, in the sense that its precision surpasses the fidelity at which landscape architects can conceptualize form and construct landscapes. With regard to the latter, ideally, the constraints of construction standardization will expand as part of a technologically driven return to craft, which has been building in other design fields for some time (with laser scanning and rapid prototyping). With regard to conceptualizing form, there is also potential for reimagining the form, or shape, of the mapping medium itself.

Unsticking Maps

The satellite urbanists' creative cartographies collaged fragments of maps, photographs, and diagrams to bridge the scale divide and to ground and unflatten their representations of landscape patterns and systems. To collage is to glue (from the French *collér*) and, given the orders of magnitude between low Earth orbit and the ground, these multimodal assemblages pasted scales and projections together. The art of collage consistently resurfaces at junctures of technological disruption within the arts, where it is deployed as a provisional, or transitional, medium that renders the disruption vivid even as it makes inroads into patching it back together.[12] The revival of collage in landscape architectural mapping and representation arguably follows this pattern, whereby the novelty of the imaging satellite (and, before that, the photocopier) disrupted, realigned, and, ultimately, rejuvenated creative practice.[13]

Given that drone mapping can be read as the latest installment in this lineage of technological imaging disruption, I am interested in developing alternative modes of creative expression that unstick the three-dimensionality of the drone's volumetric space. My intention is not to dismiss collage, which is particularly useful where there are gaps or overlaps in knowledge, whether that be site information, conceptual clarity, or multiple stakeholder viewpoints. However, as an environmental medium, collage is incomplete and two dimensional by its very structure. Moreover, with the advantage of nearness, drone maps do not need to span the orders of magnitude that drew the satellite urbanists to collage in the first place. Drone maps can be bent and stretched down to meet the ground, where the fidelity is usable, thereby bypassing the need to cut and paste.

The concept of deforming maps to convey the drone's volumetric space invokes the anachronistic mapping technique of *chorography*, which, like collage, also has a history of periodic revival. Re-popularized in the 15th century with the Latin translation of Claudius Ptolemy's *Geographia*, chorography was a style of oblique mapping that conveyed the unique personality of a locality. As the most grounded mode in Ptolemy's classical ternary mapping order, chorography sat below the Euclidean projections of *geography* and the grand structure of *cosmography*. From the Greek root *chôra* (a portion of ground, a place), the scope of chorography was the local region, where it registered features at the near scale in which human life takes place. Unlike the ichnographic (plan) Cartesian projections that typify modern maps, chorography did not purport to depict all features equally, with map space scaled and stretched according to a complex system of triangulations. And whereas quantitative geographical methods aim to eliminate the vagaries of interpretation, chorography admitted the creative contribution of the individual surveyor, who was often depicted in the foreground of the representation in the third person.[14]

With expanding horizons and worldviews, endlessly extendable and scalable Cartesian projections eventually usurped the bespoke world of the chorographic map. Stripped of geospatial agency, chorography drifted into the scenic citywide panoramas that were popular in the 19th century and endure today as tourist maps and real estate bird's-eye views.[15] Chorographic artifacts also persist in landscape architecture. Given the discipline's lasting connections to historic modes of practice, to city visioning, to overviews, and to creating pictorially immersive descriptions of the site, landscape architectural delineation aspires to the chorographic. Even landscape illustrative plans, which are ostensibly cartographic in structure, infuse the chorographic characteristics of three-dimensionality and materiality of the site through shading, shadowing, and selective emphasis.

Drone mapping potentially extends and reinvigorates this chorographic-landscape architectural lineage. Like chorography, drone mapping focuses on a portion of ground, or site, that correlates in scale to human activity. And like chorography, drone mapping places the mapper's feet on or near the site. However, unlike chorography, drone maps are typically construed ichnographically (in plan) or beheld perspectivally or in the round, like a sculpture. If we reapply Ptolemy's classical hierarchy, drone maps typically default to the measured norms of (Euclidean) geography, which is well established as the purview of satellite imagery.

Drawing on the intertwined lineage of maps and plans and of landscape and chorography, my creative work explores reshaping drone maps as a form of chorographic re-revival. The three illustrated maps depict sites that share commonalities with the Albany Bulb, in that they involve complex topography formed by some sort of erratic deposition process (landfill, landslip, and lava flow). Like the Albany Bulb, they also propagate hand-made site-specific cultural activities (homemaking, garden making, exploration, and artistic intervention) that work with the geomorphic structure of the site, as opposed to overwriting it with machines. This sense of equilibrium between geomorphological process and cultural activity resonates with chorography, which, at its historical zenith, depicted preindustrial land use patterns. I captured the drone photogrammetry for the three

Map One: Chorographic drone map of the Lava Garden, Heimaey, Iceland.

maps in-person on-site, and, true to chorographic tradition, my standing silhouette can just be made out in the upper left quadrant of the first map.

Map One charts a garden nestled into a comparatively recent lava flow on Heimaey (Home Island), off Iceland's southern coast. In 1973, lava flows from a sudden volcanic eruption threatened to block the island's only safe harbor. Months of industrious lava cooling operations redirected the flows, ultimately saving the harbor and expanding the island by 20%. When the eruption subsided, returning residents were invited to adopt a patch of the new lava field. Over the next two decades, a local couple cultivated a lava garden, which they laid out in the tradition of the *hortus conclusus*, with the nave axis aligned to the natural shape of the dell and the landform and additional windbreaks combining to form a loose enclosure. Over 100 species of plants were cultivated, and, over time, a fishpond, several follies, a gnome, a gabled wooden shed, picket fencing, and garden paths were integrated. Outside the enclosure, the garden abruptly yields to the broken basalt of the lava field.

Map Two charts Sunken City, the colloquially descriptive name given to what remains of a clifftop bungalow community in San Pedro, California, that was abandoned in 1929 due to a slow landslip. Beginning as hairline cracks in pavements and walls, and broken utilities, the slip progressed at a rate of about 30 cm per day, eventually opening a crack half a block long by four meters wide and displacing two hectares of destabilized layers of clay and ash

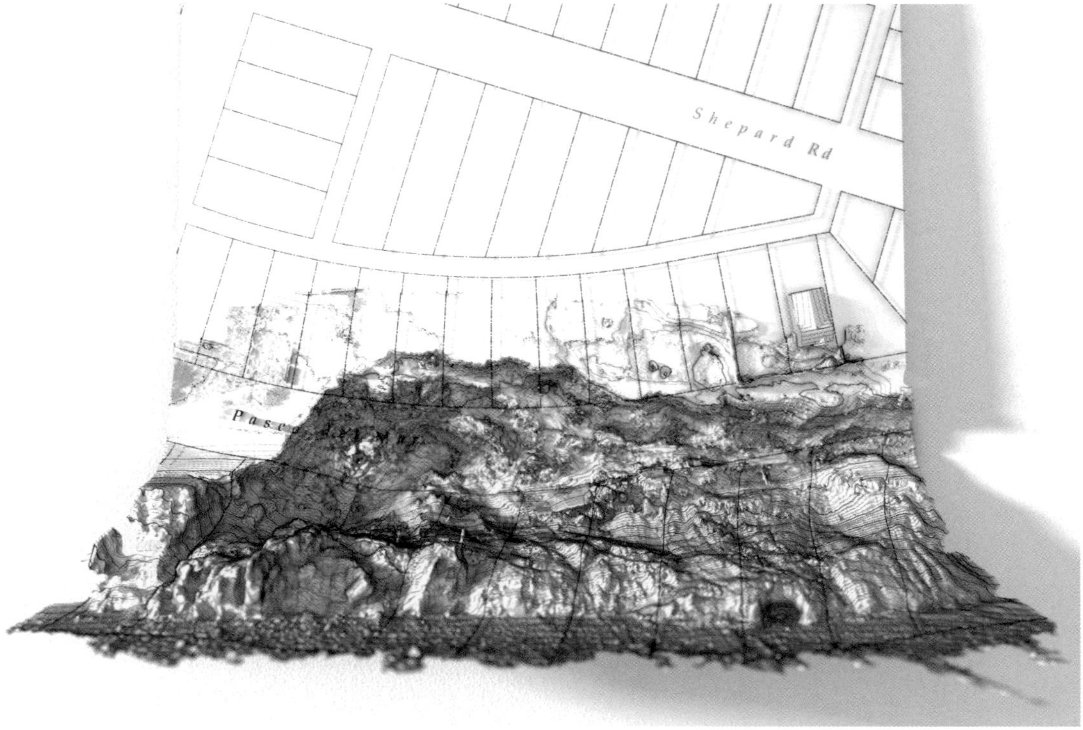

Map Two: Chorographic drone map of Sunken City, San Pedro, California.

land into the Pacific Ocean. Fragments of tram tracks, concrete slabs from roads and sidewalks, street and backyard trees, and other cultural artifacts were conveyed down with the landslip into happenstance positions on the deeply hummocked landform. Although officially sealed off, the site is heavily patinaed with graffiti and has some provenance as a Hollywood film location. More recently, fueled by the popularity on social media of desolated ruins, wastelands, and other geographical curiosities, Sunken City has become a stage set for Instagrammers who, under threat of citation, slip in through the chain link fence and risk life and limb for the most dramatic angles.

Map Three charts a resilient lava community situated on the flanks of Mount Kilauea in the heart of Hawai'i's volcanically active East Rift Zone. Originally platted as an idyllic suburb amid the runaway land speculation of the 1960s, Kalapana Gardens lasted just three decades before the largest eruption in half a millennium buried it under 15 meters of solid rock. When the lava cooled, the property parcels were extrapolated up onto the new ground level, and homesteading began. With the lava continuing to crack and settle and the threat of new lava flows always present, the eclectic mix of structures floats like life rafts. In the chorographic map, the shape and setting of the homesteads are evident, as are the access tracks that negotiate the new terrain within the confines of the old road easements. Without fences or other familiar points of reference, the distribution of dwellings and tracks appear happenstance. However, the overlaid lot lines reveal the hidden survey logic that underpins the layout.

Map Three: Chorographic drone map of Kalapana, Big Island, Hawai'i.

Across the three maps, varying degrees and shapes of curvature facilitate seamless transitions from section to perspective, to bird's eye, to plan. In transitioning from the verticality of the section to the horizontality of the plan, the maps pass through oblique angles that are the domain of chorography. As Brighenti and Pavoni observe in their interpretation of Virilio's mention of Ptolemy's ternary mapping order, the oblique angle of chorography forged a link, now lost, between the verticality of cosmography and the horizontality of geography.[16] Embodying aspects of all three mapping orders, the curved maps recall this link. Moreover, as was evident in the stretched space of Renaissance chorographic maps, the spatial variability that the curvatures create is suggestive of the elasticity that is integral to individual cognitive mapping and imaging.[17]

Depth of Field

In *The Open Sky*, Virilio identifies the diminishment of the geophysical environment's "depth of field" through the time-space compression wrought by accelerated communication and transportation technologies. For Virilio, the evaporating "optical density of the landscape" degrades our relationship with our environment and produces "confusion between the apparent horizon, which is the backdrop of all action, and the deep horizon of our collective imagination."[18] With its foundational emphasis on activating spaces and making places, landscape architecture inherently negotiates the space between Virilio's two horizons: between the shallow apparent horizon of specific actions and the deeper horizon of a shared sense of place.

As an environmental medium, drone-chorography holds potential for interceding into this space to augment landscape architecture's capacity for reframing horizons. Multiple technologies and techniques that underpin drone-chorography predispose the medium to this horizon-shaping role. First, there is the drone itself, which, as an aerial vision machine, helps us *see*—in the direct sense of providing an overview with which to situate ourselves in the landscape—and *foresee*, whereby the drone acts as a reconnaissance device that allows us to look beyond the field of view. Second, chorography's thematic connection with the bird's-eye view elevates foresight to an artform, whereby the oblique bird's-eye expands the field of view beyond the horizon to encapsulate and anticipate imagined futures.[19] And third, drone-chorography integrates characteristics of the landscape architectural illustrative plan, which traditionally fuses the existing with the proposed and casts sunlight and shadow across the page to convey time and depth.

Looking at a curved chorographic map, our eye is not drawn away to the horizon (as formed by the curvature of the Earth) or to the map frame (as dictated by the map grid or survey limits), each of which portends another time and place. In its place, the curvature folds us back into the map and draws us deeper into the site. Once on the ground, the drone-escorted return to the field (in the dual sense of a landscape site and the landscape architectural discipline) has a twist. We arrive on site, drone in hand, only to discover that the field—in the geometric sense of a two-dimensional flatland—is nowhere to be found. In its place is a volume: a field of depth, deep, thick, and rich.

Notes

1. Paul Virilio, *The Vision Machine* (Indiana University Press, 1994).
2. Ibid., 59.
3. Ibid., 59.
4. Ibid., 61.
5. This chapter builds on ideas developed in Karl Kullmann, "The Drone's Eye: Applications and Implications for Landscape Architecture," *Landscape Research* 43, no. 7 (2017): 906–21; Karl Kullmann, "The Mirage of the Metropolis: City Imaging in the Age of Digital Chorography," *Journal of Urban Design* 23, no. 1 (2017): 123–41.
6. Landscape urbanism refers to an influential environmental design and planning movement that emerged at the intersection of architecture and landscape architecture in the early 2000s. In contrast to the traditional practice of urban design, which was principally concerned with the 'bricks-and-mortar' city of housing, streets, typology, and legibility, landscape urbanism integrated ecological systems and infrastructures into the urban framework. See Karl Kullmann, "Design With (Human) Nature: Recovering the Creative Instrumentality of Social Data in Urban Design," *Journal of Urban Design* 24, no. 2 (2018): 165–82.
7. Adapted from Weizman's characterization of geopolitics as "a flat discourse" that "largely ignores the vertical dimension." Eyal Weizman, "The Politics of Verticality," *Open Democracy* (April 23, 2002), https://www.opendemocracy.net/en/article_801jsp (accessed November 18, 2023).
8. Volumetric space is a concept initially developed in political geography in response to the verticality of modern geopolitics and warfare and adapted to the sociological context of visual studies. See Stuart Elden, "Secure the Volume: Vertical Geopolitics and the Depth of Power," *Political Geography* 34 (2013): 35–51.
9. Future developments in long-range drone dispatching may dilute the practice of the operator's having feet physically planted on the site. For now, a sweet spot exists between the technique and the technology. See Karl Kullmann, "High Fidelity: Drone Mapping Fills a Missing Link in Site Representation," *Landscape Architecture Magazine* 107, no. 5 (2017): 132–39; Karen M'Closkey & Keith VanDerSys, "Behind-the-Scenes: Multispectral Imagery and Land Cover Classification," *Journal of Landscape Architecture* 17, no. 1 (2022): 22–37.
10. Pauschinger and Klauser observe that civilian drones do not actually appear to be "producing a systematic and routine surveillance gaze. Rather, civil drones...are most often employed sporadically, and, as such, indicate an activity that is not routinised." Dennis Pauschinger & Francisco R. Klauser, "Aerial Politics of Visibility: Actors, Spaces, and Drivers of Professional Drone Usage in Switzerland," *Surveillance & Society* 18, no. 4 (2020): 443–66.
11. Jorge Luis Borges, "Of Exactitude in Science," in Borges, *A Universal History of Infamy* (Penguin Books, 1954).
12. See Walter Benjamin, "The Work of Art in the Age of Mechanical Reproduction," in Benjamin, *Illuminations* (Jonathan Cape, 1970), 219–53.
13. See Karl Kullmann, "The Satellite's Progeny: Digital Chorography in the Age of Drone Vision," *Forty-Five: Journal of Outside Research* 157 (2017), http://forty-five.com/papers/157 (accessed November 18, 2023).
14. See Denis Cosgrove, *Geography and Vision: Seeing, Imagining and Representing the World* (I. B. Taurus, 2008); Edward S. Casey, "Mapping the Earth in Works of Art," in Bruce V. Foltz & Robert Frodeman (eds), *Rethinking Nature: Essays in Environmental Philosophy* (Indiana University Press, 2004), 260–70.
15. See Yve-Alain Bois, "Metamorphosis of Axonometry," *Daidalos* 1 (1981): 41–58; Lucia Nuti, "Mapping Places: Chorography and Vision in the Renaissance," in Denis Cosgrove (ed.), *Mappings* (Reaktion Books, 1999): 90–108.
16. Andrea Mubi Brighenti & Andrea Pavoni, "Vertical Vision and Atmocultural Navigation. Notes on Emerging Urban Scopic Regimes," *Visual Studies* 35, no. 5 (2020): 429–41; Jean-Marc Offner, Agnès Sander & Paul Virilio, "For a Geography of Trajectories. An Interview with Paul Virilio," *Flux* 5 (1991): 48–54.
17. See Reginald G. Golledge, "Human Wayfinding and Cognitive Maps," in Golledge (ed.), *Wayfinding Behavior: Cognitive Mapping and Other Spatial Processes* (The Johns Hopkins University Press, 1999), 5–45.
18. Paul Virilio, *Open Sky* (Verso, 1997), 22.
19. In the sense that we imagine the future as arriving from over the horizon, the bird's eye is inherently anticipatory, hence its recurrent popularity in futurist visions. See Kullmann, "The Mirage of the Metropolis."

The Patch and the Palimpsest

Heather Houser

In 1983 architecture historian André Corboz penned a germinal statement on land as story. "There is no land without imagining a land. A land can be expressed in statistical terms…, but it cannot be reduced to the quantitative. As a project the land is semanticized. It can be parsed."[1] Environmental and spatial disciplines must approach lands (and waters) as sedimented narratives inviting interpretation. In the 1980s, cartographic representation also fell under the sign of interpretation. Relationality, speculation, subjectivity, possibility, and imagination started to supplant positivist values like objectivity and universality in mapping as critical cartographers joined Corboz in treating environmental media—in both senses this collection advances—as products and expressions of narratives.[2] Critical cartographers have read stories of colonialist expansion, capitalist acquisition, extractivist ambition, and xenophobic and racist erasure in the tradition they remake. They have probed data sources such as projection and satellite imagery and design techniques such as color and borders and been overt and self-reflexive about their own choices. As cartographer Margaret Pearce (Citizen Band Potawatomi) reflects, "Approaching cartographic language as narrative… allows us to structure the map deliberately to express the particular shape of the narrative we seek to map by combining the language of graphic variables and their grammar with narrative technique."[3] Atlases especially afford intentional narrativization given their status as collections of maps.[4] Denis Wood, cartographic rebel with a cause, expressed this directly and delightfully in "Pleasure in the Idea / The Atlas as Narrative Form" (1987). The internal composition of maps as well as their "juxtaposition and sequencing" in an atlas "make something greater than any single map can be"; atlases "create a discourse, a mediation."[5] Wood urges cartographers to plumb the storytelling potential of the atlas and formally experiment with relations to space.

Map depicting the location of the Gwynns Falls watershed in the Chesapeake Bay. A sample patch is shown in detail (right).

Forty years have passed since this embrace of narrative and critique of mapping's positivist claims, and yet the persistent need to defend story suggests the case is not so settled. Well into the 21st century, those who design space and its representations advocate for attention to how mapping practices are "embedded in *specific relations of power*" and to "*what* we choose to represent, *how* we choose to represent objects..., and *what* decisions are made with those representations."[6] I focus here on these *hows* and *whats* as they pertain to atlases emerging from the fields of planning and landscape architecture and investigate how specific design techniques put pressure on what I call the usable form of environmental media. *Mississippi Floods: Designing a Shifting Landscape* (2001), by Anuradha Mathur and Dilip da Cunha, and *Patch Atlas: Integrating Design Practices and Ecological Knowledge for Cities as Complex Systems* (2019), by Victoria Marshall, Mary Cadenasso, Brian McGrath, and Steward Pickett, mediate data about landscapes—types of urban land cover in the latter and the engineered course, flow, and infrastructure of the Mississippi River in the former—to depict interdependent social and ecological forces and to capture the mutability of earth matter. Neither atlas eschews quantification, but they have varying levels of commitment to it and employ differing techniques for mediating information toward the ends of speculation and imagination. Marshall et al. use the patch of their title to disorient readers through emptiness and abundance, while Mathur and da Cunha use the palimpsest so that time, media, and data haunt each other, thereby calling out mediation and activating a historical sense. The patch leads to defamiliarization and abstraction, and the palimpsest privileges inscrutability within the excavation of memory. These formal techniques open tensions surrounding utility that persist despite the increased epistemic value of story and pleasure in environmental media-making. I argue for reading these atlases as forms about use rather than usable forms so that the epistemological possibilities of environmental media are accorded the value that practical application has received in urban design and planning.

Patchy Realism

Atlases have mediated environments for centuries and are basically defined, after Mercator's original usage, as "a collection of maps in a volume."[7] As poet-critic Susan Stewart teaches us, though, collections are never straightforward, and atlas scholars add depth to this definition.[8] Notably, geographer Aileen Buckley characterizes the medium negatively—it "is *not* a collection of *data sets*"—and elaborates that

> an atlas is a communication device that speaks primarily through maps...with a related theme...or a set of themes that relate to some selected region...[They] are like a novel. They can lead you through the story from beginning to end, they can engage you and you can become familiar with the characters (e.g., themes or locations or regions), and they can have a plot (such as historical development of a region).[9]

Buckley chimes with Wood: just as one chapter is not synecdochic for a novel, one map does not an atlas make. Atlases remain a crucial genre for information management in the 21st century precisely because they accommodate data, text, imagery, cartographic design, and creative compilation. Digital atlases have proliferated since the 1990s and are especially crucial in efforts to redress racial injustices and give epistemological priority to Indigenous, Black, and dispossessed populations.[10] However, the digital has not displaced the book, and paper atlases, especially those mediating environment and climate change, are trending.[11] If lands, waters, and other environmental matter harbor stories, that narrative is a rapidly shifting one. These transformations invite media forms that, while fixed on the page, can capture change, livingness, fluidity, and emergence as well as the quantitative and qualitative data of place.

Patch Atlas and *Mississippi Floods* embrace the book atlas for these reasons but exhibit different techniques I elaborate here. Prima facie, *Patch Atlas* seems to be that collection of data Buckley rejects, specifically the data of land cover in the Gwynns Falls watershed in Baltimore County. However, to offer a "new description of an urban region," the team of urban ecologists and designers gather that data in geographically grounded if abstract visualizations "to inspire maps that have yet to be drawn."[12] Along with this future orientation, the book has conceptual and methodological ambitions. The team creates a new urban classification system called High Ecological Resolution Classification for Urban Landscapes and Environmental Systems (HERCULES) that uses patches to differentiate and locate "the mixture and relative abundance of five elements: buildings, woody vegetation, herbaceous vegetation, paved surfaces, and bare soil."[13] (Though their focus is a watershed, water is not an element.) HERCULES aims to capture the heterogeneity of an urban ecosystem, not only what it contains but also how the components combine and can evolve. Patch is a concept from landscape ecology that designates "an area of habitat differing from its surroundings, often the smallest ecologically distinct landscape feature in a landscape mapping and classification system."[14] Marshall et al. parse land *cover* using patches as an alternative to land *use* classifications. Even though HERCULES codes vegetation and buildings separately, the authors argue their system represents the ratios and interdependence of land use combinations and thereby emphasizes the ecological impacts of the built environment.

HERCULES patches are based on false-color infrared aerial imagery of sub-meter resolution that was captured along the watershed on one day in October 1999. The atlas includes a "periodic table" of land cover elements. Small, variously colored rectangles—"swatches"—show the abundance of the five land cover types in a patch of land via the weight of each band of color corresponding to that cover. Swatches appear on the table in order of relative abundance—more than 75%, 50–75%, 35–50%, 10–35%, less than 10% of a type—so that, read vertically, the table moves from near homogeneity to degrees of heterogeneity. Thus, a swatch that is predominantly sage green has mostly bare soil; if other elements are present, they appear as narrow bands in the swatch. A swatch will be more varicolored when more cover types are present. These swatches also appear in a graph with colored bars whose height indicates the number of those patches in the watershed. Unlike a traditional atlas, however, "the journey is not directed by a map," meaning that the chapters proceed not geographically but "suite by suite from the relatively homogeneous [cover type]...down to the last suite of maximum heterogeneity" in the table.[15] That said, an abstract map rounds out the visualization toolkit and appears in each chapter.

Though the team downloaded satellite data for one day, *Patch Atlas* aspires to be a tool for historical interpretation and future-oriented design; the snapshot gives access to the bigger picture. But this

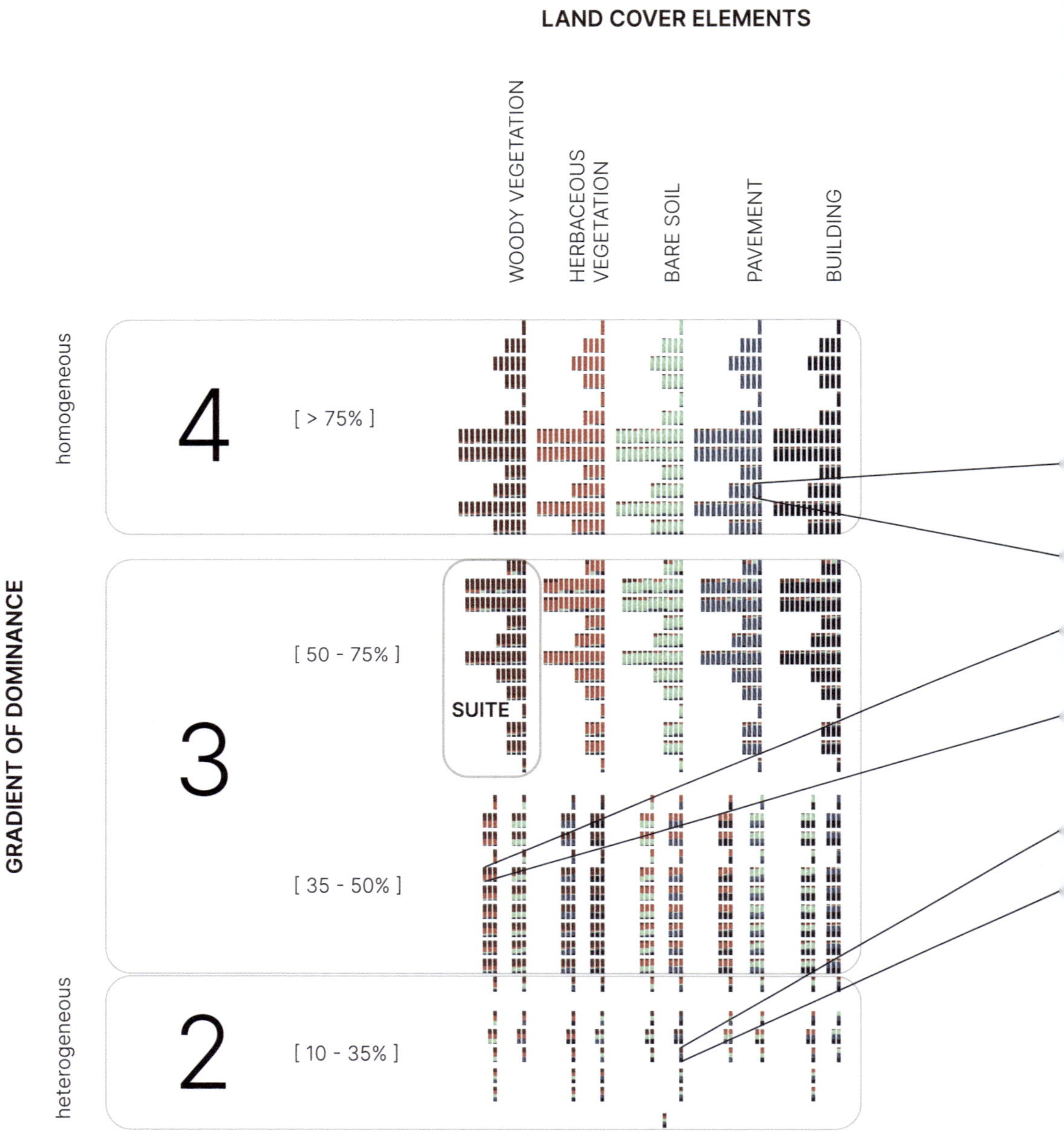

Suites of elements are arranged vertically in a gradient (above), and horizontally in a list (opposite). The enlarged diagram shows a sample of individual swatches. Each swatch defines a specific patch type identified with five numbers. Numbers in each swatch are read vertically and refer to the table numbers. A high number (e.g., 4 equals > 75%) represents a more homogeneous land cover type, while a lower number (e.g., 2 equals 10–35%) represents a mixed cover type, in decreasing degrees.

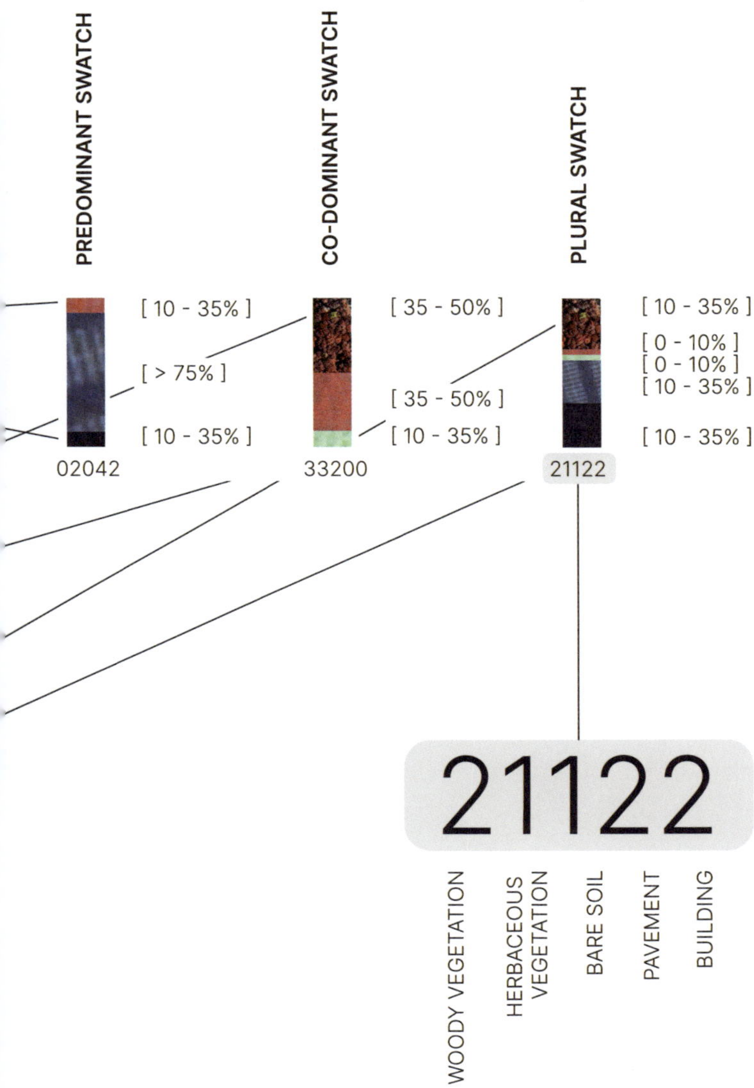
PREDOMINANT SWATCH
[10 - 35%]
[> 75%]
[10 - 35%]
02042
CO-DOMINANT SWATCH
[35 - 50%]
[35 - 50%]
[10 - 35%]
33200
PLURAL SWATCH
[10 - 35%]
[0 - 10%]
[0 - 10%]
[10 - 35%]
[10 - 35%]
21122
21122
WOODY VEGETATION
HERBACEOUS VEGETATION
BARE SOIL
PAVEMENT
BUILDING

requires interpretation, a practice Marshall et al. provoke by "slow[ing] the reader down" through "purposeful disorientation."[16] More specifically, they defamiliarize the methods of both urban design and mapmaking.[17] The authors contend that the visualization elements—swatch, graph, map—create "a pattern of abundance," but the patch and its associated visualizations also pattern emptiness.[18] White space fills the map pages, interrupted sporadically by scab-like shapes whose colors indicate the presence of the swatch types under examination. Empty rectangles are as plentiful as colored ones in the overview graphs for each chapter. Patch-making thus occurs through the classification system as well as through the images; method and visualization are therefore symmetrical. However, the relation between the visualization technique and the abundance of a cover type is asymmetrical. That is, a chapter depicting homogeneous cover (over 75% of a type) features maps with sparse coverage. Emptiness dominates the page, increasingly so as the reader flips between woody vegetation, herbaceous vegetation, bare soil, pavement, and buildings. The atlas disorients and slows readers down not only because we must learn to interpret the visualizations of HERCULES and adjust to a non-geographic chapter sequence. It also disorients by decoupling abundance and emptiness. In other words, the graphesis, Johanna Drucker's term for the study of "the meaning-producing argument structures of graphical forms," yields disorientation.[19] There is a disconnect between the data referencing environmental media in the sense of soil, trees, pavement, etc., and the formal techniques visualizing that data.

The authors correlate defamiliarization to epistemological effects that impact design and planning in the watershed. The city becomes "a patchwork that can be conceptually disassembled and reassembled in various mental ways."[20] Patchiness and defamiliarization contribute to their goal to generate complexity that elicits wonder, goads questions, and spurs investigations that are historical and speculative. How did this mix come to be? Through what processes of development, racial segregation, political influence, resident advocacy, and ecological change? What other mixes are possible and desirable and for which populations, human and more-than-human? Crucially, the atlas does not and cannot answer these questions. It instead helps users "'see' anew."

Marshall underscores this goal at the February 2022 "Instruments of Change" symposium.[21] She loosely places *Patch Atlas* in a tradition of scientific atlases that historians of science Lorraine Daston and Peter Galison describe in *Objectivity*. These atlases "train the eye to pick out certain kinds of objects as exemplary...and to regard them in a certain way...Everyone in the field addressed by the atlas must begin to learn to 'see' anew."[22] Marshall stops her engagement with *Objectivity* here, but reading deeper reveals other ways *Patch Atlas* complicates claims to objectivity. In addition to Daston and Galison's overarching argument that objectivity *has* a history and evolves to prioritize certain "epistemic virtues," one of the book's main insights is that "it is not always possible to serve truth and objectivity at the same time."[23] Marshall et al. embrace this conflict, and the patch technique exemplifies it. The patch circumscribes a domain of objectivity in that the aerial data satisfy requirements for this scientific value: "emotional detachment...automatic procedures for registering data...recourse to quantification...belief in a bedrock reality."[24] A patch also results from consistent quantitative methods of classifying, coloring, and delineating.[25] Yet the visualizations also result from "trained

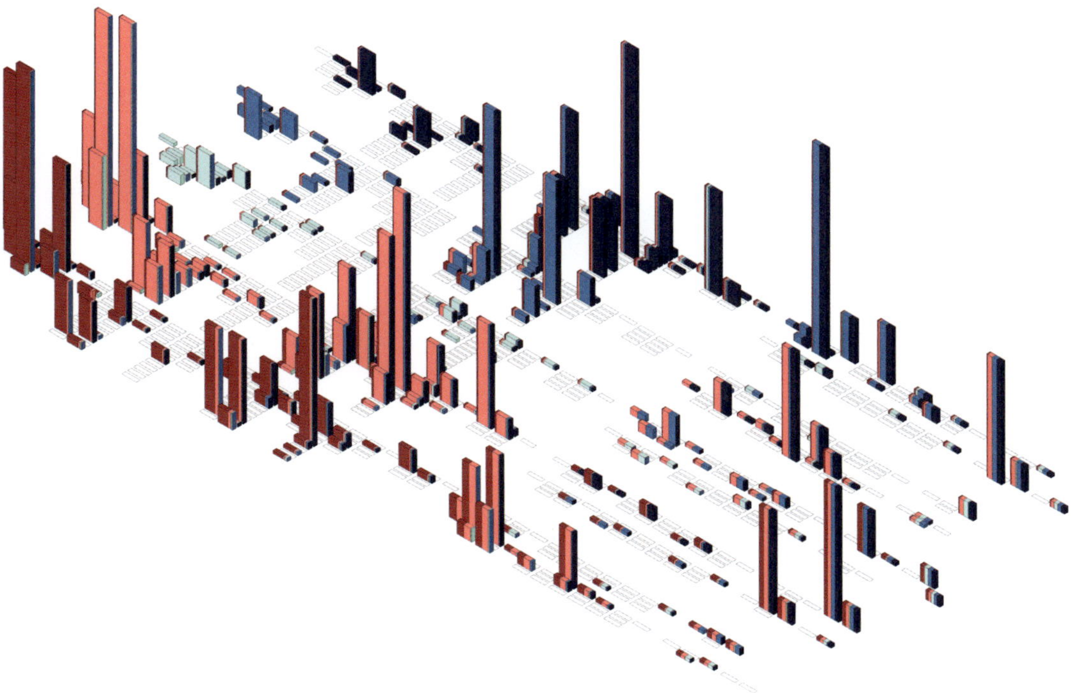

Three-dimensional graph or "signature" of the Gwynns Falls watershed patch array. As the number of patches in the watershed increases, each patch swatch increases in height.

judgment," a practice Daston and Galison locate in the evolution of objectivity. That is, the creators use "judgment to organize experience into patterns in the very act of perception"; or, in Marshall et al.'s words, they "capitalized on the exceptional skill of the human eye to recognize pattern" and colored the swatches accordingly.[26] Judgment serves truths that so-called objective data cannot, in this case the layered conditions of the Gwynns Falls watershed that are activated when designing for its future.

In the terms of historian and cartographer William Rankin, *Patch Atlas* shows a preference for realism over accuracy. He makes this distinction when sketching a transition to algorithmic mapping between the 1960s and 1990s. Rankin's study of geological and climate mapping in this period echoes the shifts that *Objectivity* tracks in scientific disciplines of other periods. Rankin demonstrates that trained eyes lost epistemic prominence and gave way to the presumed accuracy of the "fundamentally quantitative."[27] He inquires, "What is the proper role of human judgement—should mapping be 'objective,' and what is the place for an expert's subjectivity? ...Should the resulting map show something *realistic* or something *accurate*?"[28] The periodic table in *Patch Atlas* has the patina of accuracy, but the swatches, maps, and graphs insist that "the real" is accessible only through interpretation of the interplay of emptiness and abundance.

Both producing and engaging the atlas require "strategic pluralism," that is, a variety of approaches, from remote imaging, quantification, and classification, to drawing, judgment, and disorientation.[29] Marshall et al. methodologically and conceptually intervene in urban design through atlas visualizations that engender both quantification and defamiliarization; riffing off Wood, we can say that when these epistemological values collaborate, the atlas becomes "truthful in a way 'reference atlases'—hiding their messages behind the false front of 'objectivity'—never have."[30]

Palimpsesting

I will revisit my reading of *Patch Atlas* in light of use but first consider another intervention in atlas design, *Mississippi Floods*. Whereas Marshall et al. proclaim their book an atlas, Mathur and da Cunha skirt the term. They variously refer to the images in the book as "map-prints," "photoworks," and "photowalks," terminology that furthers their aim to contest the "taken-for-granted firm ground" into which official media have transformed the Mississippi River.[31] The project challenges the positivistic engineering logic that has managed the river for over 150 years. Engineers and planners continue to erect levees, gates, locks, and revetments to hold captive flow, meander, and flood. This logic has failed in the sense that the river resists control, but it has succeeded ideologically with the help of images and models. Rather than erase or ignore the visualizations that aid control, Mathur and da Cunha embed them to picture a "fluid terrain."[32]

Mississippi Floods begins with a media scene, "vivid images of a Great Flood [in 1993] across the American Midwest": "aerial photographs, satellite pictures, flood extent maps, height markers..., probability measures."[33] This recent scene returns them to a prior "great" flood, the 1927 disaster whose aftermath media such as maps, photographs, and music evoke, and then further back to the 18th- and 19th-century maps fueling colonization, settlement, commerce, chattel slavery, and ecological exhaustion. They study these documents of "capture" and take two trips wending along the Lower Mississippi to experience the alluvial valley.[34] Resistance to capture is material—water breaks through, overflows, and underflows—as well as medial: Black laborers sing the blues that document oppression and release in tune with alluvial patterns.

Like *Patch Atlas*, *Mississippi Floods* stymies expectations for an atlas and is self-reflexive about how media representing environments shape environmental matter. Chapters on "basin," "meanders," "flows," "banks," and "beds" comprise environmental, engineering, and media histories of the Mississippi that traverse data and art. The book reproduces myriad images, many of which then reappear in Mathur and da Cunha's screen-printed images. These images use maps as a base with photographs, text, timelines, newspaper clippings, technical drawings, and other media layered on top. With its media complexity spanning qualitative and quantitative sources, the project produces what I term "infowhelm." That is, it aesthetically transforms information that is abundant and readily available but also ripe for interpretation and contestation.[35] I argue that the aesthetic rendering of technical information elicits feelings that range from overwhelm and confusion to wonder and joy, and creates an epistemological complexity I explore below.

Depositing Depth, screen print on paper, 76 x 112 cm.

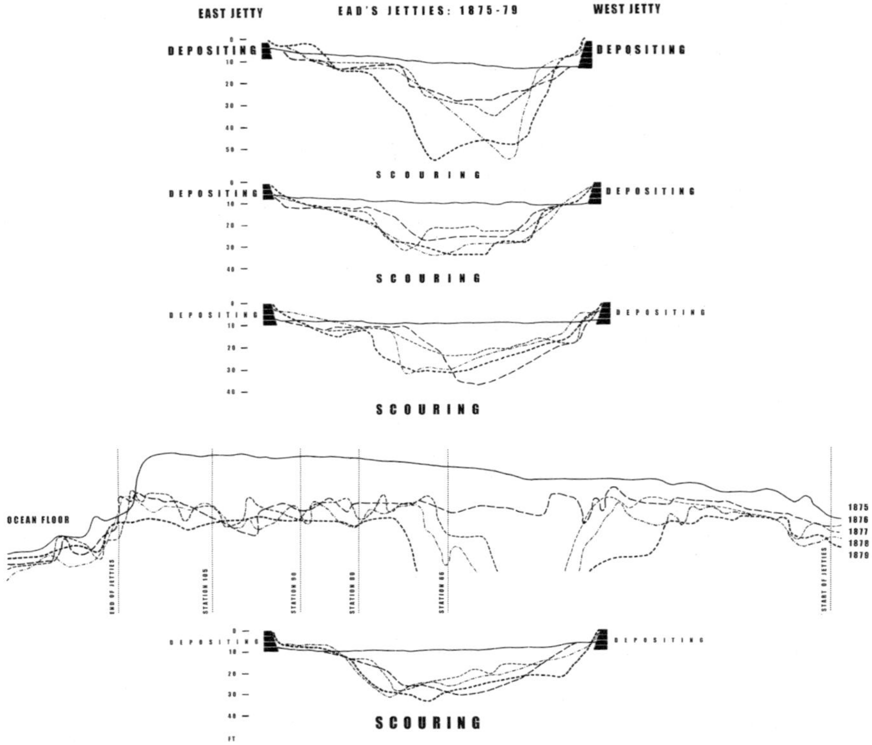

Sections through the jetties of the South Pass. This drawing comprises one layer of the *Passing Depth* screen print.

A sample from "Meanders" exhibits infowhelm and the specific techniques the creators use to invite and muddy interpretation. Information inundates with the explanation of sedimentation in the Yazoo Delta, a 220-mile expanse of the river known as the "'Mississippi's Mississippi,' famous for its politics of race and poverty"[36]: "Over a period, with all the shifts in the positions of bends, an alluvial ridge called a meander belt can form within the alluvial valley. It can be as much as fifteen feet high and fifteen miles wide. But a strong surge may change the course of the stream altogether, to abandon a meander belt and begin the formation of a new one."[37] An ode to deposition, this description identifies the actual as in a textbook explanation—"it...constructs," "deposits diminish"—but leans toward the probable hypothetical: "is liable to," "can form...can be...may change." The map-print "Depositing Depth" supplements the text and centers the Delta's curly western boundary, compared to a leaf's edge, that divides Mississippi from Arkansas and Louisiana. The image contains a "Landsat digital mosaic of the Memphis-Vicksburg region," which readers first see on page 4 layered on top of faint brushstrokes. Other remnants of pages past surround and layer on top of the image: a historical handbill (first on p. 6), an Army Corps of Engineers aerial photograph (33), an unlabeled aerial view of the 1927 flood (57), maps from Henry Fisk's influential 1944 *Geological Investigation of the Alluvial Valley of the Lower Mississippi River* (23), a photograph of a defunct "Indian Mound" (42), and graphical visualizations of the shifting river channel and of mound sites. Compelling readers to recall images from the book's past, Mathur and da Cunha encourage historical engagement. The components sequencing change (Fisk's maps, for example) anticipate a future as well as visualize the present and past. Holding together temporalities, readers must also comprehend multifarious data types and representations. The graphesis here is far from straightforward as faint, illegible text cohabits with a Landsat image lacking color signifiers, a partially visible line graph, and dots that suggest a scatterplot but actually indicate ghostly mounds.

I read this technique as a palimpsest and argue it complements the patch approach in Marshall et al. despite how distinct these artifacts are. If the patch and concomitant visualizations defamiliarize through the disjunction between abundance and emptiness, *Mississippi Floods*' palimpsesting of time, media, land/water, and human relations to them performs how mediation encrusts landscapes. Like *Patch Atlas*, the book retains commitments to data, which appear here in contexts where interpretation, for reader and for creator, is unsettled. As the authors explain, their process "begins with material specificity but extends in ways we cannot entirely predict."[38] Palimpsesting is a meander.

Narrative theorist Gérard Genette's germinal account of the palimpsest elucidates its effects in *Mississippi Floods*. "On the same parchment," he explains, "one text can become superimposed upon another, which it does not quite conceal but allows to show through."[39] The original French continues, "we can read the ancient under the new, as in a transparency...A text can always hide another, but rarely hides it completely, and usually lends itself to a double reading" or a "relational reading."[40] *Mississippi Floods*' form seeks the relationality and coexistence Genette describes. Even as the river meanders, its prior courses leave their traces. Even as Indian mounds fall victim to "'the land-levelers,'" their presence haunts.[41] Even as models, maps, and other official documents write the story of the Mississippi according to logics of control and containment, other media chart the river as a recalcitrant medium. Rhyming with Genette, *Mississippi Floods* cultivates relationality through palimpsests: "We question the tendency to understand and visualize [lines of demarcation and] these categories as separate before they are related, distinct before they are united."[42]

Mathur and da Cunha do not use *palimpsest* in *Mississippi Floods*, but the term appeals to planners and landscape architects because it suggests the environmental encoding of multiple realities. For Corboz palimpsest characterizes land as such. The complexity of media in *Mississippi Floods* engenders his argument that when people inhabit land, "the reciprocal effects of this coexistence can be observed. In other words, the land becomes the object of construction. It is a type of artifact."[43] Architects Chiara Cavalieri and Elena Cogato Lanza extend Corboz's theory and underscore the importance of semiotics and mediation. For landscape design, *palimpsest* serves

> to describe the territory as the outcome of a slow and long-term process involving multiple transformations, to deal with the evolutionary history of places, and to stress space as a conglomerate of signs, traces, and voids...upon which society can write...new chapters of its urban transformation.[44]

These "chapters" invite a multiplicity of interpretations that depend as much on absences and erasures as they do on presences. Mathur

Passing Depth, screen print on paper, 112 x 76 cm (cropped).

and da Cunha's images intimate absences such as images from past pages half-forgotten and partial or illegible text and graphs. Where *Patch Atlas* employs a visualization technique that produces emptiness and thereby a tension between abundance and absence, *Mississippi Floods* employs techniques of layering and haunting that activate memory and history. The former atlas defamiliarizes landscape and its representation, and the latter calls attention to how mediation encrusts the landscape.

Usable Form

Mississippi Floods' map-prints are beautiful, as are the paintings that supplement them, but this beauty sticks in the craw of some readers. For its aesthetic bent, the atlas received praise and faced criticism in the same breath. The citation for the 2001–2002 EDRA/*Places* Research Award notes that *Mississippi Floods* "reject[s] the oppositional logic behind calls for more river control and counter-demands that settlement be withdrawn from the flood plains" and thereby meets the "'pressing challenge for designers...to learn to see and think with appropriate complexity.'"[45] However, jurors feel lost in its innovations: "*Jacobs*: 'My problem with this is, what do you do with it?'...*Hood*: 'But as designers doing this kind of work, I wonder if we do ourselves a disservice when we couch the work as art.'...*Hanrahan*: 'Of course the pitfall is also looking at very complex diagrams...and saying, "It looks cool, but I don't understand it."'"[46] Their confusion is apt. After all, *Mississippi Floods* is about the refusal to be held captive, and it embodies that boundlessness. A readily comprehensible visual form would betray content.

But if the atlas isn't comprehensible, "'What do you do with it?'" The palimpsest technique yields multiplicity, which produces discomfort in practitioners. Mathur and da Cunha are savvy about this discomfort; they insist that "water challenges us to consider ambiguity as a condition to embrace rather than erase."[47] This awareness might not satisfy even admiring audiences. Utility preoccupies reviewers of *Patch Atlas* as well. While Marshall et al. briefly mention how urban ecologists and designers might employ the atlas, reviewers contend that it "is much less successful at exploring how design practice integrates with ecological knowledge...[and] how the system can be applied in design."[48] These reviews underscore that, no matter how visually appealing and conceptually and methodologically inventive they might be, atlases and other visualizations often bring expectations for use. The disciplinary origins, data sources, and embedded graphical forms of *Patch Atlas* and *Mississippi Floods* provoke an instrumentalist graphesis, at least with some audiences.

As a cultural critic, I do not share this orientation and cannot speak to how designers and ecologists might operationalize these atlases. I attend to the critiques about utility because they reveal a conflict between aesthetic and epistemological positioning in creative environmental media. The visualization techniques in *Patch Atlas* and *Mississippi Floods* have the affordances I elaborate above, but they simultaneously show how frictions arise between epistemological values. The atlases evince values originating in positivist science—classification, boundedness, quantification, and objectivity—as they pursue openness, speculation, storytelling, and disorientation. In *Infowhelm* I dub this "entangled epistemologies," that is, the mingling of scientific epistemologies with those rooted in imagination, speculation, and uncertainty.[49] The presence of positivist values in *Mississippi Floods* and *Patch Atlas* elicits expectations that the presence of other values undermines. In this case, utility seems to suffer as epistemologies entangle in the minds of planners, designers, and ecologists in the studio or in the field. However, we have another way of looking at this "failure": these creators innovate not so much a usable form as a form about use. They spotlight the desire for utility as an epistemological value that, while germane to their disciplines, needs to be cast aside to bring other epistemological outcomes to the fore. Or, more precisely, use needs to remain as a possible orientation toward the atlases in order to force reflection on what we expect environmental media to do.

As the atlases perturb utility, they also perturb data. This is particularly poignant in *Mississippi Floods*, which states its aim to trouble data about the Lower Mississippi, "a landscape very much in doubt not for lack of proof of what exists but because what constitutes proof is subtle and difficult."[50] Encouraging reflection about what counts as usable environmental media encourages questions of "what counts as data, what data are collected, and whose interests they serve."[51] These questions inspire environmental data justice as Lindsey Dillon et al. define it. As a tool in designers' hands, an atlas can forward "just access to, interpretation of, and control of data as important goals in and of themselves and as means to broader socioenvironmental transformations."[52] Atlases are ripe sites for this work because they are products of collaboration, accommodation, and integration of quantitative and qualitative data on environments in flux. Rather than blueprinting the course of lands and waters for the future, *Patch Atlas* and *Mississippi Floods* encourage users to halt in their design journey to ask what data and epistemologies are guiding their understanding of use, who/what has been harmed by use, and who/what might thrive from entanglement.

Notes

1. André Corboz, "The Land as Palimpsest," *Diogenes* 31, no. 121 (1983): 18.
2. See, for example, James Corner, "The Agency of Mapping," in Denis Cosgrove (ed.), *Mappings* (Reaktion Books, 1999), 213–52; Helen Couclelis, "Some Second Thoughts about Theory in the Social Sciences," *Geographical Analysis* 15, no. 1 (1983): 28–33; J. B. Harley, "Deconstructing the Map," *Cartographica* 2, no. 1 (1989): 1–20; Denis Wood, *The Power of Maps* (Guilford Press, 1992).
3. Margaret Wickens Pearce, "Framing the Days: Place and Narrative in Cartography," *Cartography and Geographic Information Science* 35, no. 1 (2008): 21.
4. I write more extensively about the atlas as narrative cartography in Heather Houser, "Drawing the Line on Oil in *Petrochemical America*," *Environmental Humanities* 13, no. 1 (2021): 21–44.
5. Denis Wood, "Pleasure in the Idea / The Atlas as Narrative Form," *Cartographica* 24, no. 1 (1987): 29.
6. Jeremy W. Crampton, *Mapping: A Critical Introduction to Cartography and GIS* (Wiley, 2010), 41. See also Sébastien Caquard, "Cartography I: Mapping Narrative Cartography," *Progress in Human Geography* 37, no. 1 (2011): 135–44; Bieke Cattoor & Chris Perkins, "Re-cartographies of Landscape: New Narratives in Architectural Atlases," *The Cartographic Journal* 51, no. 2 (2014): 166–78; Katherine McKittrick, *Demonic Grounds: Black Women and the Cartographies of Struggle* (University of Minnesota Press, 2006); Ian Muehlenhaus, "The Design and Composition of Persuasive Maps," *Cartography and Geographic Information Science* 40, no. 5 (2013): 401–14.
7. *OED Online*, s.v. "Atlas, n.1," https://www.oed.com/view/Entry/12536 (accessed August 9, 2023).
8. See Susan Stewart, *On Longing: Narratives of the Miniature, the Gigantic, the Souvenir, the Collection* (Duke University Press, 1993), 162.
9. Aileen Buckley, "Atlas Mapping in the 21st Century," *Cartography and Geographic Information Science* 30, no. 2 (2003): 149–50.
10. See, for example, the Exchange for Local Observations and Knowledge of the Arctic (ELOKA) collections and atlases (eloka-arctic.org/), Texas Freedom Colonies Project (www.thetexasfreedomcoloniesproject.com/), Decolonial Atlas (decolonialatlas.wordpress.com/), and Anti-Eviction Mapping Project (antievictionmap.com).
11. See, for example, Kirstin Dow & Thomas Downing's *The Atlas of*

Climate Change (2011); Rebecca Solnit and collaborators' trilogy *Infinite City: A San Francisco Atlas* (2010), *Unfathomable City: A New Orleans Atlas* (2013), and *Nonstop Metropolis: A New York City Atlas* (2016); and Christina Gerhardt's *Sea Change: An Atlas of Islands in a Rising Ocean* (2023), among others.
12. Victoria J. Marshall, et al., *Patch Atlas: Integrating Design Practices and Ecological Knowledge for Cities as Complex Systems* (Yale University Press, 2019), 13.
13. Ibid., 3. For more on the methodological components, see ibid., 3–4.
14. William R. Clark, "Principles of Landscape Ecology," *Nature Education Knowledge* 3, no. 10 (2010): 34.
15. Marshall, et al., *Patch Atlas*, 13.
16. Ibid., 99.
17. Viktor Shklovsky theorized modernist defamiliarization in "Art as Technique," *Russian Formalist Criticism: Four Essays* (University of Nebraska Press, 1965), 3–24.
18. Marshall, et al., *Patch Atlas*, 26.
19. Johanna Drucker, *Graphesis: Visual Forms of Knowledge Production* (Harvard University Press, 2014), 6.
20. Marshall, et al., *Patch Atlas*, 99.
21. Symposium details are at emlabupenn.com/Events/. A video of Marshall's talk is available at vimeo.com/682589891#t=2910s/.
22. Lorraine Daston & Peter Galison, *Objectivity* (Zone Books, 2007), 19.
23. Ibid., 28, 39.
24. Ibid., 29. I demonstrate the fissures in the objectivity of aerial data in Heather Houser, *Infowhelm: Environmental Art and Literature in an Age of Data* (Columbia University Press, 2020), ch. 5.
25. See Marshall, et al., *Patch Atlas*, 8.
26. Daston & Galison, *Objectivity*, 44; Marshall et al., *Patch Atlas*, 8.
27. William Rankin, "The Accuracy Trap: The Values and Meaning of Algorithmic Mapping, from Mineral Extraction to Climate Change," *Environment and History* 29, no. 1 (2023): 20.
28. Ibid., 31. While Rankin critiques strict reliance on algorithmic accuracy, he also cautions against a "single-minded critique of accuracy, since it blinds us to the more use-oriented, bottom-up trends that have accompanied it," ibid., 46.
29. Ibid., 47.
30. Wood, "Pleasure," 38.
31. Anuradha Mathur & Dilip da Cunha, *Mississippi Floods: Designing a Shifting Landscape* (Yale University Press, 2001), 11; Anu Mathur & Dilip da Cunha, "Preparing Ground," interview by Nicholas Pevzner & Sanjukta Sen, *Places*, June 2010, https://placesjournal.org/article/preparing-ground-interview; Mathur & da Cunha, *Mississippi Floods*, xi. The exhibition *Mississippi Horizons: Mapping a Shifting Terrain* complemented the book and first showed at the University of Pennsylvania in 1998.
32. Ibid., xiv.
33. Ibid., xi.
34. Ibid.
35. Houser, *Infowhelm*.
36. Mathur & da Cunha, *Mississippi Floods*, 33.
37. Ibid., 42.
38. Mathur & da Cunha, "Preparing Ground."
39. Gérard Genette, *Palimpsests: Literature in the Second Degree*, trans. Channa Newman & Claude Doubinsky (University of Nebraska Press, 1997), 398–99.
40. This explanation appears in Genette's précis of the book on the press's website, https://www.seuil.com/ouvrage/palimpsestes-la-litterature-au-second-degre-gerard-genette/9782020061162/. Gérard Genette, *Palimpsestes: La littérature au second degré* (Édition du Seuil, 1982), 618, my translations.
41. Mathur & da Cunha, *Mississippi Floods*, 43.
42. Mathur & da Cunha, "Preparing Ground."
43. Corboz, "The Land as Palimpsest," 17.
44. Chiara Cavalieri & Elena Cogato Lanza, "Territories in Time: Mapping Palimpsest Horizons," *Urban Planning* 5, no. 2 (2020): 94–95.
45. Jamie Horwitz & Todd W. Bressi, "*Mississippi Floods – Designing a Shifting Landscape* [EDRA/*Places* Awards, 2001–2002 – Research]," *Places* 15, no. 1 (2002): 40, 41.
46. Ibid., 41.
47. Mathur & da Cunha, "Preparing Ground."
48. Clinton Hindes & Julia Raxworthy, "Review of *Patch Atlas: Integrating Design Practices and Ecological Knowledge for Cities as Complex Systems*, by Victoria J. Marshall, et al.," *Journal of Landscape Architecture* 16, no. 1 (2021): 91.
49. Houser, *Infowhelm*, 13.
50. Mathur & da Cunha, *Mississippi Floods*, 153.
51. Lindsey Dillon, et al., "Environmental Data Justice and the Trump Administration: Reflections from the Environmental Data and Governance Initiative," *Environmental Justice* 10, no. 6 (2017): 187.
52. Dawn Walker, et al., "Infrastructuring Environmental Data Justice," in Jenny Goldstein & Eric Nost (eds), *The Nature of Data: Infrastructures, Environments, Politics* (University of Nebraska Press, 2022), 196.

Data, Relationships, and Action

Samantha Jo Fried

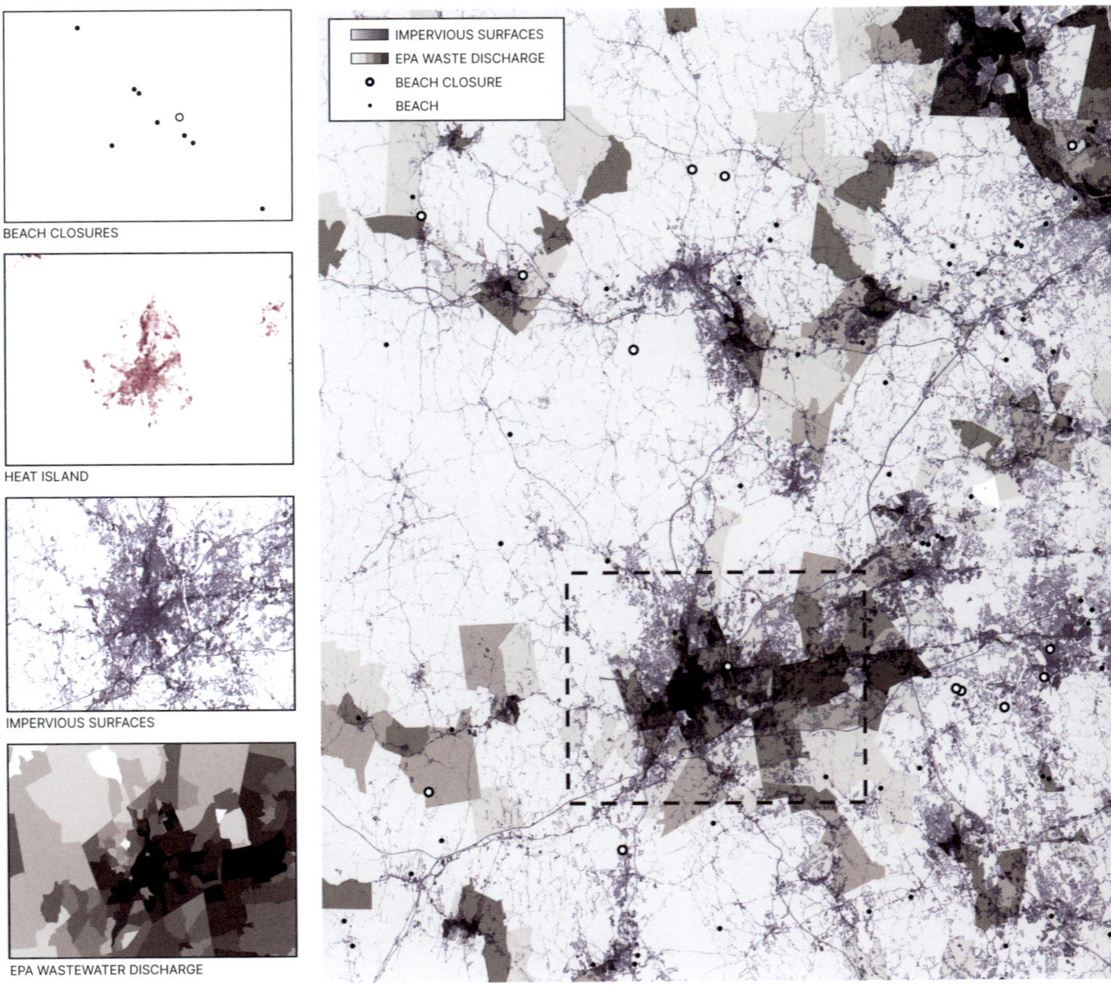

Composite and separate layers of the spatial coincidence of high-probability wastewater discharge, impervious surfaces, heat, and beach closures in Worchester, MA.

Many Earth remote sensing activities by satellite were—and still are—characterized by a "data-to-action paradigm."[1] This is a paradigm in which vast amounts of meticulous Earth data are collected with the belief that these efforts will eventually lead to action. More specifically, it is the idea that the more data about a phenomenon that experts can collect, the more apparent the best course of action on that data will become. In the data-to-action paradigm, it is not the experts' responsibility to think about action when collecting, processing, or analyzing data. It is assumed that the data speak for themselves and that collective action toward a unified goal will become obvious and inevitable once the data are in hand. In contrast, in a "civic engagement paradigm," discussions about the data are never far from

discussions about how to resolve power differentials, how to balance and accept tensions between local and global knowledge, how to resolve disputes over divergent interests (and how to live with the unresolvable), and how to acknowledge that uncertainty and unreliability can be natural parts of the knowledge-creation process.[2] People with different backgrounds, experiences, and ways of knowing have some involvement with environmental data—and ideas about how and why collective action might take place may even be intentionally imbued in data collection and analysis—however, collective action is as valuable as the existence of the data themselves. Those who have a wide range of experience in organizing collective action around environmental data are respected in the same way that technical experts are.

As someone trained in the field of Science, Technology, and Society (STS), and also as an administrator of two academic programs (STS and Civic Studies), my approach to these two ways of seeing/using data is to ask, what type of environmental advocacy *begins* with questions around remotely sensed data, especially as it pertains to highly technoscientific issues with profound consequences around democratic decision-making? In her 2020 book *Data Action*, Sarah Williams addresses the reality that "data [have] often been used—and manipulated—to make policy decisions without much stakeholder input."[3] Williams offers concrete guidance for practitioners and decision makers who collect and/or analyze data toward addressing public issues. To be clear, I do not approach what I call the "data-to-action paradigm" as someone who will ever adopt a new way of doing Earth remote sensing in terms of choosing the design of satellites to "see" Earth in a certain way, or in terms of choosing the research questions that influence data analysis. Nor do I work in a public decision-making capacity with digital Earth data. Furthermore, Earth remote sensing data analysis is highly technical and specialized in nature—the very structure and function of the field relies on proprietary knowledge. On the other hand, my role as an administrator makes me very aware of institutional logics: of processes, relationships, and systems within institutions.

In this chapter, I aim to describe a data-to-action paradigm "in the wild," so to speak. I focus on impervious surfaces as they appear on publicly available land cover mapping tools, using Worcester, Massachusetts, as a case study. This approach spotlights data as, first and foremost, a set of relationships and processes. Furthermore, this approach complicates the distinction between the local and the global. More specifically, it sits in territory between two tenuous assumptions described by Ursula Heise:

> that the local provides a familiar ground from which to expand one's awareness to larger scales and the uneasy realization that the local itself is thoroughly unfamiliar to many individuals, and may be epistemologically unfathomable in its entirety as larger entities such as the nation or the globe.[4]

Impervious surfaces, such as rooftops and paved surfaces, are terrain that water cannot penetrate or be absorbed by.[5] Impervious surfaces are at once very difficult to derive from remotely sensed satellite data and (literally) grounded and experiential. Impervious surfaces represent *and* mediate relationships—among soil, paving, water, groundwater, and local communities. Arguably, Earth remote sensing data, in general, are rich in relations because they contain information about how objects are spatially situated with respect to each other, and how objects appear over time (and at different times). In this way, data are a *product* of relationships. Anthropologist Tone Walford writes that "whilst (scientific) 'facts' can be opposed to social 'relations'...'facts' can also be seen to be themselves constituted by 'relations.'"[6] Raw data, argues Walford, contain more (and sometimes more nonsensical) relationships, and the process of cleaning and analyzing data involves cutting out superfluous relationships (or relationships the analyst deems to be superfluous). Therefore, data analysis techniques always involve choices about which relationships to bring forward and which to leave out. Likewise, media scholar Jennifer Gabrys asserts that sensing techniques say something about the relationship between people and nature, and that they produce abstractions that, in turn, inform concrete understandings. Those understandings are "not just...scientists-devices-flora-and-fauna, but also... relations that emerge through data sets and algorithmic processes, across sedimented environmental effects, and through responses to modes of ecological action."[7] In other words, data are formed by, characterize, and represent the relationships between researchers and the phenomenon they are measuring—and through the process of analyses, even more relationships come to be characterized and visually represented.

Gabrys's focus on sensing techniques as abstractions that inform and produce concrete relationalities conjures feminist physicist Evelyn Fox Keller's *dynamic objectivity*, which "aims at a form of knowledge that grants to the world around us its independent integrity but does so in a way that remains cognizant of, indeed relies on, our connectivity to the world."[8] Importantly, Keller's scientific realism is faithful to the idea that researchers *can* know valuable things through instruments like Earth remote sensing satellites and that knowledge is most accurate when researchers take both measurement *and* the relationalities brought about by that measurement into account.[9] Similarly, Jennifer Henderson's *empathetic accuracy* takes the relationship between data and their context as a matter of concern.[10] Empathetic accuracy "performs the interconnectedness of accuracy, care, and relationality" and is "a way to reframe what appears as a binary of accuracy and relationships."[11] Put simply, accuracy and relationships are not on opposite ends of a spectrum, even though many scientists have believed that neutrality is crucial to accuracy and the integrity of research and/or a way of isolating variables in experiments to remove

A zoom-in of the area shown on the previous map and postings (scraped from Google) about beach closures and Coes Pond.

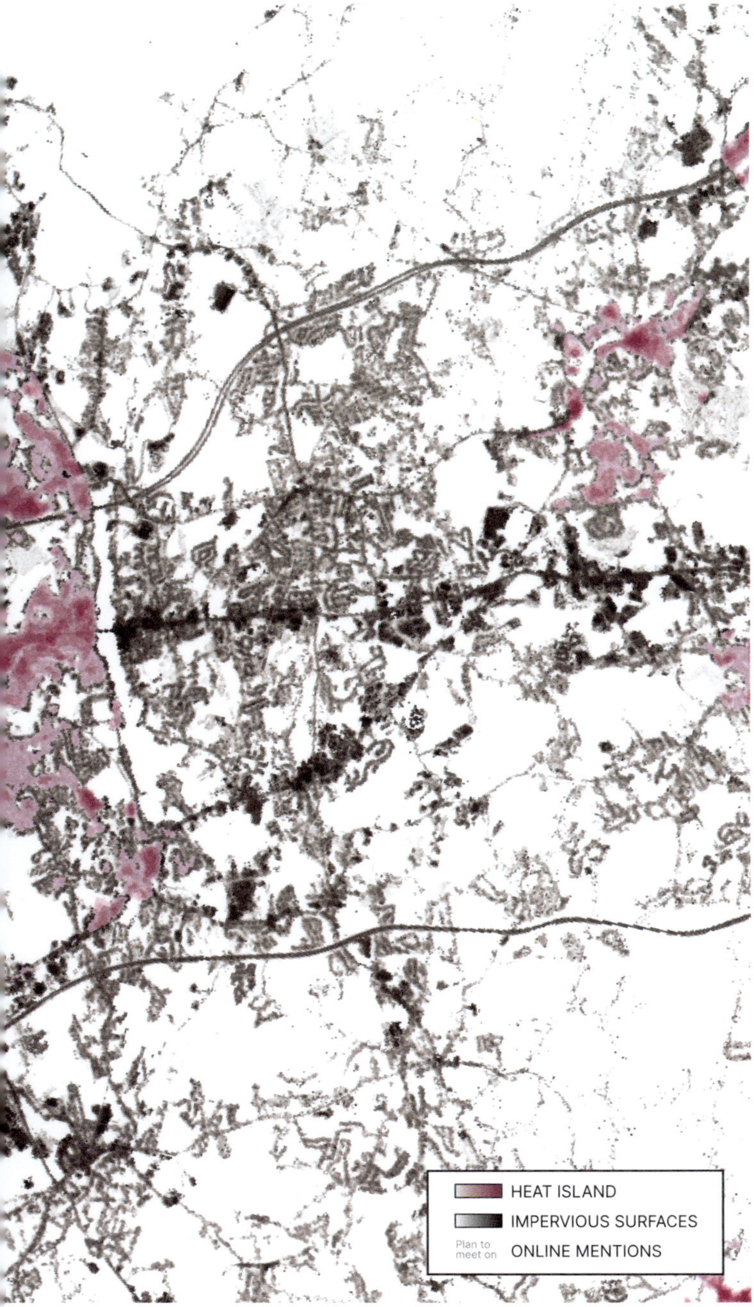
HEAT ISLAND
IMPERVIOUS SURFACES
Plan to meet on
ONLINE MENTIONS

Aerial image showing the location of the fence that separates residents from Coes Pond.

"noise."[12] Empathetic accuracy can and should be carefully extended to Earth remote sensing generally, insofar as it relates to how digital Earth data are used to make environmental predictions and direct collective action toward a perceived (and ultimately decided-upon) common good.

Remotely sensed data about impervious surfaces both characterize and visually represent relationships among roads, buildings, and people; parking lots and people; and trees (or lack thereof) and people. They also represent all that goes into those relationships (concrete, fossil fuels, carbon dioxide, trees providing oxygen and cleaning the air, trees providing shade for a nice picnic, grass and soil that can absorb water from rainfall, etc.). I am interested in an explicit connection between impervious surface maps and issues local activists might care about: high levels of imperviousness in a landscape are associated with higher levels of poverty in urban areas and more strongly felt environmental hardship when it comes to climate change. These effects are most strongly identifiable in urban heat islands and flooding. Not only do impervious surfaces create a feedback loop of heat in cities, but they also create conditions for more contaminated groundwater.[13] A common suggestion, one that sometimes comes from members of affected communities, is to balance the ill effects of impervious surfaces with trees, parks, and green spaces. This evokes questions about the kinds of strategies and actions people might owe to each other and their environments considering the presence of impervious surfaces. "Data are—and should be—imbued with norms," writes Peter Levine. "There is no such thing as a value neutral measurement, nor should we aim for one."[14] According to Levine, facts, values, and strategies are always interconnected.

By presenting viewers with new visual descriptions of land cover that causes urban heat islands and dangerous flooding, these data suggest—not specifically, but broadly—that something ought to be done to improve the quality of life for people who live on or around these geographic features. However, while imperatives to act are embedded in remotely sensed digital maps through relationship-rich facts (this surface is impervious), values (impervious surfaces can be harmful to people, and this harm should be mitigated), and strategies (different avenues for how to alter conditions based on the map), instructions about which strategy to choose are not. The best policy decisions, the most effective economic and political strategies, and the most just and equitable urban planning and development are not necessarily made clear through these data, relationship-rich as they are. Furthermore, the material conditions of people on the ground are not always elucidated through these relationships.

Impervious Surfaces

I walk through a parking lot at least once a day, yet the process of identifying something as a parking lot through digital Earth data is wildly difficult. Impervious surfaces have been of interest in the Earth remote sensing community since the 1970s and are an ongoing challenge for researchers in terms of data analysis.[15] Impervious surface data are a kind of data that analysts can only produce when they determine what is nonsensical through classification techniques. For instance, boundaries of different land cover types within cities are made very challenging by the way light reflects off objects, and soil and water have a spectral reflectance that appears very similar to that of some kinds of impervious surfaces.[16] Impervious surface data need to be derived algorithmically to fulfill the scale of an existing remotely sensed image. Direct per-pixel classification does not suffice for moderate- and low-resolution Earth data, as a single pixel in such an image often contains multiple kinds of land cover.[17] Researchers are still learning different methods of extracting information about imperviousness from images. Importantly, different extraction methods are used for different data types, but what exactly leads to the most ideal impervious surface map is not yet understood.[18]

Worcester, where I lived from 2019–2021, is swelteringly hot in the summer. Its downtown area has little greenspace, and it is comprised largely of renters, not homeowners. By comparing a handful of publicly available maps of Worcester—some remotely sensed, and some GIS- and/or census-based—I show the tenuous relationship between the local and the global and ask how this relationship can be more fully addressed. This is an important line of inquiry because the best strategies and courses of action exist within a more holistic understanding of relationships between climate as it appears on a map and as it is felt by people on the ground. I use a publicly available tool—the Multi-Resolution Land Characteristics (MRLC) National Land Cover Dataset (NLCD) viewer—which is an interactive map that utilizes Landsat imagery and allows users to navigate to any location in the United States to learn about its land cover characteristics. I compare this with maps describing urban heat islands, obtained from ArcGIS and the Trust for Public Land. Recent heavy rain in Massachusetts allows me to compare MRLC impervious surface maps with statewide beach closures and EPA environmental justice maps describing unsanitary runoff risks.

The sweltering heat I felt at the peak of Worcester summers can be understood on a larger scale by comparing impervious surface maps and heat island maps, between which there is a direct relationship. Land surface temperature "is strongly positively correlated with" the existence and extent of impervious surfaces, and land surface temperature causes urban heat islands.[19] Urban heat islands increase the energy burden for inner-city residents. The proliferation of air conditioning units pumping hot air into the city adds to the collecting heat, ultimately creating unsafe conditions for those without air conditioning or a cool, shaded place to rest and rehydrate.[20] Heat, like the kind created in urban heat islands, "is the most deadly weather-related risk here and abroad."[21] There is also a relationship between urban heat islands and air pollution.[22] Tree cover is known to be an effective source of coolness on very hot days (and of pollution reduction); however, diverse, low-income areas do not have access to the cooling tree cover that wealthier white neighborhoods do.[23]

Like the MRLC viewer, the urban heat island map utilizes Landsat data. However, unlike the MRLC, which combines data from a number of different public sources and Landsat decadal surveys, the ArcGIS urban heat island viewer utilizes only Landsat 8 imagery from 2018 and 2019. Landsat can measure surface temperature for the ground and for tops of buildings, or for whatever material is facing the sky. These temperatures are discretely classified (using a scale of one to five, with one being mild heat and five being severe heat), and sorted and imaged by a proprietary, Python-coded platform called the Descartes Lab.[24] This allows for faster image processing and, therefore, faster creation of urban heat island maps.[25] Here is a clear example of the data-to-action paradigm: while this urban heat island map is crucial for visualizing the extent of the issue, the creation of the map itself only identifies the problem. As McDonald, Biswas, and Spotwood make clear, "Any serious effort at climate adaptation [with respect to urban heat islands] must address the linked issue of inequality among different neighborhoods."[26]

Flooding—sometimes called urban waterlogging—is another issue on which impervious surface maps can shed light.[27] This happens when drainage and sewage infrastructure fails to support a growing population. When it rains heavily, there is nowhere for water to drain.[28] In these instances, rain falls and then makes its way into local bodies of water, along with a myriad of pollutants, including pesticides, pathogens, nutrients, and sediment.[29] Alternatively, the soil may absorb water, which acts as a filter for pollutants.[30] As I write this, Eastern Massachusetts is experiencing heavy rain that is flowing into, and contaminating, water bodies: over 50 Massachusetts beaches are "posted."[31] This means that the water is deemed unsafe for swimming. Creating a map of the swimming locations listed on the Massachusetts state website on July 10, 2023, offers its own challenges, as a number of the posted locations are described in ways that locals will understand, but in ways that are not searchable on Google Maps. For instance, one Salem beach is listed simply as "Steps." However, a search on Google Maps yields no results for a beach called "Steps," and there is no clear landmark for that location.

As seen in the figures on pages 194–95, the visual relationships within the map of "posted" beaches, the MLCD map of impervious surfaces, and an EPA map of areas prone to wastewater discharge is clear—even without the sort of calibration that would make the relationships among these maps more quantitative. However, the quantitative context is not the only kind of evidence missing from this assortment of datapoints. While the relationships among imperviousness, more populated areas, and contamination of swimming areas from rainfall may be obvious, the courses of action—increase surfaces that absorb water (e.g., soil and trees) or implement city-sanctioned clean-up projects for contaminated waters—are not so straightforward. In practice, as many researchers have noted, being environmentally friendly does not equate to being environmentally just.

Sometimes, areas posing health hazards and community risks are not so easily identifiable, and what communities in the surrounding area want is nuanced and unmappable. In late 2020 and early 2021, the City of Worcester announced plans to replace Hillside Beach—one beach on the otherwise publicly managed Coes Pond—with a boardwalk and wooded areas. The beach backed up to a publicly funded housing project, Lakeside Apartments. Several Worcester city signs were posted on the beach, warning of the dangers of swimming and deeming it closed. As local journalist and activist Bill Shaner quips, "Signs saying not to swim of course have always famously prevented people from swimming."[32] A fence prevented apartment residents from Lakeside Apartments from accessing Coes Pond by way of Hillside Beach. If children living in the apartments wanted to swim in Coes Pond, they needed to walk onto a state highway (Route 12) and then swim to it from a publicly owned beach on the other side.

Photograph of warning signs posted at one of the few access points to Coes Pond. Image by Rick CinClair – USA Today Network.

Kids living in the Lakeside Apartments had a choice between climbing a chain-link fence or crossing a busy highway to swim.[33]

Ultimately, the city planned to replace Hillside Beach with a boardwalk and close it for good, instead of attending to Lakeside Apartments families' wishes to have a clean and accessible city-controlled beach. The reasons were cost and environment: making the beach a safe and accessible place for residents to swim was $4.5 million more expensive than replacing the beach with a boardwalk, and the city was incentivized to replace the beach with a wetland.[34] Shaner points out that the city obtains money for the project through census data, which reports Lakeside Apartments and surrounding areas as an Environmental Justice (EJ) population. In an ideal world, the purpose of doing this is to ensure that historically disadvantaged communities are receiving the benefits of environmental projects.[35] While (non-remotely sensed) maps describing community demographics are crucial to just planning, they are not adequate on their own. In the case of Hillside Beach, local activists rallied to supplement the EJ demographics with their own perspectives. After months of sustained pressure (and years of activism around the issue), they managed to get the city to open the gate and build the boardwalk on another side of the public housing complex.[36] Nonetheless, this is a key example of how a literal top-down view of urban-environmental issues is a partial story—and that, if planners are not careful, maps can usurp community voice and perspective. As Sarah Williams notes while exploring the history of the 1901 Royal Housing Commission in London, "the maps may have simply created rational evidence to garner public support for policies the city government already wanted to enact."[37]

This case is significant because it is about safety and greenspace in an area with an underserved population. Yet, the case defies categorization in several key ways: the Hillside Beach area itself does not stand out on any of the impervious surface maps; it is not an area with significant imperviousness (though there is some), nor is it overlayed by a blotchy heat island in the ArcGIS map. It is not in a census tract with particularly remarkable levels of wastewater discharge—granted, if the city is not responsible for the care and keeping of Hillside Beach, there may be other safety issues for people who swim. Hillside Beach and Coes Reservoir (the larger body of water to which it connects) were not posted areas on July 10, 2023 (however, there have been instances of cyanobacteria closing Coes Reservoir in the summer and fall of 2022).[38] Furthermore, according to the EPA's EJ map, the area is not particularly prone to flooding.[39] Given all of this, this debacle—which has just as much to do with a community's desire for access to a particular kind of clean, natural space in an urban area—would be significantly more difficult to learn about if one did not follow local politics and activism in Worcester.

Conclusion

It is a lost opportunity when communities are brought into planning and discussion of urban environmental projects after the fact and, ultimately, it is a failure to build relationships. Sarah Williams puts forth the idea that government-led sensing projects (and mapping and data projects writ large) are trust-building opportunities between officials and communities.[40] This idea is in the same vein as Fox Keller's dynamic objectivity, which "is not unlike empathy, a form of knowledge of other persons that draws explicitly on the commonality of feelings and experience in order to enrich one's understanding of another in [their] own right."[41] Williams advocates for more participatory sensing projects that foster collective knowledge bases and that "lead participants to truly ask and understand what the data [mean]."[42]

Williams also makes a strong argument for publicly owned data, which is increasingly becoming proprietary.[43] Likewise, I would add that, even when data are public, sometimes their highly technical nature and bureaucratic frameworks make them nearly as inaccessible as proprietary data. While census-based EJ maps are easier to understand and navigate, remotely sensed data collected by satellites are deeply technical—as are the resultant impervious surface data. General audiences do not have the context to interpret relationships that are bound up in this data. There is a mismatch, too, between the need for more technically advanced impervious surface data and the need to figure out what action to take on that data. This is intended to be less of a criticism and more of an observation about how complicated it is to create action-oriented knowledge about the local and the global simultaneously. I do not think this is only a communication problem, only a scientific research problem, or only a problem that people who study the limits of the scientific method can solve: arguably, it is all three of these problems at once.[44] That data are relationship-rich, permeating so many facets of life, both technical and social, makes it all the more necessary to treat the issue of action on environmental data as a scientific/critical/rhetorical issue; to treat these components of the issues as inseparable.

Dosemagen et al. offer four lessons that attend to this inseparability of the scientific/critical/rhetorical, which I will extend to these cases: emphasizing social explanations for impervious surface data, how sociotechnical systems that create impervious surfaces "influence distribution of social power and inequality," attunement to how these kinds of power relations proliferate even in action and justice-oriented work, and a critical eye toward the ideas, funding, and even professionalization of this action-oriented work.[45] Dosemagen et al.'s recommendations involve an extension of the theme that environmental data are relationship-rich: by maintaining what they call "self-reflexivity," researchers and activists commit to recognizing all the relationships bound up in environmental data; and by refocusing work on the power dynamics undergirding sociotechnical systems, people must ask themselves how to foster relationships among motley and unexpected groups of people, reflecting the complexity of the relationships in the data. This is an antidote to what Fox Keller reasons is a struggle to locate oneself in scientific pursuits, which has resulted in a dominance-based mentality that has not actually been good for the pursuit of objective knowledge.[46] The pursuit of environmental data magnifies these anxieties: about knowing how ecology works, knowing how people work, and knowing what the future will look like. I advocate for reframing: use the relationships tangled up in data as a jumping-off point to foster relationships that transcend data.

Acknowledgment

The author would like to acknowledge Peter Levine and Nick Seaver for their generous engagement with, and thoughtful edits for, this chapter. Thanks are also owed to Matt Lacroix for reading the first draft and listening to my learning process around impervious surfaces.

Notes

1. Samantha Jo Fried, "Landsat in Contexts: Deconstructing and Reconstructing the Data-to-Action Paradigm in Earth Remote Sensing," (Doctoral dissertation, Virginia Tech, 2019); Samantha Jo Fried, "How Climate Science Could Lead to Action," *American Scientist* 108, no. 1 (2020): 34–42; Samantha Jo Fried, "Satellites, War, Climate Change, and the Environment: Are We at Risk for Environmental Deskilling?" *AI & Society* (2020): 1–9.
2. Fried, "How Climate Science Could Lead to Action."
3. Sarah Williams, "Introduction: Using Data Action," in *Data Action: Using Data for Public Good* (MIT Press, 2020), x.
4. Ursula K. Heise, "From the Blue Planet to Google Earth," in *Sense of Place and Sense of Planet: The Environmental Imagination of the Global* (Oxford University Press, 2008), 41.
5. Qihao Weng, "Remote Sensing of Impervious Surfaces: An Overview," in Qihao Weng (ed.), *Remote Sensing of Impervious Surfaces* (CRC Press, 2007), 1.
6. Antonia Walford, "Raw Data: Making Relations Matter," *Social Analysis* 61, no. 2 (2017): 68.
7. Jennifer Gabrys, "Sensing an Experimental Forest: Processing Environments and Distributing Relations," *Computational Culture* 2 (2012): 5–6.
8. Evelyn Fox Keller, "Dynamic Objectivity: Love, Power, and Knowledge," in *Reflections on Gender and Science* (Yale University Press, 1985), 117.
9. According to Ian Hacking, scientific realism "says that the entities, states and processes described by correct theories really do exist. Protons, photons, fields of force, and black holes are as real as toe-nails, turbines, eddies in a stream, and volcanoes. The weak interactions of small particle physics are as real as falling in love." In other words, things that are not directly observable or experienced by people are real when they are studied through a combination of theories and instruments developed by the scientific community. Water pixels viewed through an infrared remote sensing device are as real as the feeling of water itself on our skin and as real as love. Ian Hacking, *Representing and Intervening: Introductory Topics in the Philosophy of Natural Science* (Cambridge University Press, 1983), 21.
10. This term was coined by Bruno Latour. "A thing is," he writes, "in one sense, an object out there and, in another sense, an *issue* very much *in* there, at any rate, a *gathering*...The same word *thing* designates matters of fact and matters of concern." In other words, anything that we want to learn about out in the world—whether it is trees, parking lots, roads, or urban heat islands—is connected to many other things and issues. Every curiosity brings with it a set of relationships, which are worthy of study. See Bruno Latour, "Why Has Critique Run Out of Steam? From Matters of Fact to Matters of Concern," *Critical Inquiry* 30, no. 2 (2004): 233.
11. Jennifer Henderson, "Weather-Ready Nation or Ready-Weather Agency? Emphatic Accuracy and Sociotechnical Resilience in the National Weather Service," in Sulfikar Amir (ed.), *The Sociotechnical Constitution of Resilience* (Palgrave MacMillan, 2018), 93–95.
12. Robert K. Merton, "A Note on Science and Democracy," *Journal of Legal & Political Sociology* 1 (1942): 115–26.
13. James D. Hurd & Daniel L. Civco, "Temporal Characterization of Impervious Surfaces for the State of Connecticut," in *ASPRS Annual Conference Proceedings* (Denver, Colorado, May 2004).
14. Peter Levine, "Guest Editor's Introduction: On Reintegrating Facts, Values, Strategies," *The Good Society* 26, no. 2 (2017): 196.
15. Dengsheng Lu, Emilio Moran & Scott Hetrick, "Detection of Impervious Surface Change with Multitemporal Landsat Images in an Urban–Rural Frontier," *ISPRS Journal of Photogrammetry and Remote Sensing* 66, no. 3 (2011): 299.
16. Yuliang Wang & Mingshi Li, "Urban Impervious Surface Detection from Remote Sensing Images: A Review of the Methods and Challenges," *IEEE Geoscience and Remote Sensing Magazine* 7, no. 3 (2019): 65.
17. Lu, Moran & Hetrick, "Detection of Impervious Surface Change," 304.
18. Shanshan Feng & Fenglei Fan, "Impervious Surface Extraction Based on Different Methods from Multiple Spatial Resolution Images: A Comprehensive Comparison," *International Journal of Digital Earth* 14, no. 9 (2021): 1,151.
19. Lizhong Hua, et al., "The Impacts of the Expansion of Urban Impervious Surfaces on Urban Heat Islands in a Coastal City in China," *Sustainability* 12, no. 2 (2020): 475; Patricia Wanjiku Mwangi, Faith Njoki Karanja & Peter Kariuki Kamau, "Analysis of the Relationship Between Land's Surface Temperature and Vegetation and Built-up Indices in Upper-Hill, Nairobi," *Journal of Geoscience and Environment Protection* 6, no. 1 (2018): 1.
20. United States Environmental Protection Agency, "Learn About Heat Islands," https://www.epa.gov/heatislands/learn-about-heat-islands (accessed July 10, 2023).
21. Robert McDonald, Tanushree Biswas & Erica Spotswood, "Throwing Shade at the Green New Deal," *LA+ Interdisciplinary Journal of Landscape Architecture*, 15 (2022): 67.
22. Patricia Wanjiku Mwangi, et al., "Analysis of the relationship between land surface temperature and vegetation," 1; Bakhtiar Feizizadeh & Thomas Blaschke, "Examining Urban Heat Island Relations to Land Use and Air Pollution: Multiple Endmember Spectral Mixture Analysis for Thermal Remote Sensing," *IEEE Journal of Selected Topics in Applied Earth Observations and Remote Sensing* 6, no. 3 (2013): 1,749.
23. McDonald, Biswas & Spotswood, "Throwing Shade at the Green New Deal," 67; Theobermanine Cherry, "Air Pollution: Boston" (poster presented at the Jonathan M. Tisch College of Civic Life Leadership for Social Change Residential Program, Medford, July 21, 2023).

24. The Descartes Lab appears to be a data analytics company specializing in geospatial mapping, though it is difficult to find much information about it written for non-experts who are not using its product.
25. ArcGIS.com, "Urban Heat Island Severity for U.S. cities—2019," https://www.arcgis.com/home/item.html?id=4f6d-72903c9741a6a6ee6349f5393572 (accessed June 28, 2023).
26. McDonald, Biswas & Spotswood, "Throwing Shade at the Green New Deal," 73.
27. Shanshan Feng & Fenglei Fan, "Impervious Surface Extraction Based on Different Methods," 1,148.
28. Lanjun Zou, et al., "The Rain-Induced Urban Waterlogging Risk and Its Evaluation: A Case Study in the Central City of Shanghai," *Water* 14, no. 22 (2022): 3,780.
29. Yuliang Wang & Mingshi Li, "Urban Impervious Surface Detection from Remote Sensing Images," 65.
30. Scientific American, "How Dirt Cleans Water," https://www.scientificamerican.com/article/how-dirt-cleans-water/ (accessed July 29, 2023).
31. Government of Massachusetts, "Current public beach postings," https://www.mass.gov/info-details/current-public-beach-postings (accessed July 10, 2023).
32. Bill Shaner, "The Hillside Beach Situation," *Worcester Sucks and I Love It* (February 8, 2021), https://www.worcestersucks.email/p/the-hillside-beach-situation.
33. Ibid.
34. According to the state, wetland replacement is important because wetlands naturally detoxify water, and they were looking for a location to "replace" wetlands that had been destroyed elsewhere. The process of replacing wetlands "typically involves excavation of upland soils to a depth where the naturally occurring water table can support wetland vegetation." The city of Worcester wanted to make Hillside Beach greener and leafier by adding a boardwalk partially surrounded by wetlands. To an outsider, this might seem like an indisputably good decision. However, Lakeside Apartment residents felt differently. As Shaner states: "It looks a lot like the city is taking away their beach, and they're right about that. That's what the city is doing." Scott Jackson, et al.. "Massachusetts Inland Wetland Replacement Guidelines," (Massachusetts Department of Environmental Protection, Bureau of Water Resources, Wetlands Program, 2022), 1; Bill Shaner, "The Hillside Beach Situation."
35. To be considered an EJ area, a census tract must meet at least one of the following criteria (quoted from mass.gov): "The annual median household income is 65 percent or less of the statewide annual median household income; minorities make up 40 percent or more of the population; 25 percent or more of households identify as speaking English less than 'very well'; minorities make up 25 percent or more of the population and the annual median household income of the municipality in which the neighborhood is located does not exceed 150 percent of the statewide annual median household income." Government of Massachusetts, "Environmental Justice Populations in Massachusetts," https://www.mass.gov/info-details/environmental-justice-populations-in-massachusetts (accessed July 22, 2023).
36. Save Hillside Beach on Coes Reservoir, "Lakeside Community Celebration," https://www.facebook.com/events/610463113259503/ (accessed July 22, 2023).
37. Sarah Williams, "Big Data for Cities is Not New," 17.
38. City of Worcester, "Blue Green Algae Presence Closes Coes Reservoir, Binienda Beach," July 20, 2022, https://www.worcesterma.gov/announcements/blue-green-algae-presence-closes-coes-reservoir-binienda-beach (accessed July 22, 2023); City of Worcester, "Coes Reservoir Closed Due to Cyanobacteria," October 5, 2022, https://www.worcesterma.gov/announcements/coes-reservoir-closed-due-to-cyanobacteria (accessed July 22, 2023).
39. Environmental Protection Agency, "EJScreen," https://ejscreen.epa.gov/mapper/ (accessed July 22, 2023).
40. Williams, "Build It! Data Is Never Raw, It's Collected," 79.
41. Fox Keller, "Dynamic Objectivity: Love, Power, and Knowledge," 117.
42. Williams, "Build It! Data Is Never Raw, It's Collected," 86–87.
43. Williams, "Data as a Public Good," 191.
44. Bruno Latour, "Crisis," in *We Have Never Been Modern* (Harvard University Press, 1993), 1–11.
45. Shannon Dosemagen, et al., "Disaster, Participatory Science, and Infrastructure," *Citizen Science: Theory and Practice* 7, no. 1 (2022): 4–5.
46. Fox Keller, "Dynamic Objectivity: Love, Power, and Knowledge," 124.

The Environmental Gaze: Visual Perspectives on Monitoring Landscapes of Ecological Devastation

Lila Lee-Morrison

Film stills from *The Remote Sensation of Disintegration* by Imani Jacqueline Brown, 2020.

The increasing application of monitoring technologies, and the specific perspectives afforded through them, are transforming our understanding of and relationship to our environment. Through systems of mass data accrual, the physical processes and elemental attributes of regional and planetary landscapes are transformed into media, such as digital multi-layered maps, graphs, thermal imaging, models, and 3D simulations. Yet, aside from this transformation of environmental processes into data, there is also the recognition that the physical landscape and its attributes are themselves forms of media, which can mediate between temporalities of past and present and relationships between a subject and an object. To this end, this chapter examines the aesthetics of environmental monitoring through a visual culture and art historical perspective by focusing on the enactment of an *environmental gaze* as a theoretical intervention into the ways in which physical landscapes are seen, represented, and transformed into information through the visual field of environmental monitoring technologies.

This examination focuses on narratives that emerge from the artworks of Imani Jacqueline Brown and her critical approach toward visualizations of the coastal wetlands of Louisiana, a site of ecological devastation with a history of intense extractivism. These are explored against the backdrop of two other sources of data imaging and environmental monitoring of the same landscape: the multilayered data maps of a federal conservation project, the Coastwide Reference Monitoring System (CRMS), and the cross-referencing of multiple visual data sources by Forensic Architecture in collaboration with the non-profit RISE St James. Together, these examples of environmental data production help to define present environmental problems—such as toxic pollution, biodiversity loss, and climate change. Using both remote and local views, and with a specific framing of temporal relations and outcomes, these two sources enact forms of an all-encompassing environmental gaze that can be associated with scientific and militaristic contexts. In contrast, Brown's artworks have an open-ended outcome that questions the potentialities of such an environmental gaze. Her works do this through addressing how notions of landscape can instead be understood through embodiment, expanding the contexts of its temporal scales and foregrounding meaning *in situ*ated and partial views.

The Environmental Gaze

Imaging technologies such as satellite imaging, automated recognition systems, statistical and 3D modeling programs, simulations, drones equipped with lidar, and other sensing technologies with visual outputs are central to monitoring environments. The development of and dependence on these advanced visual technologies brings about an expansion of the perceptual scope of landscapes and their material processes. Developed and primarily implemented within the contexts of military and scientific observation, these technologies are designed to produce a landscape made intelligible and legible for analysis within multiple arenas.[1] Through this technological form of seeing, recent perspectives of earth and climate monitoring continue a characteristic view from nowhere, yet also purport to see everywhere.

This all-encompassing view, which underscores scientific authority and its knowledge production, is famously critiqued by Donna Haraway. Aerial views afforded by drone and satellite systems provide what Haraway has described as a "conquering gaze from nowhere."[2] Haraway's call for a "feminist objectivity" within the field of science and technology counters this view by insisting on reclaiming an embodied vision that gives saliency to the production of meaning through a partial and "situated perspective"; that is, a perspective that accounts for its "limited location" and specificity of context and view.[3] In this way, Haraway is not interested so much in challenging vision through technologies but in shifting our understanding of objectivity to one that incorporates the truth of its always partial, limited, and situated registers. Vision is metaphorical in Haraway's reconfiguration. It is an arena that evades binaries. She states that feminist objectivity leaves behind the desires of an objective view in that it is "not about transcendence and splitting of subject and object" but rather about understanding scientific accounts of phenomena, which have highly limited specific visual possibilities that help to organize worlds. In other words, her attention is on *specificity* rather than generality, a characteristic that so often frames our understanding and application of objectivity. In this way, specificity allows for accountability for "what we learn how to see."[4] However, vision for Haraway is also a sense perception that she wishes to reclaim from unmarked bodies (and positions) – a kind of re-embodiment of the visual sense that accounts for the knowledge produced therein. Haraway's call for feminist objectivity through an inquiry into the sensory systems of vision and visual technologies, i.e., "how these visual systems work, technically, socially and psychically," can contribute to an expanded understanding of knowledge accrual when placed in the specific context of environmental monitoring technologies.[5]

In referencing a splitting of a subject and object, Haraway points toward the formations that structure the concept of the gaze, which addresses an act of looking as a social organization and a power relation resulting from it between a subject who is doing the looking and the object that is being looked at. Jean-Paul Sartre's original description of this concept (*le regard*) uses a metaphor of "the watcher in the park" to situate a subject who observes a landscape that opens up for him to regard.[6] The object observed is a landscape, and the neutrality of the surrounding environment situates a subject at the center of the observer's visual field. Art historian Norman Bryson expands the notion of the gaze by critically examining the limitations of Western philosophy and discussions of visuality against the intervention of Eastern thought, questioning "where the subject resides." Bryson proposes a philosophical move toward a radical decentering of the subject by reflecting on how a reliance on the binary between subject and object limits its possibilities.[7] Drawing on the work of Japanese philosopher Keiji Nishitani, Bryson describes the concept of śūnyatā, which translates to radical impermanence or emptiness. Śūnyatā dissolves the illusion of any stand-alone permanence of an object by recognizing it as part of a "mobile continuum" in a momentary phase of transformation.[8] Recognizing an inherent śūnyatā quality of the object of the gaze reveals the role of other agencies in the gaze, such as the visual framing devices utilized to construct and arrest the object's form. The technologies of environmental monitoring and the visual output of these technologies can be understood in this way, as having agency in the ways in which they create arresting forms in the environment and thereby construct images, which in turn define its meaning.

Contexts of Monitoring a Landscape: Land and Air

One source of environmental monitoring in the area of Louisiana's coastal wetlands is the CRMS, which monitors the effectiveness of restoration and protection projects along the entire coast.[9] The projects that this system monitors are founded upon the need to respond to a crisis of land loss in the area of Louisiana's coastal wetlands and focus on tracking the chemical compositions of the soil, vegetation, and the shifting conditions of swamp and salt marsh habitats. Monitoring at multiple spatial scales, CRMS collects data from 390 sites that include 218 restoration project sites. It utilizes indexical methods of tracking the changing conditions of its projects. CRMS operates on what could be called ground truth, that is, the collection of information known to be real or true because it is done through direct observation, field measurements, and regularly scheduled collection of physical samples that track the composition of soils and vegetation, salinity, temperature, and elevation levels of water. It also includes photographs of sites to document vegetation growth in its data collection. Data are collected to produce a holistic visualization in the form of an extensive, multilayered digital map that includes categorical layers of data, marked by color. The multilayered map of CRMS and its diverse forms of visualization show the digital translation of a collected ground truth that tracks temporally specified physical attributes of the area. The data categories that one can choose to make visible on the map include the locations of CRMS stations, locations of restoration project sites, elevation surveys, areas of hydrologic basins and vegetation, land indices, and areas designated as public. The visualizations of both the map, with its embedded layers, and the photographs give an observer an informatic overview of the region and provide temporal indices that make visible before and after changes that have been introduced and affect the land. Although the categorical features of the CRMS map delineate spatial and temporal parameters, providing, for example, data about the specificity of locations, the overall mediated product of the map reproduces what appears and enacts an environmental gaze with an all-encompassing view - a holistic image of a landscape made legible through its multiple layers of data.

In the CRMS map, the data layer that tracks vegetation, once clicked on, visualizes color-coded layers onto the map that mark the soil composition as salinized, brackish, freshwater, swamp, water, and other. These areas coincide with the sites of CRMS stations. When zooming into the area known as Death Alley or Cancer Alley—named so because of the amount of toxins produced through the petrochemical companies that inhabit the landscape along the Mississippi River between Baton Rouge and New Orleans—one sees blocks of bright yellow that encase the entirety of the length of the river and its tributaries. The bright yellow color marks the areas of vegetation known as *other* on the map legend or, in other words, unknown. Like a neon marker, which, instead of highlighting signals a redaction, this area of "other" vegetation marks blind spots of data on the map that coincide with a lack of CRMS sites along this stretch of the Mississippi River. In an otherwise informatically comprehensive form of environmental media, what is

Film stills from *What Remains at the Ends of the Earth?* by Imani Jacqueline Brown, 2022.

this broad area of "other" and how does it point toward contextual limitations of environmental monitoring? How can its (in)visibility be accounted for? What other sources of data and meaning can account for this blind spot?

One answer is the type of environmental monitoring conducted by the collaborative, investigative group Forensic Architecture, located at Goldsmiths University, in partnership with RISE St James, a community environmental justice organization. Together they trace the composition of land and its air quality in a project titled "Environmental Racism in Death Alley, Louisiana."[10] An aim of Forensic Architecture is to produce visualizations through the cross referencing of multiple data sources and media formats to bring visibility to state violence and violations of human rights that otherwise would go unseen and therefore unaccounted for; in this case, the toxic air pollution and lethal airborne pollutants emitted from the more than 200 petrochemical industrial giants that inhabit the area along the Mississippi River. The privatization of land by the petrochemical industry in this area coincides with the area that is highlighted as "other" in the color-coded maps of CRMS. Yet, this industry's activity predominantly affects the physical and material landscape of the surrounding area, which CRMS tracks and monitors. Forensic Architecture fills in a gap in visual knowledge that also speaks to the ethical and evidentiary implications of its production. Forensic Architecture relies on multiple sources of data and imaging techniques. Like CRMS, it produces digital maps but, instead of tracking the ground composition, these maps track the composition and movement of the air in this region. This approach perhaps circumvents the lack of access due to land privatization and instead sources multiple, publicly available data sources, including wind indices, which show the speed and direction of the wind on specific dates, and cross-references them with records that list the percentages of chemical toxins present in specifically located petrochemical tanks. These sources of data are pieced together with other

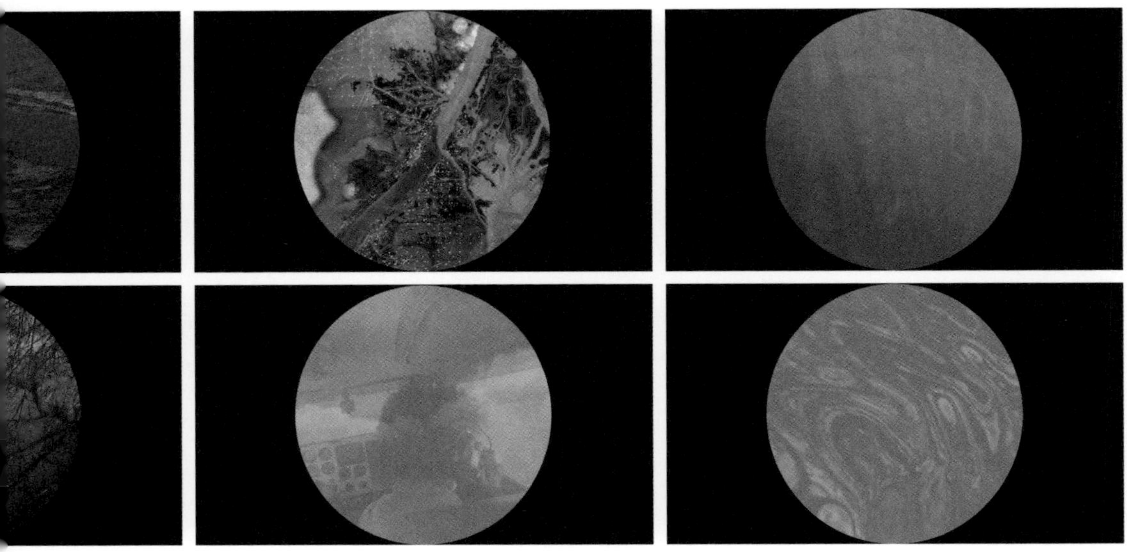

digital imaging techniques, such as meteorological models, 3D fluid dynamic simulation, and thermal imaging, which can trace the presence of toxic emissions. The resulting evidentiary visualizations of Forensic Architecture are an example of what Abelardo Gil-Fournier and Jussi Parikka call "synthetic geographies," geographies produced through datasets and mobilized in machine-learning techniques for visual ends. They argue that their production and use shift the "ground" in ground truth to the ground of the surface of the image. In other words, ground truths are read from the synthetic AI images and through the ways in which datasets are mobilized in machine-learning techniques.[11] Gil-Fournier and Parikka argue that the ground "becomes synthesized with meaningful aesthetic and epistemological consequences."[12] This distinguishes between the map produced by CRMS and the maps of Forensic Architecture in how data and visualization are mobilized; specifically, in how the latter is *grounded* within sociopolitical contexts of meaning. Nevertheless, these two examples of environmental visualizations exemplify what Gil-Fournier and Parikka characterize as a central aspect of the important role of ground truth as having "both a technical and symbolic meaning in how it negotiates relations between images, material surfaces (geographical, landscape, territorial) and their entangled relations...in various institutional arrangements of power and knowledge."[13] Through the cross-referencing of multiple data and digitally mediated image sources, Forensic Architecture produces an environmental gaze through the construction of what can be considered holistic, evidentiary images that track the existence of toxic cloud emissions. This results in the construction of evidence that directly relates the activities of the petrochemical industry to the decline of living standards and health of the neighboring Black communities that inhabit the areas in and around Death Alley, which has the highest levels of cancer in the United States.

Critical Aesthetics of Landscape

Through two multimedia artworks titled, *What Remains at the Ends of the Earth?* (2022) and *The Remote Sensation of Disintegration* (2020), the artist, Imani Jacqueline Brown (who worked as a researcher with Forensic Architecture on the Death Alley project, among others), addresses the ways in which images of the environment of Death Alley have been represented, seen, and experienced. Brown situates this landscape within a broader sociocultural and historical context, drawing on the evidentiary aesthetics of environmental data, landscape, and mapping, yet does so through a lens of open-ended critical inquiry into the perspectives afforded through them. In this, Brown highlights the role of an observing subject within the framing of a techno-environmental gaze. The loss of coastal wetlands and gradual devastation of land in the region is directly related by Brown to the digging of wells and canals by the petrochemical corporations. The temporal continuities of this shifting landscape are extended by Brown to prehistoric times. At the beginning of *What Remains at the Ends of the Earth?* one hears Brown's voice describe the practices of present fossil fuel industries as "drill[ing] 10,000 feet and 65 million years deep," referring to a space-time continuum marked by the extinction of dinosaurs.[14] Working with a circular cinematic projection, we see points of light against a black backdrop that resemble a constellation of stars in the night sky. Yet as straight lines begin to emit from each, these points transform into a systematic network and, according to the narration, illustrate pipelines that overlay a satellite image of the earth. What appears as an image of the cosmos shifts into a system of technical design that structures practices of ecological extraction and natural resource accrual. The narrator's voice states, "They raise colonies of primordial bacteria from their slumber and put them to work powering a trillion electric stars."[15] The invocation of beyond-human temporal scales decenters an anthropogenic frame of reference to the environment and brings into focus other agencies. Scales of temporality are extended beyond an era of capitalist extraction to wider narratives of relational geological forces, which puts the former's agency into question.

Brown critically reflects on ways of seeing landscape through mediated and techno-scientific framings that are categorized into local vs. remote views, and how they each have different affordances in representing ecological devastation. In *The Remote Sensation of Disintegration* (2020), Brown asks, on "what position and scale do we sense our disintegration?" Utilizing a visual methodology of split-screen video, she juxtaposes the on-the-ground view (which represents the local view) of video footage filmed by the artist while floating down the Mississippi River with remote views of aerial footage also taken by the artist from inside a small plane as well as publicly available satellite imagery of the same region. Brown reflects upon the binary of local and remote in relation to the ways in which we see and sense landscape. At one point, addressing a relationship of visual proximity, Brown asks, "Absent a face, is the human still present in the image of the ecosystem?"[16] She references the media images that were widely distributed after Hurricane Katrina, images that one could describe as depicting a perspective that is on the ground and local. As Brown (and others) argues, the wide distribution and reception of these images in the news media "fetishized suffering," transforming the event into a spectacle of racialized, ecological catastrophe while at the same time "obscuring the cosmologies, systems, and corporations that perpetrate said suffering."[17] These images and the localized perspective afforded through them enabled a kind of distanced view of disaster voyeurism for an audience. Instead, Brown's speculative approach to the aerial perspective offers alternatives to the ways in which environment and ecological devastation are sensed and where a sense of embodiment in relation to landscape is present.

Brown critically approaches the aerial perspective and its historical alignment within scientific, military, and colonial and racial hierarchies and notions of an objective truth. She references this perspective in her work through satellite images and historical maps as well as her own video footage taken from within an airplane. She states, "To ascend is simply to bear witness to the lie, to the catastrophe," recognizing the role of remote viewing as a form of testimony while also dismissing a direct relation to the production of an objective truth.[18] Brown describes through narration and image that this view from above makes possible a new sensibility within her own body in relation to the land and its history. In *What Remains at the Ends of the Earth?* we see aerial footage of the scarred land around Death Alley, described by Brown as "the whiplashed skin" of the earth, drawing on a history of the region as a site of trauma and enslavement of African bodies. This figurative reference merges body and land through a violent history of the extractivism of both. The possibility of visualizing this connection is afforded through an aerial view by Brown. It, in part, makes it possible for Brown to visualize what she terms the "ecological body," which is the body that is a convergence of myriad forms, influences, and entanglements—the microbial, individual, community, and environmental body.[19] Brown references this regarding her own body when she describes growing up within the coastal wetlands of this area—the toxins of the region are in her own cells. As the artist states,

> I am from Louisiana, experienced Katrina, and am therefore bodily, as well as culturally, spiritually, etc., connected to the place. My understanding of the 'ecological body' came very much from locating my childhood home, which was destroyed by Katrina, in the satellite image and recognizing its proximity to the fraying wetlands. As well as [from] recognizing that my health problems—which I attribute to environmental pollution—abated after moving to London.[20]

Brown describes how these factors are pertinent to an understanding of "being-in-and-becoming-place." This experience in coming to terms with the ecological body describes a hybrid of person and place and, in turn, expands an understanding of the body that is doing the observing and sensing.

Returning to an expanded notion of the gaze as outlined by Bryson and Nishitani, I see Brown's intervention as countering the binaries of a subject/object through an expanded notion of the observing subject. In this way, Brown's artworks present an example of śūnyatā applied to the role of the observer. Yet, rather than *applied to* the object being viewed, as Bryson references the concept, it is the observer *in relation to* the object that enters "a mobile continuum." Brown's reference to the ecological body is an expanded notion of the observing body in the way śūnyatā inscribes existing in relation to the landscape as a "mobile continuum." Referencing the framing devices of scientific and military contexts to construct and arrest the landscape form, Brown appropriates and recontextualizes its image output and perspective to construct an expression of a gaze. Instead of a gaze that concretizes the power relations of a centralized observer dominant above the landscape, which continues and validates practices of natural resource extraction, Brown speculates about redefining or, one could say, *taking back* the aerial perspective to align it with ways of seeing that relate to other contexts—ones that merge the aerial perspective with other forms of intelligence such as ancestral myth and with nonhuman ways of seeing and knowing. She states that seeing from above is "seeing like an ancestor, like a bird with a map of home behind my eyes," referring to folktales from the artist's enslaved ancestors in which "birds are messengers from the spirit world" and "Black humans can fly."[21] Brown's work could be said to outline another form of an environmental gaze that expresses the limits of an omnipresent view, while also utilizing a composite approach (like that of the CRMS map and Forensic Architecture) that pieces together situated perspectives of landscape. Yet, unlike the previous examples of environmental visualization, Brown foregrounds the limitations of the partial views that both remote and local perspectives entail. Her use of multiple image sources of the coastal wetlands environment addresses the gaps of knowledge and data that exist between and within contemporary landscapes and environmental visualizations. Like the environmental visualizations of both CRMS and Forensic Architecture, environmental imaging for Brown can also provide witness, but one in which a truth is found from multiple situated registers and most centrally derives from and through expanded notions of an embodied sense of the observer in relation to an environment. An environmental gaze that constitutes a sense

Film stills from *The Remote Sensation of Disintegration* by Imani Jacqueline Brown, 2020.

of "being in place" shifts toward a condition of "being place." Brown's work, with its focus on the aesthetics of a landscape of ecological devastation, draws on a geological prehistory, sociopolitical contexts, ancestral knowledge, and myth that expand the contexts of knowledge production in environmental monitoring.

Conclusion

Haraway and Bryson and their discussions of situated and partial perspectives and the gaze as situating a subject in relation to an object that can extend beyond a visual field provide perspectives on the different approaches in which environment is increasingly viewed through technological forms of seeing. Two sources of the visual framing of environmental monitoring, CRMS and Forensic Architecture, are discussed as an inquiry into the production of environmental media and the environmental gaze within the contexts of scientific inquiry and evidence, respectively. Both are designed to produce holistic images of the ecologically devastated landscape known as Death Alley. Their methods and image practices are juxtaposed against the artworks of Imani Jacqueline Brown, which address the gaps in knowledge and views of landscape through cultural, lived, and subjective experience, foregrounding meaning in perspectives that are both situated and embodied, if not complete. Her works expand an understanding of the sociopolitical and historical implications of the role of technologies in seeing the environment and its conditions anew. Specifically, her work critically explores the role of the gaze through techno-mediated ways of seeing the environment and its representative accounts of its remote and localized enactment. Within the context of an environmental gaze, her work, as I see it, applies Nishitani's notion of śūnyatā toward the object being viewed, i.e., the devastated landscapes of the coastal wetlands of Louisiana, as well as toward the observing viewer. *In situ*ating this landscape within a geological history of dispossession, Brown's work appropriates the framing of a technological aerial gaze through an embodied and situated approach, enacting a distribution of power in environmental monitoring. This approach is especially necessary for addressing present contexts of environmental (in)justices and how the effects of ecological devastation and the increasing widespread subsidence caused by agencies of extraction are unevenly distributed and affecting communities that inhabit these areas. Brown produces a representation of landscape that not only addresses the gaps in seeing and knowing, but also repairs an interdependence of relations between bodies and land. The environmental gaze as a conduit of how we see and know the landscape can expand to include the bodies, lives, and histories that constitute it and which it constitutes.

Acknowledgment

Many thanks to Alison Gerber, Isak Engdahl, and Tobias Olofsson, my colleagues at Lund University, for their informed feedback and discussions on the development of this text. This article is part of *Show & Tell*, a project funded by the European Research Council (ERC) under the European Union's Horizon 2020 research and innovation program (Grant agreement No. 949050).

Notes

1. For more on the nexus of the military/scientific framing in environmental monitoring, see William J. Broad, "Inside the C.I.A., She Became a Spy for Planet Earth," *New York Times* (Jan 5, 2021), https://www.nytimes.com/2021/01/05/science/linda-zall-cia.html.
2. Donna Haraway, "Situated Knowledges: The Science Question in Feminism and the Privilege of Partial Perspective," *Feminist Studies* 14, no. 3 (1988): 581.
3. Ibid., 583.
4. Ibid.
5. Ibid.
6. Jean-Paul Sartre, *Being and Nothingness*, trans. Hazel E. Barnes (New York Philosophical Library, 1956): 254–302.
7. Norman Bryson, "The Gaze in the Expanded Field," in Hal Foster (ed.), *Vision and Visuality* (Bay Press, 1986), 87.
8. Ibid., 97.
9. Coastwide Reference Monitoring System, "CRMS Viewer," https://lacoast.gov/crms_viewer/Map/CRMSViewer (accessed November 13, 2023).
10. Forensic Architecture, "Environmental Racism in Death Alley, Louisiana," https://forensic-architecture.org/investigation/environmental-racism-in-death-alley-louisiana (accessed November 11, 2023).
11. Abelardo Gil-Fournier & Jussi Parikka, "Ground Truth to Fake Geographies: Machine Vision and Learning in Visual Practices," *AI & Society* 36, (2021): 1,254. For more on ground truthing and machine learning, see Florian Jaton, *The Constitution of Algorithms: Ground Truthing, Programming, and Formulation* (MIT Press, 2021).
12. Gil-Fournier & Jussi Parikka, "Ground Truth to Fake Geographies," 1,254.
13. Ibid., 1,253–34.
14. Imani Jacqueline Brown, "What Remains at the Ends of the Earth?" https://imanijacquelinebrown.net/What-remains-at-the-ends-of-the-earth (accessed October 12, 2023), 0:37.
15. Ibid., 1:01.
16. Imani Jacqueline Brown, "The Remote Sensation of Disintegration," https://imanijacquelinebrown.net/The-Remote-Sensation-of-Disintegration (accessed October 12, 2023).
17. See Douglas Kellner, "The Katrina Hurricane Spectacle and Crisis of the Bush Presidency," *Cultural Studies ↔ Critical Methodologies* 7, no. 2 (2007): 222–34.
18. Imani Jacqueline Brown, "What Remains at the Ends of the Earth?" 2:42.
19. Brown, "The Remote Sensation of Disintegration."
20. Imani Jacqueline Brown, email message to author, March 11, 2024.
21. Sophia Nahli Allison states, "Flight became a secret language for runaway slaves, and it continues to represent black mobility toward liberation." For more on myth and Black flight, see Sophia Nahli Allison, "Revisiting the Legend of Flying Africans," *New Yorker* (March 7, 2019), https://www.newyorker.com/culture/culture-desk/revisiting-the-legend-of-flying-africans; Lorna McDaniel, "The Flying Africans: Extent and Strength of the Myth in the Americas," *Nieuwe West-Indische Gids/New West Indian Guide* 64, no. 1/2 (1990): 28–40.

Acknowledgments

The inspiration for this edited volume came from the "Instruments of Change" symposium held in February 2022. This event marked the official launch of the Environmental Modeling Lab (EMLab), co-founded with our colleague Sean Burkholder under the auspices of the Department of Landscape Architecture's McHarg Center at the University of Pennsylvania Stuart Weitzman School of Design. While not all symposium participants contributed to this collection, the stimulating conversations that arose from that event guided the spirit of this book. We extend our gratitude to Bradley Cantrell, Monica Chasten, Anya Domlesky, Iryna Dronova, John E. Fernández, Jennifer Gabrys, Ilmar Hurkxkens, Victoria Jane Marshall, Brett Milligan, Fatemeh Nasrollahi, Robert Gerard Pietrusko, and Sarah Williams. Special thanks to Sean Burkholder for the fruitful and ongoing collaborations and discussions within the EMLab and beyond. We would also like to thank our former chair and co-director of the McHarg Center, Richard Weller, for supporting the event, and Billy Fleming, the former Wilks Family Director of the McHarg Center, for logistical assistance in hosting the symposium. Our appreciation also extends to our outstanding research assistant, Youzi Olivia Xu, for her help with the graphics related to the event.

This publication would not have been possible without the financial support of the McHarg Center for our many talented graduate research assistants. We would especially like to thank Maura McDaniel and Michelle Chan Syl Yeng, who lent their creative energies to making images and providing visual consistency for each chapter—a challenging task given the diversity of topics and projects. We are grateful to our Dean, Fritz Steiner, for providing funds to support the publication of this book and to our publishers, ORO Editions / AR+D—in particular, Jake Anderson, for his early support and ongoing assistance. We also thank Luke Bulman for his patience and for designing a visually engaging and thoughtfully crafted book.

Above all, we are indebted to the many artists, designers, engineers, and scientists who generously permitted us to use their work and to the authors for their thoughtful contributions and generosity of time.

Karen M'Closkey and Keith VanDerSys (eds) are faculty in landscape architecture at the University of Pennsylvania Weitzman School of Design and co-founders of PEG office of landscape + architecture and Penn's Environmental Modeling Lab (EMLab). Their work in the EMLab specializes in environmental simulation modeling and remote sensing related to designing and monitoring natural infrastructure in coastal environments. Their work has been acknowledged through numerous awards, exhibitions, and fellowships, including a PEW Fellowship in the Arts, and has appeared in over 70 design publications. They are guest editors of *LA+ GEO* (2020) and *LA+ Simulation* (2016), and authors of *Dynamic Patterns: Visualizing Landscapes in a Digital Age* (2017). M'Closkey is also the author of *Unearthed: The Landscapes of Hargreaves Associates* (2013), which received the J. B. Jackson Book Award from the Foundation for Landscape Studies; co-curator and co-editor of the symposium and book *Design with Nature Now* (2019); and, since 2023, is editor in chief of *LA+ Interdisciplinary Journal of Landscape Architecture*.

Jeffrey Moro is an assistant clinical professor with the African American Digital and Experimental Humanities (AADHum) Initiative at the University of Maryland, College Park. His research focuses on how media technologies facilitate our cultural apprehension of the natural world, with particular interest in the creative and technical applications of environmental data in contemporary cultural production. His work has appeared in the journals *Amodern*, *Media Fields*, and *Digital Humanities Quarterly*, and he has contributed reviews to *ISLE*, the *Journal of Environmental Media*, and the *Los Angeles Review of Books*. He is working on a book project titled *Cloud Studies*, which explores how technical and creative media capture, interpret, and compute the air, and such media's consequent relationship to climate change. Before joining AADHum, he completed a PhD in English with a certificate in Digital Studies at the University of Maryland and worked as a post-Baccalaureate Resident with Five College Digital Humanities in western Massachusetts.

Wilko Graf von Hardenberg is a historian of science and the environment at Humboldt University in Berlin. He has been a guest professor at the same university and the University of Wisconsin-Madison, as well as a senior research scholar at the Max Planck Institute for the History of Science in Berlin. He is the author of the first history of the Gran Paradiso National Park in Italy in the years of the fascist regime: *A Monastery for the Ibex. Conservation, State, and Conflict on the Gran Paradiso, 1919–1949* (2021). He also co-authored *Mussolini's Nature: An Environmental History of Italian Fascism* (2022) and authored *Sea Level: A History* (2024) on the concept of sea level from the 18th century to the Anthropocene.

Brian D. Harris and Justin Shawler both hold research positions with the US Army Engineer Research and Development Center's Coastal and Hydraulics Lab in the Coastal Engineering Branch. Dr. Harris received a doctorate in Civil and Environmental Engineering with a concentration in Geotechnical Engineering from Louisiana State University, where his dissertation focused on natural coastal infrastructure. Harris's research interests include the geotechnical design, construction, performance, and monitoring techniques of Natural and Nature Based Features (wetlands, headlands, mangroves, islands) and the beneficial use of dredged material. Dr. Shawler holds a PhD in Geological Oceanography from the Virginia Institute of Marine

Science. Shawler's research interests include coastal geology and the drivers of change along barrier islands and in estuaries. He previously worked as a coastal scientist for the Delaware Department of Natural Resources and Environmental Control where he led projects focused on the beneficial use of dredged material.

Matthew Jull and Leena Cho are founding directors of ARCTIC DESIGN GROUP, and co-authors of *Mediating Environments* (2019). Jull is an associate professor of architecture at the University of Virginia, and a geophysicist. His research focuses on systems and processes of architecture and urbanization in extreme environments, specifically in Arctic Russia and North America. Cho is an assistant professor of Landscape Architecture at the University of Virginia whose research investigates the conception, representation, and design instrumentation of weather phenomena and climates in built environments. They practice under the moniker KUTONOTUK, a firm that has received international recognition in 17 prestigious design competitions and has been featured in over 30 publications and 20 exhibitions in North America, Asia, and Europe.

Ilmar Hurkxkens is an architect and researcher interested in digital terrain modeling technologies and the development of new design and construction processes with natural granular material. He is a postdoctoral researcher at Gramazio Kohler Research and lecturer at the Master of Science in Landscape Architecture at the ETH Zürich. Previously, Hurkxkens worked at the chair of Landscape Architecture of Prof. Girot, where he directed design research studios and developed digital tools for large-scale landscape design. He is co-founder of LANDSKIP, a laboratory for landscape transformation, and he practices landscape architecture with projects in Switzerland, the Netherlands, and Greece. In 2020 Hurkxkens was nominated for the ETH Medal of outstanding doctoral research for his dissertation "Robotic Landscapes: Topological Approaches to Terrain, Design, and Fabrication," which was recently published as the book *Robotic Landscapes—Designing the Unfinished* (2021).

Christopher Streb, PE, is a practice leader with Biohabitats, leading the firm's research and development effort called Bioworks. He is an ecological engineer with 20 years of experience in restoration and regenerative design. Combining engineering and ecological design through a biomimicry lens, he approaches every project as an opportunity to create and restore functional life support systems. Recognizing that best intentions in design and implementation are not verification of outcomes, Streb is charged with developing methods for monitoring and evaluating projects to determine whether ecological goals are being realized. Over the past decade, he has designed and developed ecological interventions to restore functional habitat along urban waterfronts. He has been awarded a patent for a floating wetland technology and was the ecological team lead on the National Aquarium Floating Wetland Prototype, which earned the 2018 Honor Award for Research from the American Society of Landscape Architects.

David Blersch is an associate professor of ecological engineering in the Biosystems Engineering Department at Auburn University. His work focuses on developing ecotechnology for water and wastewater remediation, approaches for ecological restoration in aquatic ecosystems, and aspects of self-organization in designed techno-ecosystems at multiple scales. Dr. Blersch has been a leader in ecological engineering projects and research totaling over $10 million, with recent projects in ecological-based food production in aquaponics systems, optimization of algae cultivation systems for nutrient recovery from wastewater, and development of wetland systems for remediation of wastewater from agricultural production. He remains a leader in the development of ecological engineering as a field of practice, recently as president of the American Ecological Engineering Society, which includes the development of a university-level curriculum for ecological engineering education and assisting in the development of professional certification of ecological engineering practitioners and ecosystem designers.

Jennifer Gabrys is chair in Media, Culture and Environment in the Department of Sociology at the University of Cambridge. She leads the Planetary Praxis research group and is principal investigator on the European Research Council (ERC)–funded project, "Smart Forests: Transforming Environments into Social-Political Technologies." She also leads Citizen Sense and AirKit, which are participatory and practice-based research projects funded by the ERC that address air pollution and citizen engagement. Gabrys writes on digital technologies, environments, and social life. Her publications include *How to Do Things with Sensors* (2019) and *Program Earth: Environmental Sensing Technology and the Making of a Computational Planet* (2016). Her newest book, *Citizens of Worlds: Open-Air Toolkits for Environmental Struggle* (2022) was published by University of Minnesota Press and is available on Manifold. She also co-edits the "Planetarities" short-monograph series published through Goldsmiths Press. Her work can be found at jennifergabrys.net.

Paolo Patelli is currently a postdoctoral researcher with the "Design and Aesthetics for Environmental Data" project headed by Jussi Parikka under the Digital Design and Information Studies department at Aarhus University, Denmark. Previously, he was a Research Associate at the Research Center for Material Culture in Leiden (2020–22), a fellow at the Akademie Schloss Solitude (2020–21), a research fellow at Het Nieuwe Instituut (2019–20), and an artist-in-residence at the Jan van Eyck Academie in Maastricht (2017–18). He collaborated with the Programme d'Expérimentation en Arts Politiques (SPEAP) at Sciences Po (2016–18) and taught at The New School's Parsons Paris, Design Academy Eindhoven (2017–21), and Sandberg Instituut (2019–22). With a background in architecture and an interest in multimodal methods, he developed artistic research projects investigating the materialities, scenes, and atmospheres at the intersections of space and society, technologies, and environments. He holds a PhD in Architecture and Urban Design from Politecnico di Milano (2015).

Jussi Parikka is a professor in Digital Aesthetics and Culture at Aarhus University in Denmark where he is director of the Digital Aesthetics Research Centre (DARC). He is also a visiting professor at Winchester School of Art (University of Southampton) and at FAMU at the Academy of Performing Arts in Prague, where he leads the project Operational Images and Visual Culture (2019–23, funded by the Czech Science Foundation). In 2021, he was elected as a member of Academia Europaea. His published books include *Insect Media* (2010), *Digital Contagions* (2007/2016), *A Geology of Media* (2015), and *A Slow, Contemporary Violence* (2016). Recently, he co-edited *Photography Off the Scale* (2021) and is co-author of *The Lab Book: Situated Practices in Media Studies* (2022). His most recent books are *Living*

Surfaces: Images, Plants, and Environments of Media, with Abelardo Gil-Fournier (2024), and *Operational Images* (2023). Parikka's books have been translated into 11 languages, including Japanese, Korean, Chinese, Czech, Italian, French, Spanish, and Portuguese. His work can be found at jussiparikka.net.

Iryna Dronova is an associate professor jointly appointed in the Departments of Landscape Architecture & Environmental Planning (College of Environmental Design) and Environmental Science, Policy & Management (College of Natural Resources) at the University of California, Berkeley. Her research combines landscape ecology with remote sensing and geographic information science to investigate multi-scale dynamics of human-dominated landscapes and improve the monitoring and assessment of ecological restoration outcomes, with particular emphasis on wetlands and land-water interfaces. She is particularly interested in how the increasing accessibility, spatial resolution, and temporal frequency of remote sensing products can facilitate landscape planning and decision-making and strategically complement ground-based data collection and monitoring. Besides wetlands, Dronova also works on questions related to nature-based climate solutions in cities, particularly the important potential of urban green spaces to provide microclimatic cooling together with various social, public health, and ecological benefits.

Karl Kullmann is a landscape architect, urban designer, and associate professor at the College of Environmental Design, University of California, Berkeley. Karl's scholarship and creative work explore the cultural agency of topographically complex landscapes in the context of landscape and urban design. Karl has published widely on this subject through diverse lenses, including green infrastructure, design modeling and visualization, and mapping and datascaping. He has been published in top journals, including *PLACES*, *Journal of Landscape Architecture*, *Studies in the History of Gardens and Designed Landscapes*, *Landscape Research*, and *Journal of Architectural Education.* This research is actively applied through design practice, with built, urban, and landscape projects in China, Australia, and Germany and numerous design competition prizes and exhibitions.

Heather Houser is professor of English at the University of Texas at Austin where she co-founded Planet Texas 2050, UT Austin's inaugural grand research challenge focused on climate resilience. She writes on contemporary culture, the environment, and science. Her books include *Infowhelm: Environmental Art & Literature in an Age of Data* (2020) and *Ecosickness in Contemporary U.S. Fiction: Environment and Affect* (2014), which won the 2015 Association for the Study of the Arts of the Present Book Prize and was shortlisted for the 2014 British Society for Literature and Science Book Prize. She writes for both academic and public audiences. Her academic articles have appeared in top journals including *New Literary History*, *Environmental Humanities*, *Modern Fiction Studies*, *American Literary History*, *American Literature*, *Public Culture*, and *Contemporary Literature.* Her writing for more general audiences has been published in *New York Review Daily*, *Yes! Magazine*, *LitHub*, *Public Books*, and *Los Angeles Review of Books*.

Samantha Jo Fried is the program manager for Science, Technology, and Society (STS) and the Civic Studies Program at the Jonathan M. Tisch College of Civic Life at Tufts University. Her research interests combine STS, civic studies, activism and political organizing, critical data studies, science and technology policy, and Earth remote sensing, among others. Her dissertation "Landsat in Contexts: Deconstructing and Reconstructing the Data-to-Action Paradigm in Environmental Remote Sensing," which traces the history of the development of Landsat satellites and multispectral imaging, questions the "data to action" narrative around which much rhetoric on environmental data collection is structured. She is co-author of the book *Postphenomenology and Imaging: How To Read Technology*, and her articles have appeared in *AI and Society, American Scientist,* and *Techné: Research in Philosophy and Technology.*

Lila Lee-Morrison is a postdoctoral researcher at Lund University on the ERC funded project titled, "Show and Tell: Scientific representation, algorithmically generated visualizations, and evidence across epistemic cultures." Her research interests include investigating the visuality of contemporary technologies of machinic and algorithmic perception and the sociopolitical and cultural contexts of its application and material infrastructures. She is a recent recipient of the Andy Warhol Art Writers Grant (2023) and is working on a book project titled, *Machinic Landscapes: Technology, Art and Environment in an Age of Planetarity* which updates the art historical genre of landscape against the backdrop of the Anthropocene and through the work of contemporary artists whose practices address the figuring of diverse subjectivities as enmeshed in both technical and environmental processes. She has published with MIT Press, Artforum, Liverpool University Press, and Brill Publishing.

Image Credits

Introduction

9 Joseph Liesganig, *Dimensio graduum meridiani Viennensis et Hungarici, 1770*.
10 James Corner and Alex S. MacLean, *Taking Measures Across the American Landscape* (Yale University Press, 1996), 171. Used with permission.
12 Image courtesy of NASA's Earth Observatory, https://earthobservatory.nasa.gov/images/43401/50th-anniversary-of-the-tiros-satellite.
13 Image courtesy of NOAA.
14 Image by Keith VanDerSys.
15 Image by Keith VanDerSys.
16 Courtesy of The Architectural Archives, University of Pennsylvania.
18 Image by Atticus E. L. Stovall.
20 NASA public domain data compiled by Nathan Bergey.

Moro

30 Drawing by Michelle Chan Syl Yeng.
33 Photograph by Joshua Jensen. Image courtesy of the artist.
34 Image by Michelle Chan Syl Yeng generated using Matt Dzugan's Weather Data Art at Observable, https://observablehq.com/@mattdzugan/here-with-the-wind-using-wind-data-to-make-art-part-2-all-done-i.
36 Photograph by Joshua Jensen. Image courtesy of the artist.

Hardenberg

42 Traugott Bromme, *Atlas zu Alex. v. Humboldt's Kosmos in zweiundvierzig Tafeln mit erläuterndem Texte* (Stuttgart: Krais & Hoffmann, 1851), pl. 18, https://doi.org/10.5962/bhl.title.39968.
44 Images courtesy of NASA's Earth Observatory, https://earthobservatory.nasa.gov/world-of-change/AralSea/show-all.
46 E. G. Ravenstein, "The Lake-Level of the Victoria Nyanza," *The Geographical Journal* 18, no. 4 (1901): 405, https://doi.org/10.2307/1775726.
50 Sir John Kirk, *Lake Nyassa, the River Shire &c. (South Eastern Africa) from the M.S. map by Dr. Kirk*. London: published for the journal of the Royal Geographical Society by J. Murray, Albemarle Street, 1865, https://maps.princeton.edu/catalog/princeton-gf06g513t.

M'Closkey and VanDerSys

54 Image courtesy of Keith VanDerSys.
57 Image courtesy of Keith VanDerSys.
59 Image courtesy of Keith VanDerSys.
62 Image courtesy of Keith VanDerSys.

Harris and Shawler

68 Maps generated from the CPRA's 2023 Louisiana Coastal Master Plan Data Access Portal, https://mpdap.coastal.la.gov/#chart=2-52. Redrawn by Maura McDaniel.
71 Maps generated from the CPRA's 2023 Louisiana Coastal Master Plan Data Access Portal, https://mpdap.coastal.la.gov/#chart=2-52. Redrawn by Maura McDaniel.
72 Image courtesy of Louisiana's Coastal Protection and Restoration Authority (CPRA) program.
74 Image courtesy of Michael O. Snyder.
78 Image courtesy of Brian Harris.

Jull and Cho

82 Image courtesy of Arctic Design Group, 2023.
84 Image by Matthew Jull / Arctic Design Group, 2020.
86 Image by Leena Cho / Arctic Design Group, June 2020.
88 Image by Leena Cho / Arctic Design Group, 2020.
90 Data from UVA Arctic Research Center, 2022. Image by Nita Wareechatchai / Arctic Design Group, 2023.

Hurkxkens

95 Model created by students Caspar Trueb and Lorin Wiedemeier. Image courtesy of the author.
96 Image by Girts Apskalns. Courtesy of Gramazio Kohler Research, Robotic Systems Lab, Prof. Christophe Girot and Ilmar Hurkxkens, ETH Zurich.
98 Simulation by students Caspar Trueb and Lorin Wiedemeier. Image courtesy of the author.
102 Simulation by students Caspar Trueb and Lorin Wiedemeier. Image courtesy of the author.
104 Illustration by Caspar Trueb and Lorin Wiedemeier. Image courtesy of the author.

Streb and Blersch

110 Image courtesy of The Pask Estate.
112 Image drawn by Maura McDaniel, interpreted from an image by Kevin J. Beiler, Daniel M. Durall, Suzanne W. Simard, Sheri A. Maxwell, Annette M. Kretzer, "Architecture of the Wood-Wide Web: *Rhizopogon* spp. genets link multiple Douglas-fir cohorts," *New Phytologist* 185 (2010): 546.
116 Project lead – Nelson Byrd Woltz Landscape Architects; Ecology Consultant – Biohabitats. Image by Nick Hubbard.
120 Project lead – Ayer Saint Gross; Ecology Consultant (concept phase) – Biohabitats. Image by David Coffey.

Gabrys

124 Image courtesy of the author.
127 Image courtesy of the author.
128 Images by Andrew Ellicott Douglass, 1919. Public domain, via Wiki Commons.

Patelli and Parikka

135 Diagram redrawn by Maura McDaniel. Originally created by Jinyi Liu and Menghan Zhang, "The Evolution and Impacts of 'Complexity Notions' in Landscape Architecture," *Landscape Research* 48, no. 6 (2023): 797. Used with permission.
138 Diagram redrawn by Maura McDaniel. Originally created by Chris J. Topping, et al., "ALMaSS, An Agent-Based Model for Animals in Temperate European Landscapes," *Ecological Modeling*, 167 (2013): 71. Used with permission.
141 Diagram redrawn by Maura McDaniel. Originally created by Chris J. Topping, et al., "ALMaSS, An Agent-Based Model for Animals in Temperate European Landscapes,"

Ecological Modeling, 167 (2013): 76. Used with permission.

144 Diagram redrawn by Maura McDaniel. Originally created by Chris J. Topping, et al., "ALMaSS, An Agent-Based Model for Animals in Temperate European Landscapes," *Ecological Modeling*, 167 (2013): 73. Used with permission.

Dronova

150 Image courtesy of the author.
152 Image courtesy of the author.
156 Author's maps redrawn by Keith VanDerSys. Used with permission.
160 Image source from USGS Earth Explorer for July 2014; digital raster stretching by Keith VanDerSys.

Kullmann

164 Public domain, https://archive.org/details/fabricaetususins00zubl [accessed August 02, 2024].
168 Image by Michelle Chan Syl Yeng / Keith VanDerSys.
172 Image courtesy of the author.
173 Image courtesy of the author.
174 Image courtesy of the author.

Houser

179 Images courtesy of Victoria J. Marshall, Mary L. Cadenasso, Brian P. McGrath, and Steward T. A. Pickett.
182 Images courtesy of Victoria J. Marshall, Mary L. Cadenasso, Brian P. McGrath, and Steward T. A. Pickett.
185 Images courtesy of Victoria J. Marshall, Mary L. Cadenasso, Brian P. McGrath, and Steward T. A. Pickett.
187 Image courtesy of Anuradha Mathur and Dilip da Cunha.
188 Image courtesy of Anuradha Mathur and Dilip da Cunha.
190 Image courtesy of Anuradha Mathur and Dilip da Cunha.

Fried

194 Impervious surface data accessed through the Multi-Resolution Land Characteristics (MRLC). Watershed data accessed from the EPA's Environmental Justice Screening and Mapping Tool (EJScreen). Beach closure locations are accessed from the Mass.gov website. Images drawn by Maura McDaniel based on information from the author's maps.
198 Images drawn by Maura McDaniel based on information from the author's maps.
200 Image courtesy of Maura McDaniel, using imagery from Google Earth Pro (Version 10.69.0.1), 42°14′59″ N 71°50′02″ W (accessed, 09/14/2022).

Lee-Morrison

208 Images courtesy of Imani Jacqueline Brown.
212 Images courtesy of Imani Jacqueline Brown.
217 Images courtesy of Imani Jacqueline Brown.

Index